BY THE ATLANTIC

The Food and Cooking of South West France and Spain

Caroline Conran

PROSPECT
BOOKS
2016

This edition published in 2016 by Prospect Books at
26 Parke Road, London, SW13 9NG

British Library Cataloguing in Publication Data:
A catalogue entry for this book is available from the British Library.

ISBN 978-1-909248-47-2

Set in Cochin, Gill Sans and Adobe Garamond Pro by Catheryn Kilgarriff and Rebecca Gillieron.

Printed by T.J. International, United Kingdom.

Contents

Foreword

I managed to find a most exacting project in writing *By The Atlantic*. Much of it involved travelling to the South West Coast of France and the Basque Country. Here the job was hard.

I had to spend as much time as possible in fabled, teeming market halls, finding out about the produce. It was necessary to keep renting a flat with a kitchen on the beach at Biarritz, with the Atlantic pounding outside the window. Friends came to help try out the fish restaurants and bistros. I had to have several stays in Bordeaux, Bayonne, Cap Ferret, Pau, St Jean de Luz, Souillac, San Sebastian and Bilbao.

Then came The Road Trip, a phenomenal journey up into the Pyrenees with Kate Hill of Camont Cookery School, my friend and mentor on all things Gascon. There I inspected fat pigs and shoals of trout long and hard and had the picnic of my life.

With Kate I learned grilling techniques from Basque gentlemen, and found out how to make a ham and we wandered with friends Bill Law, Cate McGuire and Lee Knox round the deep dark streets of San Sebastian looking for and finding the best pinchos and tapas in town. We explored the extraordinary menu at Asador Extebarri where everything is cooked in essence of wood smoke. We ate ice cream with cream puffs by the sea and drank hot chocolate in the mountains. It was all the hardest work imaginable.

Then with Beth Coventry and Julian Biggs, both talented chefs, we tried out every one of the recipes that had accumulated and we sat down and ate them all.

I have learned that its always important to have a good lawyer at hand and we could not have done better than to share these dishes with solicitor Michael Seifert, who was the essential critic to have on board, as he loved every single dish.

So many thanks to all my friends who have cheered me on and to editor, author and friend Carmen Callil, who started me off on this long road. And thanks once again to all the other knowledgeable and talented writers whose books have inspired me and whose names are in the Bibliography.

Lastly, my thanks to my publisher Catheryn Kilgarriff, without whom this book would not have been written.

Introduction

Experiencing the lively world of the pavement restaurant in South West France, where you listen to the laughter and watch the diners, you would be forgiven for thinking that the locals are loud. They are explosive! Even their names are explosive. Berasategui, Arbalaitz, Arzak, Eneko Atxa (four top Basque chefs), Xirikadis, Urraca, Darroze, Ramounada (four top Gascon chefs). Everyone likes to talk, shout to the next table or across the street, bring in another chair, another pushchair; they epitomise an enviable, full on, cheerful, friendly enjoyment of life and, hard to define, something Edmond Rostand called, in his classic Gascon play Cyrano de Bergerac, *panache.*[1]*

As we find out in Rostand's play, Cyrano and his cadets had plenty of *panache;* we also discover that food is very, very important to Gascons and today, 120 years on, the South West of France has some of the finest food and the most outstanding restaurants in the world. There are 25 starred restaurants in Gascony, 37 in the Pays Basque - the highest concentration of Michelin stars per capita in the world. One, La Tupina in Bordeaux, matches exactly the description from the opening scene in Act Two of *Cyrano de Bergerac* which takes place in Ragueneau's bakery.

> "*In the middle of the shop an iron hoop hangs from the ceiling. It can be drawn up and down; game hangs from it. The ovens in the shadow of the stairs glow red, The copper pans shine. The spits are turning. Heaps of food piled pyramidally. Hams hanging. Bustle and scurry…*"

La Tupina, whose motto is "*between the kitchen garden and the fireplace*", is a gem, with chickens cooking on spits in front of a wood fire, fish from the Gironde, including local caviar, and counters piled with the

---

1 *Panache in its primary sense means a plume of feathers on a helmet, but in its figurative sense is display, swagger, verve, but also a grace.*

very biggest spring asparagus, tomatoes or, in autumn, fresh ceps. It represents to me a certain local trait of generosity.

This is the South, as far South as the Mediterranean coast: Bordeaux is level with Valence, both on the latitude where the true Midi begins; Biarritz is, surprisingly, further South than Nice and the French Riviera. But the climate, although summers are very hot, is softer than the Mediterranean, governed by the weather coming off the sea and the mountains, the Atlantic Ocean and the Pyrenees, halcyon in summer, with plenty of sunshine, but also copious rains and, except for the high mountains, rather mild winters. The produce and the cooking are based on the fortunate coming together of that Atlantic climate, the influence of those mountains with their warm South wind, the splendid large rivers, and the immense fertility of the Garonne valley and the Béarn with its happy seasons.

This book is about the food and cooking of South West France, but I am also including some aspects of Spanish Basque cooking in my book, since the two parts of the Basque country, French and Spanish, sharing a language of their own, are really one nation and have been so since before history began. I also find a symbiotic relationship between the French *Maître Cuisiniers* and the renowned chefs of Euskalda (the Basque Country) who openly acknowledge that some thirty years ago, at the start of their mission to improve the status of Basque food - when twelve chefs formed a group, agreeing to share every idea and invention, and deliberately set out to create a new style of Basque cooking - they were enthused by the ideas of the French Nouvelle Cuisine, a movement co-founded and nurtured by Gascony's favourite chef, Michel Gúerard of Eugénie-les-Bains.

This approach worked brilliantly, although they confess there were some failures - for example they tried to introduce cooking with lots of butter and cream, but people did not like it and still don't. These chefs felt that what the French chefs were doing - freshening, lightening and innovating traditional cuisine, introducing new techniques, combinations and ingredients, turning themselves into celebrities - could easily be reproduced and even improved upon, in the Basque Country. They succeeded beyond their expectations and they consider their success is due more to their ability to work together, sharing everything, and to their invention of Basque Nouvelle Cuisine, than to traditional dishes. However they emphasize that it is important to bear in mind that modern and classic cuisine are one and the same - cooperation and continuity, a very Basque point of view.

One thing chefs and home cooks in Gascony and Basqueland always insist upon is good, fresh, seasonal local ingredients, and the South West, with its warm, temperate, sunny-but-showery Atlantic climate, is the place for the best of everything. The food they cook can be summed up as vibrant, and to get the appetite going, many offer counters packed with irresistible tapas and pinchos, each one a powerful miniature taste-explosion, and an inviting ham or several hams, hanging from the ceiling, ready to be sliced. This is the breadbasket of France and country dwellers here are proud to be producers, supplying the finest asparagus, tomatoes, prunes, and fruits. Along the 200 km of coast, fishing boats still go out daily, although in decreasing numbers, and many families are working the oyster farms of the salty Arcachon Basin, and running oyster shacks, where you can taste the freshest oysters by the blue lagoon. The best free range poultry, grass fed beef, acorn fed pork, hams, charcuterie and cheeses are produced here to inspire home cooks at the daily markets and to satisfy the exacting standards of the chefs.

It is not hard to be enthusiastic about a recent taste amongst cooks, chefs, food journalists, restaurant critics, lunchers and diners for strong, vibrant, challenging flavours - for acidic or vinegary notes, a hit of smoke from grilling over wood, fermented aged saltiness, fresh sourness, *umami* tanginess, briny anchovy fishiness, earthy beets and chard or bitter chicory, or grapefruits, or mineral notes from seaweed, samphire or kale, stingingly hot mustard, horseradish and pungent garlic, raw onion and shallots, powerful chilli heat - we love it all and bland, creamy and understated flavours are often essential, now, in helping to counterbalance the impact of some of these very powerful tastes.

Traditional French cooking avoided challenging or overwhelming the palate and looked for balanced, harmonious flavours that pleased the taste buds without scaring (or scarring) them. I was eating dinner with three star Burgundian chef Georges Blanc, when he had a fearful tantrum because he was served a Thai soup with chilli in it at Simon

Hopkinson's *Hilaire* Restaurant in London. *"Do you want to ruin my palate?'* he screamed. But in South West France, vibrant, heightened tastes have always been at the core of their cooking. Gascons and Basques love strong flavours: it's the only part of France where they traditionally use hot chillies in their food. They love smoke and grilling on vast grills, using different woods; they love rare meat, raw fish, grilled fish and salt fish - anchovies and salt cod, salted goose, duck, pork and sausages cooked in fat, extra deep-flavoured beef from very aged animals. They also love strong, salty sheep cheeses, cured foods of all kinds and very intense-flavoured charcuterie, which they serve with pickled chillies; they are master ham makers. They love salt - who else would put a salty piece of ham on top of a croûton spread with tangy, ultra-aged blue cheese or wrap a salty olive and a pickled chilli in a brined anchovy?

These well-liked, traditional local tastes come from the means of preserving foods, an age-old skill essential for survival. This was a regular job for women and girls in every household. They knew how to preserve with salt, with fermentation, with smoke, with air-drying or fire-drying on racks. They preserved *en confit* (salted and slow-cooked in pork or poultry fat), with alcohol, with sugar or in a pickle with vinegar, and by distillation. A short drive into the mountains from cosmopolitan Biarritz, it is easy to find many Basque women who continue to make superb artisan sheep's cheeses, an inherited occupation, and small co-operative charcuteries of the highest quality.

As in the rest of Europe, the family pig was, over the centuries, a lifesaver. Every single bit was eaten, including the ears, tails, guts, blood and feet: these still feature in soups and stews. Everyone knew how to make chorizo or dried saucisson, while the hams were hung up in a reasonably cool place, having been rubbed with hot pepper on the cut side to keep the flies away. This still imparts a delicious characteristic flavour to Bayonne hams. Because salt from Béarn was cheap and plentiful and the warm *foehn* wind on the French side of the Pyrenees creates a climate perfect for curing meats, this region became renowned for its charcuterie. Some of the unusual local combinations, such as shellfish with meat in rice dishes, also came originally from necessity. If what you had to feed your family was a couple of cabbages or a wild rabbit, a bit of chorizo or confit sausage and a few wild mushrooms, or perhaps a few small fish or snails, then they can be put together to make a potato laden soup, or a bean or rice dish. A local dish that crops up in the Médoc, Cap Ferret and in Arcachon is a surprising combination of hot and cold - burning hot *crépinettes,* (coarse little pork patties covered in pig's caul,) or little, sizzling chipolatas, served with icy cold oysters, a lovely contrast.

Kipling declared that he could detect two essential characteristics in the smell of a country; the type of wood that people burnt, and the condiments they used in the kitchen. In the Médoc, look out for the smell of game, especially pigeons, and for beefsteak and bone marrow cooking over vine prunings or vine stumps. In the Pyrenees look for spicy sausages, lamb cutlets and whole heads of garlic on glowing oak wood, or fish, generously salted, crisping over a vast grill. In the Basque country prawn whiskers are singed on a *plancha*, where the condiment is paprika or their own fierce red pepper, *piment d'Espelette,* often partnered with a simple sauce of olive oil pungent with slices of gently fried garlic. In the South West, a region as vivid in its food as it is in its landscape, after millions of years of cooking on wood, people have not given up on char grilling, which the Basques call *Erretegia*. Just about every household with an outdoor space has a barbecue. In some *Erretegia* restaurants the fire is played like a theatre organ, with grids that can be raised and lowered, grills shaped to hold different types of fish, special perforated pots with wide funnels for delicate foods, and various instruments for moving pieces of wood around. Smoking can be applied to butter, to chestnuts, to chorizo, to potatoes, to razor clams, to fresh shrimp, to almost anything at all.

In Extebarri, a now world-renowned restaurant in the village of Axpe in the Spanish Basque country, it is the essence of smoke that the inspirational figure behind this exciting food is looking for. Not too much actual, billowy smoke but intense aromas from the heart of the wood. Bittor Arginzoniz, the owner, chef and fanatic grill master, hates charcoal and the coarse flavour it gives. For him grilling over wood is an atavistic activity, one in which he can recover something intensely ingrained in human beings over millennia. He is correct - some European households did not achieve their first gas or electric stove until the 1970s - not even a tiny dot in the timetable of human history - and it has to be admitted that although it would now be hard to go back, the price we paid was the loss of a certain flavour. Cooking with fire is also, for Bittor, about the logs - he uses vine stumps, orange wood, olive or oak and differentiates their flavours.

"For me it is the most natural form of cooking there is," he says. *"And it has the greatest potential to improve the flavour of any ingredient".*

If you want the best results for your outdoor grill, forget charcoal from the supermarket, or even worse, the compressed nuts from commercial packs or - *quelle horreur* - gas bombs, only acceptable under a *plancha,* Spanish style. If you can, always cook over hardwood. It takes longer but if you can do it, it is worth it for the flavour.

The *plancha* is another Spanish influenced institution. According to Basques it should be a massive iron plate, heated from below. They do not agree that a portable one on top of the cooker will do. Slightly inclined, it has a cup to collect the fat, and is a brilliant way of flash-cooking lots of small pieces of food very fast for a very short time, so they retain all their juices. It is perfect for small fish such as red mullet, squid, prawns, mussels, scallops, sliced aubergines, artichokes, mushrooms - anything that can be cooked quickly, even *foie gras*. Yes, fresh *foie gras*, fattened goose liver, is an unavoidable item on every menu. Here there is no ban, it is a favourite local food and people eat it without a pang, in fact it is a trigger for feeling special and having fun. In the South West, people are having lots of fun wherever you go, whether it's Bordeaux or Cap Ferret, the lush Dordogne valley or the high Pyrenees, the unspoiled villages of the Basque country, or the heart of Gascony, the Guyenne, and they really are enjoying themselves completely, even if all they are doing is swopping recipes with a neighbour or buying a few leeks or downing a few oysters and that glass of white wine on the way home from work. In places, particularly by the sea, there will also be tourists having fun, but apart from the surfers this stunning coast remains very much a French travel destination, although there are always some sturdy foreign hikers and cyclists getting ready to explore the Pyrenees.

But travelling in South West France for entertainment (casinos, golf, tennis and hunting) and health (sea bathing at Biarritz and taking the waters in the Pyrenees) has at times been very fashionable. In the nineteenth and first half of the twentieth century Biarritz was made fashionable by Napoleon III and his wife Eugénie, and became the place to go for well-connected people, particularly Russian and British, including, at the peak of its popularity, their Royal families. Queen Victoria, Edward VII and even the Czar and his entourage loved to get together in Biarritz. The fashion was to journey South, perambulating through Bordeaux, the Médoc, les Landes and Gascony, the Pays Basque and the Pyrenees. Notable amongst all the travellers were several writers who jotted down their impressions as, travelling by coach and horses, they discovered the Midi for the first time. Their impressions were fresh, as this journey South was a novelty - and not an easy voyage.

The roads were often very bad, which lengthened the journey interminably. According to the poet, Théophile Gautier, the travellers in his coach, having run out of biscuits and chocolate, started to feel as if they were on the raft of the Medusa, and were ready to eat their breeches, the soles of their boots and their top hats. When the passengers finally arrived at the coaching-stop in Bordeaux, there were abundant inns and throngs of pushy hotel porters, grabbing at legs and coat tails and shouting insults about rival establishments. *"Monsieur they never clean their pans!" "They cook with lard!" "They will rob you!"* And there were desperate dining rooms. In 1838 Stendhal found:

> *"A fairly good dinner and fairly good company in the hotel I was staying in; but this dinner, which started at quarter past five, took place in a vast room on the ground floor, black, without light, low ceilinged and such a sad room as does not exist anywhere in Geneva probably, and we are in Bordeaux, the centre of Gascon vivacity, and more méridionale than Valence."*

But he still decided *"Bordeaux is, without contradiction, the most beautiful town in France"*. At Lesparre, the former capital of bas-Médoc, he ate at the Lion d'Or, which I find is still there. He asked for something to eat and the wife of the patron replied

"Nous vous donnerons Monsieur, un morceau de confit - at this word I trembled". (my guess is that he thought it was jam) *"Monsieur c'est du canard confit"*. *"The little dinner was exquisite, composed as it was strictly*

of a leg of duck confit and rather few potatoes. I asked for lots more".

It seems people did not over eat. He stated that in the whole of Bordeaux he saw only one fat person, unlike Paris where people's noses disappeared in rolls of fat. He made several unfavourable remarks about Paris, which was stiff, proud and affected in comparison. However the German philosopher Schopenhauer, who came to stay in Bordeaux with his parents in 1804 aged 15, was taken to a crowded ball and was appalled to note that people of Bordeaux had a characteristic smell, *'very disagreeable to a foreigner':* they all, even in elegant, very well dressed society, stank strongly of garlic. In spite of bad roads, dark rooms, small portions and bad smells, the writers' journals show their liking of beautiful Bordeaux, and their affection for the warmth and relaxed attitude of the dazzling South. Stendhal loved the Bordelais, particularly the finesse of the women with their lovely eye lashes and lack of affectation, and remarked:

> *"The good-sense Bordelais do not get worked up about anything except to be in a state that will give them the means to lead a joyful life. 'Joyeuse Vie'."*

Flaubert was beguiled by the children. *"As young children, still new and unselfconscious* (peu modest*) the effect is charming with their white bonnets. Their intelligent gaiety is very pleasing."* Bordeaux, he says, is *"magnificent and gay, people only think of amusing themselves".*

Crossing les Landes on his voyage to Spain in 1840, with his friend Eugène Piot, Théophile Gautier was less than enthusiastic*:*

> *"One comes across the first of les Landes; these are immense sweeps of grey, violet and blueish earth, with more or less noticeable undulations. A short sparse moss, some russet coloured heather and stunted broom, are the only vegetation. It has the sadness of the Egyptian Thébiade, and at any minute you expect to see a file of dromedaries and camels; you cannot imagine that man has ever been here…"*

Nobel Prize winning author François Mauriac lived, as a youngish man, in his family house Malagar, near Saint Méxant, Gironde; he adored the valley of the Garonne, which, he said, *"spread out its riches in an excess of light"*. In 1924 he writes to a friend about *"the ravishing beauty of the end of Spring"*. And later of *"the strange sweetness of Autumn, which perfuses, saturates and penetrates the landscape"*. In 1926 he was eating interminable meals in Arcachon where his children would fall asleep between the turbot and the roast and he describes the beaches as *"swarming with naked bodies like the banks of Ganges. This generation knows how to live without clothes, the children and adolescents play ball clad only in suntan."*

Like us, when we go South, most voyagers were seduced not only by the landscape but by the people as Henry James, aged 24, was, by the Basques:

"Strong and brown, such as I have seen many times in Biarritz, with their soft round haircut, their white espadrilles and their air of fulfilling a pledge. One has never seen a race so tough, so enduring."

Although the Biarritz of Henry James, of Coco Chanel and Charlie Chaplin is long gone and today, Biarritz is no longer loved by the smart set, it remains a gay, sunny little place with amazing beaches and Bordeaux is still the most beautiful town in France. The Gascon spirit and the enduring quality of the Basque, even after terrible persecution by Franco, lives on, and they have indeed renewed themselves. And throughout the South West, the Médoc, Gascony and the Basque country, you still find people concentrating on enjoying themselves, and eating and drinking are a very great part of the enjoyment. The food they enjoy, and the way they cook it, is the subject of this book.

Chapter One

The Taste of South West France

SEA AND MOUNTAINS

The food is good, the drink flows free
At lunchtime, suppertime and tea.
Its true without a doubt, I swear
No earthly country can compare;
Under heaven no land but this
Has such abundant joy and bliss.
(The land of Cockaygne, 1330s, anonymous)

The South West of France, bordered by the flawless, sandy beaches of the Atlantic, runs South from the vast Gironde estuary, the valley of the Garonne bathed in light and the dramatic Dordogne, winding through limestone cliffs. After les Landes – many hundreds of kilometres of pine woods, grey sand and heather – it ends in those high mountains, the Pyrenees. This is all Aquitaine and it encompasses the

Médoc, the Dordogne, the Agenais and Lot-et-Garonne, les Landes, the Pays Basque and the Béarn.

Wherever there are river valleys there are vegetables and fruits, and wherever there are mountains there are cheeses and hams. *Terroir* is the secret of this and *terroir* is the lovely evocative word that describes the special flavours and qualities that come uniquely and specifically from the matrix of local conditions.

Character comes from the breeze blowing off the Atlantic which gives the Basque wine Txacoli its fresh, salty tang; the South wind called a *foehn* from the Pyrenees that helps dry and cure the air-dried hams of the mountains, the oak and pine trees that grow in the grey sands of les Landes that are favourable to ceps and all kinds of wild mushrooms, the moisture-holding properties of deep river valley soil in the Garonne valley that makes it perfect for growing melons and tomatoes, the way that water runs straight through limestone in Périgord, providing ideal conditions for the truffle.

In one area of the Pyrenees a liquorice plant, *herbe réglisse*, grows abundantly in the high pastures and gives a special flavour to the milk of the sheep that graze there – this in turn flavours the Ossau Iraty cheese, while on the Atlantic side of the Pyrenees the cheesemakers use alder wood – which grows freely by their mountain streams – to give an unusually subtle flavour of smoke to their sheep's cheeses.

Each area has its own unique breed of animals, poultry, special means of preserving fish or pork, unusual dairy products, vegetables, and fruit and each has a unique flavour that comes from the very land itself, in all of its aspects.

Until recently, people had forgotten a good deal about the importance of their local specialities, and in particular their breeds of cows, sheep and pigs, their local tomatoes or plums. But when cheap pork imported from Brittany and goodness knows where else, flooded the ham industry in Bayonne, many people became alarmed.

Rare old local breeds suddenly gained a new respect and their unique strengths were appreciated again. Many were saved from the brink; *pie noir* (black and white) pigs, *Gascon porc noir* (black pigs) and brindled Bazas beef cattle were almost gone; to lose these marvellous animals, bred to thrive in local conditions, would have been a tragedy. Now people take pride in their local species and in the way they are reared, and cherish old indigenous varieties of fruit trees and vegetables.

There are fêtes and festivals to celebrate these cattle, pigs, cheeses, asparagus, peppers, garlic or plums. In this chapter (and throughout the book), I have tried to describe just some of the extraordinary, beautiful and unique foods that are a true reflection of the *terroirs* of the South West.

CHEESE

La transhumance is the romantic tradition of herdsmen leading their beasts, decorated with jingling bells, up to the mountain pastures of the Pyrenees for the summer. It may sound archaic, but it still continues, many still go on foot, and at the last count there were still *transhumeurs* (seasonal movers of livestock) on 300,000 hectares of the Haute Pyrénées on the French side, more on the Spanish side.

In mid-June, as the lowland pastures of the Béarn and the Pays Basque dry up in the heat, herdsmen and shepherds take up 35,000 cows, 120,000 sheep, a few goats and 2,300 horses.

The shepherds and cowmen are happy to go up in June, when the South Wind suddenly starts to blow and the snow begins to melt, and just as happy to come down in September when the evenings draw in.

In the past, the shepherds lived up in the mountain pastures throughout the summer, in groups of stone cabins, called *cayolars,* in which the men, whose job it was to milk the sheep twice a day, slept, cooked, ate and drank and made cheeses. In the Béarn, some two hundred still follow the tradition.

The cheeses, mostly large wheels or cylinders called *Tommes,* can be made of sheep's milk or cow's milk or a mixture of the two – the flowers and herbs of the mountains give fragrance to the milk.

The men have a community system called the *tchotch*, agreed on over a glass or two in the inn the night before the departure, which includes taking turns to keep watch for predators such as bears (there are still a few dozen roaming the mountains).

Some of these shepherds still spend summer in their stone dwellings, milking and making cheeses, although they may now have microwaves to cook their dinner, electric milking parlours and computers to keep tabs on their straying sheep and lambs, by means of a device clipped onto the sheep's ears.

Some of the living cabins may also provide a refuge for walkers and climbers.

But today many farmers drive up to the high pastures to milk and check over the sheep during the day and then shut them into pens, sending the milk to the cheese makers in chilled vans and getting back to the comfort of home at night.

When the sheep come down at the end of the summer, the ewes start to have their lambs, the custom is then to butcher the lambs between 15th December and 1st March. The ewes, bedded on dried bracken, continue to produce milk and once the young milk-fed lambs have gone, are milked twice a day; much of the milk from the ewes goes to a farm dairy, to the Roquefort cheesemakers or to local cheesemakers.

Ossau Iraty, Fromage d'Estive, Tomme d'Estive

In three valleys of the Béarn mountains, Aspe, Barétous and Ossau, the Ossau Iraty cheese is made.

This Basque sheep's milk cheese has a long history, one that predates Christianity, and it was mentioned by the Roman writer Martial in the first century, by which time it was already well known.

Traditionally, it is made from the rich milk of just two breeds of sheep. The animals of choice are the Basco-Béarnaise and the Red-faced or Black-faced Manech sheep, with curling horns, bred to thrive in the mountains, and to give large quantities of particularly rich milk which is ideal for cheese making. In the high Iraty forest area, where they stay for the summer months, pastures are rich with wild flowers, wild thyme and a type of liquorice plant, *herbe réglisse*, and the cheese is subtly charged with their fragrance; it has a beautiful nutty and herby flavour.

Ossau Iraty has been given an *aoc*. It can only be made from milk from the area of the Ossau river valleys in Béarn, where the sheep overwinter, and the highlands and forests of Iraty in the summer.

The best cheeses are made between June and September when the grass is at its richest.

The pressed, hard cheeses are matured for at least 60 days; they are drum-shaped, weighing from 2 kilos (4½ pounds) up to 7 kilos (15½ pounds). Buttery but firm, they are eaten in every possible way, and are the favourite 'farmer's dessert', served with black cherry jam or quince cheese, or with walnuts and hazelnuts. It is a *'fromage de garde'* which means cheese that will keep in perfect condition over the winter, necessary in this region to feed the mountain villages cut off by snow. This cheese is long-matured.

Keep it wrapped in cling film or a damp cloth in a cold place, and remove it from the refrigerator an hour before serving.

Look for the label Fromage de Brébis Agour; this dairy makes prize winning cheeses.

Ardi Gasna

If you drive south from the coast at St Jean de Luz, you are soon in the green foothills of the Pyrenees, and you are bound to see signs saying 'Ardi Gasna' which means sheep's milk cheese.

Follow these, and you will come to remote farms where the fences are made of huge slabs of stone that remind one of Asterix.

In one quite large farm, I found a charming schoolgirl, with black hair and dark eyes. She showed me the dairy where the sheep's cheeses are made. It is she who gets up early in the morning to milk the family's flock of sheep before she goes off to school. When she comes home she milks them again and she makes the cheeses. They are small wheels of a delicate and flowery flavour, perfectly delicious and just the cheese to eat in thin slices with home made black cherry jam, which is also made on the farm. By the way, not surprisingly, she does not like cheese.

Pur Brebis de l'Abbaye de Belloc

Made by Benedictine monks since the seventeenth century at the Abbey of Belloc and Urt, in the French Basque mountains, this fabulous cheese is one of the great Pyrenean ewe's cheeses. The high meadows, close to the Atlantic, and under its influence, are always green and ideal for pasturing milking sheep. The texture of the cheese, which comes in large wheels, is smooth and supple, and the flavour is described variously as nutty, fruity and with a taste of caramelised brown sugar.

Cabrit des Pyrénées

Made from the milk of an ancient and very imposing race of goats, (the Billy goats are majestic with massive curling horns) is *la chèvre des Pyrénées*. The nannies are rustic and shaggy, and produce milk that is rich and gives a taste of flowers to the creamy white cheeses.

Chaumes

Although this cow's milk cheese has been made in Périgord, East of Bordeaux, for less than 50 years, it is said to be similar in style to the Monastery cheeses made by Trappist monks throughout Europe since the Middle Ages. It is firm but supple, rich and creamy with a flavour of hazelnuts. It is also a good melting cheese.

Idiazábal

Another Basque raw sheep's milk cheese, Idiazábal is made by sheep farmers and shepherds in the high pastures, some 60 miles south of San Sebastian. Their large flocks of shaggy Latxa sheep are pastured all summer on the Spanish side of the Pyrenees in the highlands known as Goierri. Many of the artisan cheesemakers smoke their cheeses over alder wood, which gives a much finer flavour than the usual commercial smoked cheese.

Roncal Cheese

If you like strong cheese, this is for you, a whole milk, unpasteurised mountain cheese, made in the Roncal valley in north Navarre, on the Spanish side of the Pyrenees, by small farmers, from December to July. Made mainly with the milk of Latxa sheep, it comes in cylinders of up to 3½ kilos (8 pounds). It has a strong, piquant, spicy flavour and is good served with walnuts and a glass of wine.

Cabécou de Périgord - Cabécous

These are the small white goat's cheeses of Périgord.

Always and only made by hand, they have the flavour of meadows. The goats are allowed to forage at large in the stony hills and find all sorts of wild herbs to eat there, including a type of mint and wild marjoram. It is a creamy cheese that melts in the mouth – available all year round, it is particularly good for cooking when young. Eat it hot on a piece of toast with a splash of olive oil. Some people rub the toast with garlic or spread it with jam.

La Compostelle or *Fromage Compostela*

An outstanding deep-flavoured, creamy goat's cheese with a slight kick. One of many strong little goat's cheeses made on the Causses of the Lot, near the spectacular vertical village of Rocamadour from May onwards. The fromagerie is near the Pilgrim's Way to Compostella, hence the scallop shell impression on the top. The flavour is subtle, as the well-fed goats are either out in the pastures eating wild marjoram, mint and tough little grasses, or inside eating dried peas, barley and locally made hay.

Bleu des Basques

This is a rather successful mountain cheese of rich, unpasteurised ewe's milk introduced recently by a young cooperative, high in the Pyrenees. It has a hard rind and a creamy interior with greeny-blue veins. The flavour is creamy, earthy and salty. Accompany it with a sweet white wine such as Sauternes and fresh figs.

Cochonaille
Everything in the pig is good

Andouille Béarnaise

If you like the taste of garlic sausage, pepper and tripe, then you will like this. Milder than most *andouille* or *andouillette* and quite succulent, it is made with pork chitterlings, cut in strips and salted in a mixture of salt, pepper and garlic for four days, then stuffed into casings and hung up to dry. The air drying process is similar to the drying of Bayonne hams. The *andouille* was traditionally eaten at the annual pig killing – *pèle-porc* – after maturing for a year. It can be eaten sliced, like salami or cooked. Fry thick slices with a shallot for one minute. Mix cream and mustard together and stir into the pan, cover and cook for 5 minutes.

Salade de Museau

Fromage de tête, a jellied terrine of pig's tongue, cheek and ears, is sliced thinly and then into little pieces the size of large postage stamps. These are mixed with thinly sliced gherkins, finely chopped onions or shallot, pepper, oil and vinegar.

Hure is similar to *fromage de tête* but usually made with wild boar.

Gratton de Lormont

Well liked throughout the Gironde, this *gratton* is nothing like the normal, crunchy *grattons* or scratchings made of skin and tissue with the fat rendered out. It is more like a *jambon persillée*, and is made with pork shoulder, back fat and throat meat, cooked with white wine, garlic, black pepper, nutmeg, cloves and bay leaves. It is eaten sliced.

Grillons d'Oie, Grillons de Canard

A speciality from Périgord, *grillons* are made with shredded, long cooked duck or goose and the fat and remnants of tissue in which they were cooked, mashed together to make a rough spread for a *tartine* (slice of bread or toast) and are similar to rillettes.

Galabard or *Boudin Béarnais*

This not a blood sausage, it is a hot spicy sausage with some blood in it, together with pig's head and offal, especially the tongue, heart, lungs and teats. These meats are simmered until soft and then chopped and mixed with lightly sautéed onions and leeks, lots of chilli powder and flakes, salt and enough blood to bind and colour the mixture. It is then stuffed into intestines and tied with string. The sausages are simmered gently at 87 – 90°C.

Grill this splendid sausage over a wood fire, or slice and fry it, and serve it with fried apples and mashed potatoes.

Alan Davidson enjoyed a Basque version of the Galabard describing it as, 'A huge black pudding with tiny pig's tongues embedded in it. Sliced it gives the impression of two pink eyes staring out of a round black face.'

The Boudin Landais is a pure black pudding, flavoured with hot chilli and stuffed into a large intestine, hence its impressive size and irregular shape.

Boudin de Burgos

This is the best of black puddings, a speciality from Northern Spain, extremely tender, speckled with rice, flavoured with cumin, paprika and pepper and air dried. Use it in cooking or fry in slices and put it on pieces of toast for tapas, perhaps with a fried quail's egg on top.

Bayonne Ham

Jambon de Bayonne is probably the most famous product of all Basque charcuterie, if not the best. It is an example of how *terroir* affects the ways in which man conspires with nature. Salt is necessary to preserve meat and preserved meat was essential for winter survival, before refrigeration and deep-freezing were available to everyone.

Without local salt, the ham industry would never have become what it is. Sel de Bayonne came from Mouguerre, by the river Adour, and salt was mined there until 2010. Very white rock salt also came from Briscous, a village about 15 kilometres from Bayonne. Fossil salt from Saliés, a bit further away, in the Béarn, is also used. More about Saliés in a minute (see page 33).

Most Bayonne ham is made outside Bayonne, but there is one artisan, Pierre Ibaïalde, making good ham at his *saloir* right in the heart of the old city.

He uses the dry-mined salt from the deep mines of Saliés de Béarn and mixes it with sweet paprika, pepper and vinegar. It is said that this cure combined with the warm, strong *foehn* give the characteristic Bayonne flavour. The *foehn* is a wind that flows down the sheltered Northern, French, side of the Pyrenees making it warmer by some degrees than the windward Spanish side. The puzzle is to see how the *vent* gets into the temperature controlled curing rooms at all.

The sizeable hams and shoulders of pork are massaged daily with handfuls of the salt mixture and left on wooden shelves for 12 days in a humid salting room (100% humidity) kept at a temperature of 2°C (35°F). The hams are pressed by hand to squeeze out any blood.

They are then hung up in rows, in a curing room and kept there to air-dry for 9 months (at 60% humidity) and next the cut side is rubbed with a mixture of flour, black pepper, and pork fat, to protect it and the hams are hung in a drying chamber for 3 months. Finally they are boned and pressed for 2 – 3 days and the cut side is scraped clean and powdered with *piment d'Espelette* to keep off the flies. During this year of curing, they shrink from 12 kilos (26½ pounds) down to 8 kilos (17½ pounds). They will keep well, but toughen as they age. If offered a slice of aged ham that has become dry, sprinkle it with olive oil.

According to a Gault et Millau *'Guide Gourmande de France'*, Bayonne ham was sometimes cooked whole and then cut in slices almost as thick as a beef steak; even raw ham was cut into much thicker slices (hard to cut it thin by hand) and you needed good teeth. Nowadays it is cut paper thin.

For most of the twentieth century across the South West, *jambon crû*, which is served at every opportunity in every restaurant throughout

Aquitaine, was mostly hard, dry and salty, and very inferior to Parma ham.

Disappointingly, the famous Bayonne ham is still mostly made from pigs reared in Normandy, but things are changing.

Ibaiama Ham

In the 1980s, a group of pig farmers and charcutiers decided to get together and return to the traditional Basque way of rearing pigs, and old ways of making ham; the result is intensely flavoured ham, dark ruby in colour with copious amounts of really delicious, soft fat.

The pigs, some of them the indigenous old Basque black-foot breed, are kept outside on the mountain slopes, where they share their woods and meadows with milking sheep, ponies and cows.

Here, in the Autumn, they forage for acorns, beech mast and chestnuts, which give the meat good fat and a characteristic, deep flavour. They are also fattened far longer than normal, eating only organic foods; all these pigs must be reared in the Pays Basque.

The hams are aged for 15 – 20 months.

The result is silky, velvety ham, and richly flavoured charcuterie, well-marbled with fat, delicate and juicy. They make traditional *saucisson sec, chorizo, txirula de porc* (a long thin hot salami) and *lomo*, (cured loin) from their beautiful pigs.

Eric Ospital, who, with Christian Etchebert, has written a useful book called *Tout Est Bon Dans le Cochon*, was one of these entrepreneurs. He has a magnificent charcuterie in Hasparren, high in the Pyrenees, where he sells their wonderful Ibaiona or Ibaiama ham.

And in the large and airy room where his hams hang to mature – a visitor will see that they are marked with the names of all the smartest restaurants in Paris, plus the Elysée Palace.

Kintoa Ham

Another branch of Basque pig farmers is the collective who make Kintoa ham. The Kintoa was the tax of one in five pigs which once had to be given to the king from every herd.

Kintoa pigs are reared in Les Aldudes in the hills of the Pyrenees, a lush farming commune, half French and half tied to Spain, where 20 pig breeders have revived an ancient, almost extinct race of Basque pigs.

In the Autumn, towards the end of the fattening, the pigs are sent to graze in the high meadows and forage under the oak, chestnut and beech trees.

I visited a farm in les Aldudes rearing the old Basque black and white Pie Noir pigs (not the same as Spanish *patta negra* – black feet – *pie* means magpie and also black and white or piebald). The sows were lolling under the apple trees with their piglets, while older pigs were to be seen trotting high on the mountain slopes; 30% of what the pigs eat comes from foraging.

This diet and the fact that the pigs are allowed to get big and fat, and are not slaughtered until over a year old, gives a characteristic deep flavour, softer more delicious fat, juicier meat and a deeper red colour.

Look for Basque Kintoa ham; Patriana import these hams from Pierre Oteiza.

Baïgorri Ham

At St. Étienne de Baigorri nearby, the hams from *pie noir* pigs are dry cured with salt from the Adour gemme (fossil) salt works, rubbed lavishly with paprika and dried, hanging in temperature controlled sheds for the first six months and then traditionally, in draughty wooden lofts, with the warm *foehn* wind from the South and the Atlantic breezes from the North whistling through (these have mostly given way to temperature and humidity controlled sheds).

They mature altogether for a minimum of 16 months.

By now the hams have developed a beautiful, tender, velvety feel and a sweet flavour of caramelised hazelnuts and spice; such hams are true rivals to the Pata Negra Iberico hams of Spain.

Copeaux de Jambon

In Les Halles de Biarritz you can choose from a range of wonderful hams and take home a box of very thin, delicate shavings of ham cut in *copeaux*, (about ⅓ of a slice). You can choose dark Pie Noir ham or pink Bayonne ham and the skilled *charcutière* will slice it for you. To serve, buy a *ficelle* (thin breadstick). Cut it in half and pile the lower half with *copeaux* of ham. Put the top back on, cut into four and serve as a heavenly breakfast or lunch or, very important, just spread out the ham on a board or a slate as tapas.

Lomo

Served hot or cold, *lomo* is salt cured loin of pork with a paprika and olive oil mix on the outside (to make it see page 235) – try it with salsa de piquillos.

Cecina

Cecina is meat cured with salt and air-dried, much like ham, but not made with pork – it can be made with beef, with goat or mutton or with donkey, mule or horsemeat.

Grenier Médoquin

A sausage made with pork chitterlings, seasoned with an unprecedented amount of spice, garlic and pepper, compressed into a natural skin (more intestines) and then cooked in broth, this is *saucisson* with a 'burning soul'. It is served thinly sliced, either by itself or with other local charcuterie and a glass of red Médoc.

Locals feel it is ready to be discovered by the world, and recently I saw it offered up in Pau with a little floral salad. Crimped tripe sausage scattered with little blue pansies and pink prawns – who could resist?

L'Assiette Ibérique

A slate or wooden board for two or more people to share, on which are arranged some or all of the following, in thin overlapping slices:

Chorizo, jambon de Bayonne or other local ham, sheep's cheese, a slice of Pâte Basque, which is a coarse pâté seasoned with hot red pepper. There will be pickled guindillo peppers or gherkins, good bread and possibly some radishes to accompany it.

Saffron and Yellow Powders

Paëlla, chick peas, mussels, potatoes, tripe, fish soups, aïoli, all get a new vibrancy with the addition of saffron. The warm, velvety flavour and singing yellow colour add a certain class to any dish. But it takes 20,000 of the stigmata of the crocus plant *crocus sativa* to get 125 grams (4½ ounces) of the spice and each one has to be gathered by hand; consequently this spice is always regarded as precious.

In the fourteenth century, saffron was much prized and the price became terrifically high, encouraging a trade in false saffron, '*safran bastard*'. This was so severely frowned upon that the penalty for this passing off, if you were caught, was death.

Today, whether in stamen form or powder, saffron is still prohibitively expensive.

However there are substitutes which are much cheaper. I find they work quite well; they are quite different but they taste good and give a beautiful colour.

Spigol, invented by Spaniard Anton Espig in 1876, and made in France, contains 3% saffron plus turmeric, sweet paprika, unnamed spices and salt. Traditionally an edible yellow dye E102 – E124 is included but a new version has only natural ingredients.

Spigol gives a bright and beautiful yellow colour and adds spice and perfume to rice, potatoes, paella, chicken or fish. You can put it in aïoli and mayonnaise and in all kinds of fish and shellfish soups.

La Dalia is specifically meant for making paëlla but can be used in any other dishes where saffron might be used except mayonnaise and aïoli or other uncooked dishes.

Made in Spain since 1913, La Dalia also contains saffron, (but only 1%), paprika, cornflour and other spices, and yellow colourings, E102 – E110.

SALT

Salt is the white gold mined from the earth beneath the Adour valley.

It has an ancient history; salt has been mined here for more than 3,000 years and has been a commodity since the Middle Ages, when a salt tax was imposed; it is essential to the salting of cod and the curing of Bayonne ham, charcuterie, anchovies, tuna and sardines.

300 million years ago, this valley was under the ocean; as it retreated it left an enormous salt pan. This was then covered and the salt remains there, in some places as much as quarter of a mile underground, fresh and unpolluted.

Rock salt – *sel gemme* – has always been precious, since it can be used to preserve food for the winter when fresh food is scarce, an essential technique before refrigeration.

There are also naturally saline waters ten times saltier than sea water, springing up at Saliés-de-Béarn near Pau. A legend tells us that a wild boar, escaping from Gaston Phoebus, fourteenth century Count of Foix and author of *Livre de Chasse (Book of the Hunt),* fell into a spring at Saliés de Béarn and was found months later in a state of perfect preservation, hence the salting of hams began.

The history of Saliés was shaped by salt – for centuries salt water ruled the waking hours of the inhabitants; at set intervals the *tiradous* (drawers) would draw salt water from an open air pool in the centre of the town and run through the town, emptying their wooden buckets into troughs placed outside the salt makers sheds. Today, at the annual Festival in September, there are races for women, running as fast as they can with big wooden buckets of salt on their heads. The salt made here is vital for the local trades of brining and preserving meat and fish and in fact must be included in the making of Bayonne ham.

FAT

The Cooking Medium of the South West

The fact is that animal fats were the main cooking medium of the whole South West over the centuries.

Ham fat, bacon fat and pork fat were popular in the Pyrenees for most dishes, while in Gascony and les Landes, goose and duck fat were the favourites. In Périgueux and the Lot it was again pork fat and goose fat. Not olive oil - although this is the Midi, it is not the Mediterranean and winters here are too tough for olive trees.

However they do have local oils that they often prefer today, to replace the traditional animal fats, which although healthy and natural, can sometimes be heavy.

Now cooking is mainly done with large quantities of sunflower oil, and of course corn oil. For salads, there are walnut and hazelnut oils.

But in the Pays Basque and now along the West Coast, the easy connection with Spain means that olive oil has long been an everyday commodity; a real taste for it has developed and it is much in use for cooking too.

THE TASTE OF THE VINE COUNTRY

The banks of the Gironde – croaking frogs in green meadows, a golden brown river glowing with light, misty grey sky. On the water, a dark huge ship. Three fishing cabins in blues or greys on stilts above the flood of water. Yellow vines behind.

This is the Médoc – every few hundred yards another château, all the familiar names flashing by, followed by neat rows of well-groomed vines. All the vine workers seem to congregate at a riverside restaurant, Le Port de la Grange at Parempuyre, happy with its no-frills, 'lets get this good food on the table' attitude and 13 euro menu.

It is packed with outdoor guys and they are eating piquillo peppers stuffed with brandade, followed by *lamelles d'encornets* (squid) or *lomo* (cured pork loin) served with, can it be cauliflower cheese? The desserts include *crumble de fruits*. Surely these are imports from Britain?

Quite a few of the châteaux, for example Château Loudenne, for a long time had English or Irish owners. The British were always lovers of good claret and the top châteaux have always entertained a great number of English buyers. Many have chefs in the kitchen who are trained to understand the importance of serving food which flatters and showcases the wine.

Over the years of serving this kind of food to potential wine buyers, wine journalists and other guests, bizarrely, some of the British or Irish recipes such as steak pie, le rosbif of course, cauliflower cheese, apple crumble – have deeply taken root.

I asked about this when I went to stay at Château Loudenne and my hostess explained that the best dishes may be rich but should be somewhat bland, free of strong flavours – no strong fiery red pepper, a top favourite taste further South, a mere hint of garlic, no vinegar or other acids, no astringent vegetables such as spinach or artichokes, shallots in preference to onions. Mashed potatoes, a local favourite, are very good!

For the fish course, you were allowed fresh sole, or the local white fish *maigre*, from the Gironde, plainly grilled and served with creamy cep-flavoured rice, the fresh ceps chopped very fine. The next day, I seem to remember, it was sea bass in a creamy sauce, also with mushrooms - morels or *champignons de Paris*.

For the main course, red meat such as fillet of beef *en croûte* or roast venison works well. Game such as partridge or pheasant is great, as is beef daube in a red wine sauce, roast veal, perhaps with carrots, and roast chicken with truffles. Pasta has been a favourite for over 100 years according to Christian Coulon and tagliatelle can be served with daubes or civets of wild boar or pigeon. No citrus fruits or eggs are allowed but cream and chocolate are both acceptable, as is cheese; with a big strong St Emilion serve a non-tannic, well ripened Chaumes, not a young cheese. With a sweet wine such as Sauternes serve salty Roquefort and choose nutty Ossau Iraty with a younger, lighter red.

La Plancha
A Whiff of Spanish Smoke
(or how to singe a prawn)

In the Pays Basque, ideas have always been shared readily across the borders because they can be explained and described in a shared language (Basque or Euskadi). When it comes to cooking, one great shared invention is undoubtedly *La Plancha*.

I first came across the *plancha*, and specifically *gambas alla plancha*, at a club called Madame Zozo's in Catalonia, a sixties scene of great euphoria, and have felt very romantic about the gadget ever since those heady days.

Often used outdoors, as there can be plenty of smoke, it can quickly cook large quantities of little things such as small squid, sliced octopus, *gambas* (prawns), that might slip through the bars of an open grill, kidneys, tiny lamb cutlets, sausages, sliced peppers or other vegetables and toasted *pain de campagne* can be moved around individually on a flat plate, but not in a wire sandwich grill.

Cooking on a *plancha*, it turns out, is pretty ubiquitous throughout Atlantic Spain; happily the French South West Atlantic coast has adopted the *plancha* too, and the smell of singeing prawn whiskers wanders at will in the streets of St Jean de Luz and Cap Ferret alike.

Originally a metal plate or griddle placed over a wood fire, on which food was grilled quickly in seconds, the *plancha*, now described as a flat top grill, eventually became a sophisticated gadget, a massive piece of equipment weighing a ton, consisting, basically, of a heated, slightly sloping metal hotplate on a stand.

The cook, provided with a metal scraper and a pair of tongs, flips small morsels of food over and then onto a dish, while larger pieces of meat or fish are drizzled from a bottle containing lemon juice and water or lemon juice and oil, and sprinkled liberally with fine salt beforehand or while they cook.

There is also a mixture called Xipister (pronounced chipister) which contains hot red pepper from Espelette, vinegar and various herbs and spices, plus a little olive oil (see recipe page 39). This can be sprinkled onto grilled fish, chicken, steaks and chops and anything cooked on a *plancha*.

If you want to do it the Basque way, according to the lady in the hardware shop by Biarritz covered market, you get a big, hefty one – no Basque worth his salt would use the small stove top *planchas* that she has on sale there – in fact she almost begged me not to buy one.

A good *plancha* has a bowl at one side into which the fat and juices flow, so these do not get wasted or burned. It is a very quick, easy, healthy way to cook; it uses little fat, just a brushing of olive oil, and the food cooks in its own juice.

According to Cedric Béchade of the classy, one star restaurant l'Auberge Basque, outside St Pée sur Nivelle, the *plancha* is 'un art de vivre', in fact he has written two books about it and he even uses it for cooking fruit. And there is hardly a popular restaurant in coastal Pays Basque that doesn't have *calamars* or *sardines à la plancha* on the menu.

If you want to improvise, use a metal grill plate with a handle, or even a large iron frying pan and place it, without fat, on a fire, a barbecue or even on the gas, but watch out for the smoke.

Let it get very hot.

Be prepared with tongs, a hot dish, and a bowl of olive oil and a brush – you can start with small squid, sardines, prawns in their shells and sliced vegetables such courgettes, peppers and aubergines; all easy to cook on the *plancha*. Brush the food lightly with olive oil, place it on the *plancha* and season with salt while it cooks. Turn the pieces individually with tongs. A squeeze of lemon finishes the cooking.

Chapter Two

Basic Sauces and Accompaniments

These recipes reflect some local tastes. As any visitor to the Atlantic coast, to Gascony or the Pays Basque, will know, certain flavours are omnipresent. One important one, which stands out, is the use of the tingling condiment, ground hot red peppers, the *piment d'Espelette*, made from special *aoc* chillies with just the perfect amount of bite; it is far superior to any normal chilli product and far more expensive. The plastic string of red peppers found in any local bistrot is mimicking the strings of real peppers that hang on the outside walls of the timbered red and white houses to dry in Espelette village.

Espelette pepper crops up in everything, including some of the following sauces, and even in bread, and it is definitely addictive. Basque men use it in large quantities without flinching. It can be bought online.

The nearest thing to it would be chilli flakes, cayenne pepper or hot paprika, all of which can be substituted, but do not always give that exactly perfect balance of heat and flavour.

Fresh red and, particularly, many varieties of green sweet peppers are superb in the region and are used all the time, you might say indiscriminately. They are eaten on their own fried in olive oil and sprinkled with salt as tapas, or roasted, or simmered with beef, lamb, chicken or pork, in mellow daubes. They also add their sweetness to the wonderful Sauce Basquaise, which is regularly served with meat or fish, with eggs and with ham.

When it comes to salads, dressings are often powerful, and cider vinegar which is a little stronger and a little deeper in flavour, can replace wine vinegar, while sherry vinegar, perfumed and mellow but with quite a strong buzz, adds character to a dressing or a sauce.

Many sauces are sharp and freshened up further with raw shallots, mustard, capers, or cornichons.

There are a number of Red and also Red and Green sauces, containing tomatoes and herbs, which add colour as well as flavour to popular dishes such as *Pot au Feu* and *Poule au Pot*.

Garlic is ubiquitous and is not used in small amounts, but in mighty quantities. The pink garlic of Lautrec, sweet, juicy, tender and long lasting, is the variety most favoured and after that, the stripey violet garlic of Cadours, hot, strong and sweet, from the Haute Garonne or white garlic from Lomagne, in Gascony. There are also the green leaves of wild garlic, which make a spicy tasting green oil used for enlivening soups.

Local pickles are simple and easy to make. Particularly good with cheese and with duck are pickled cherries, while as an accompaniment to charcuterie, pickled peppers are popular.

In this chapter, I have tried to capture a few of these local flavours and to describe sauces and condiments that help to give food and cooking that particularly smack of the South West.

Sauce Xipister

Known in the Béarn as Sauce Goxoki, this hot and sour sauce is sprinkled on grilled fish, used as a marinade for fish or mixed with the juices of a fish cooked in the oven. It can also accompany roasted *Agneau de Lait* and may be used without moderation to accompany *Pot au Feu*.

It usually contains vinegar, garlic, sprigs of thyme, chilli flakes or *piment d'Espelette*, black peppercorns. Other spices and herbs are sometimes added. Mix the ingredients, pour into bottles and keep it for a month, shaking from time to time, before using.

A more complex version is recommended by Pierre Henri Vannieuwenhuyse, author of several books on cooking *à la plancha*, including *Recettes et Cuisine à la Plancha*.

1 teaspoon chopped red chillies
½ teaspoon chilli flakes or Espelette pepper
350ml (12 fl oz) cider vinegar
50ml (2 fl oz) olive oil
1 teaspoon coriander seeds
1 teaspoon mustard seeds
2 cloves garlic cut in half lengthwise
1 bay leaf
1 sprig rosemary
2 sprigs thyme
10 black peppercorns
1 small teaspoon salt

Stir the fresh chilli and Espelette pepper or other chilli into the vinegar. Add the olive oil.

Toast the coriander seeds and mustard seeds lightly in a dry frying pan to bring out the flavour

Put the spices, garlic, herbs, peppercorns and salt into a bottle. Pour the vinegar and chilli mixture into the bottle, cork it and shake it well. Leave it in the refrigerator for 2 weeks, shaking it every 2 or 3 days. It will keep for 2 months or more. (Makes a small bottle.)

Chorizo Sauce

Chorizo brings a characteristic glow to any dish and this sauce is much in use to liven up plain white fish, particularly fillets of bream or cod fried lightly in olive oil.

2 tablespoons olive oil
I small onion chopped
3 cloves garlic
70g (2½ oz) chorizo, skinned and finely diced
50ml (2 fl oz) dry white wine
300ml (10 fl oz) chicken stock
2 tablespoons cider vinegar
250g (9oz) canned chopped tomatoes
1½ teaspoons sweet paprika
½ – I teaspoon *piment d'Espelette* or ground chilli
3 sprigs thyme
salt

Heat the oil in a medium saucepan and soften the onion for 5–10 minutes, until its starts to be transparent.

Add the garlic and chorizo and cook gently for 5 minutes. Add the wine and let it bubble until the alcohol evaporates, 2–3 minutes.

Add the chicken stock, vinegar, tomatoes, paprika, piment or chilli and thyme. Add salt and simmer for 20 minutes or until it reaches the right consistency.

Béarnaise Red Sauce
Sauce Rouge

Brilliant and easy, *Sauce Rouge*, from Pau, is eaten with vegetables, poultry or fish; I had it at the Henri IV Restaurant with their *Poule au Pot*; it gives a lift and rich colour to a plate of plain poached chicken. You can also use it in other dishes, where tomato sauce is wanted. Add chopped chives, parsley or shredded fresh basil leaves to the sauce if you want to.

7 large plum tomatoes or 2 x 400g (14 oz) tins plum tomatoes, drained
I tablespoon olive oil
½ – I teaspoon smoked paprika, to taste
sea salt and freshly ground black pepper

Heat the grill and put the tomatoes in a small roasting tin lined with oiled foil. Grill them for 30 minutes until they are blackened and soft. Allow them to cool and remove the skins. Chop the tomatoes and blend them with olive oil, paprika, a little salt and some fresh black pepper. (Serves 4)

Green Sauce

This sauce is from les Landes; in Bazas, home of some of the world's finest beef; they serve it at their big cattle fair with *Pot au Feu*, and it is also excellent with hot ox-tongue.

2 tablespoons white wine vinegar
5 tablespoons olive oil
I clove garlic
3 teaspoons tomato paste
2 tablespoons chopped parsley
2 tablespoons chopped chives
2 shallots, finely chopped
4 chopped cornichons
salt and pepper

To make the sauce, put the vinegar, olive oil, garlic and tomato paste into a small blender and whizz them together. Season and stir in the herbs, chopped shallots and cornichons. Season generously.
(Serves 4 – 6)

Chilli Oil

2 teaspoons chilli flakes
2 tablespoons olive oil
125ml (4 fl oz) light olive oil

Heat the chilli flakes in a small frying pan, watch out for the fumes. When the flakes are hot but not toasted pour in 2 tablespoons of olive oil and leave over night. Dilute with the remaining olive oil. Keep for a week before using. (Makes a small cupful.)

Eskualdun Salsa
Sauce Basquaise

At its best, this beautiful deep red sauce (almost as useful as tomato sauce, which we could never live without), is rich and flavourful. I make it entirely without green peppers, although authentically these should be added along with the red. The trouble is, Basque green peppers, *piments doux* or *piments du Pays*, are quite sweet and tender, while ours taste a bit unripe and are less sweet in flavour, so, if you are north of Bordeaux, stick to the red.

The sauce Basquaise is good with fried eggs, with such vegetables as courgettes and aubergines, with fish – cod or hake or tuna – with fishcakes and with pork. It goes particularly well with barbecued lamb cutlets. You can also cook chicken or quails with it, and the Hôtel des Pyrénées serves this with a *Piéce de Boeuf* (onglet), together with chopped shallots and Béarnaise Sauce.

If you add a bit of vinegar, it makes a perfect alternative to tomato ketchup! (Serves 4)

1 large or 2 medium banana shallots
2 large red peppers, peeled with a potato peeler and chopped
2 large cloves garlic, chopped
3 tablespoons olive oil
1 large or 2 medium tomatoes, skinned, seeded and chopped
1 tablespoon tomato purée
50ml (2 fl oz) water
½ teaspoon Espelette pepper, hot paprika or cayenne
2 bay leaves
sea salt, pinch of sugar

Heat the oil in a frying pan over a low heat and soften the shallots, peppers and garlic for 15 minutes. Add the tomatoes, tomato purée dissolved in the water, hot red pepper, bay leaves and seasoning.

Simmer for 25 minutes, stirring from time to time; cover the pan when some of the water has evaporated and the sauce has started to thicken. Add a dash of water if it seems to be sticking, but the sauce must not be watery. (Serves 4)

Sauce of Preserved Piquillo Peppers
Salsa de Piquillos

Piquillo peppers are small, intensely red, spicy-sweet peppers from the Ribera del Rioja in the Navarra region of Northern Spain. They are grilled over a fire to give a smoky taste; sometimes this is done out in the fields, where they are being picked, and they are then skinned by hand and preserved in jars. Piquillos are like little pockets that can be stuffed to make a good starter (see page 278).

They can also be used to make a beautiful, bright orange, piquant sauce to go with squid, roasted fish or cold beef, lamb or pork. In every jar there will be some damaged ones, so use the whole ones for stuffing and the broken ones for sauce.

12 piquillo peppers, from a jar, cut in pieces
1 small shallot, finely chopped
1 large clove garlic, chopped
2 tablespoons olive oil
1 tablespoon red wine vinegar
½ teaspoon sugar
½ teaspoon hot paprika or *piment d'Espelette*
salt

Sweat the shallot and garlic in olive oil, over a low heat, until soft. Add the vinegar and cook gently for 5 minutes, then add the piquillo peppers and sugar and cook for 5 more minutes. Season with paprika or *piment d'Espelette* and salt, cook, stirring for 2 or 3 minutes, and blitz in a small blender until smooth.

Variations:
~ Add a tablespoon of fresh tomato sauce to the finished sauce and

blend it in.

~ Add a tablespoon of cream to the finished sauce and blend it in.

~ Add both. (Serves 4)

Tomato Sauce

Tomatoes love the climate of the South West, and Marmande, in Lot-et-Garonne, is famous for its enormous juicy tomatoes with a strong, sweet flavour.

In mid to late summer, when they are at their best, and cheapest, tomatoes are piled on market stalls in dozens of varieties, and in rainbow colours. Many country households make a point of cooking and bottling or freezing large quantities while they are in season, but if you are freezing the sauce, leave out the garlic and add it later. You can use this sauce on its own or in any dishes needing tomato concentrate, coulis, etc.

1kg (2¼ lb) ripe, red tomatoes, skinned, or 2 x 400g (14 oz) tins of plum tomatoes
4 tablespoons olive oil
2 white onions, finely chopped
2 – 3 large cloves garlic, finely chopped
generous pinch thyme leaves
1 bay leaf
salt, sugar

Skin and quarter the tomatoes and put them in a bowl. Gently heat the olive oil in a heavy pan and sweat the onion, without browning, stirring it occasionally. After 20 minutes, add the garlic and cook gently for a further 5 minutes.

Add the tomatoes and their juice to the onion, the thyme, the bay leaf and a little salt, cover the pan and simmer for an hour. Check the sauce from time to time and add a tablespoon or two of water if necessary.

Remove the bay leaf and sieve or purée the sauce in a blender. (Serves 4 – 6)

Green Olive Sauce

Easy to make, easy to eat, particularly good with fried cod or grilled monk fish. It is also perfect as a spread or a dip.

175g (6 oz) stoned green olives, plain or anchovy flavoured
½ white onion finely chopped
2 cloves garlic
3 tablespoons olive oil
sprigs of thyme
125ml (4 fl oz) chicken stock

Gently soften the onion and garlic in one tablespoon of olive oil for 10 minutes without browning. Add the olives, thyme and stock and simmer for 5 minutes. Allow to cool and purée in a blender, slowly adding the remaining 2 tablespoons of olive oil; blend until smooth. (Serves 4)

Easy Béarnaise Sauce

One story tells us that Chef Jules Colette at the Paris restaurant called Le Pavillon Henri IV invented Béarnaise sauce in the nineteenth century. It was named in Henri's honour, as he was born in Pau in the Béarn.

I never really understood the role of Béarnaise Sauce until food writer Michael Ruhlman (*Translating the chef's craft for every kitchen,* 2011 on his blog) explained it as follows:

"If you cook a steak on a grill, the problem is that there is no juice, no gravy. Ditto a hamburger – the result can be dry. So what is needed? Béarnaise Sauce."

Béarnaise takes the place of pan juices and gravy, so make it loose and almost pourable; it is a divine combination of lemon, shallot, tarragon and butter, held together with egg yolks. This is my lemon flavoured take on Michael Ruhlman's quick, easy version. Make it shortly before you cook the steak or burgers.

2 tablespoons lemon juice
1 tablespoon finely chopped shallot
2 egg yolks
200g (7 oz) salted butter
½ tablespoon chopped French tarragon
salt, freshly ground pepper

Put the lemon juice and chopped shallot, salt and pepper into a deep bowl or jug that you can use with a hand held blender, let them infuse together for 10 minutes.

Blend the egg yolks into the lemon juice and shallot and whizz them until you have a smooth mixture.

Melt the butter until it just starts to foam, it must not brown. Turn off the heat, wait 1 minute.

Now pour the butter into the egg yolks in a slow, steady trickle, whisking with a hand held whisk or a wire whisk as you do so. Stir in the tarragon and keep the sauce warm until needed, stirring often. (Serves 4-6)

Sauce Gribiche

One of the two sauces served with Beef *Pot au Feu* at the once famous Brasserie Goxoki in Pau. The other was the *Sauce Rouge* on page 41.

This is a very Southern version – plenty of vinegar, no cream.

It goes splendidly with lobster, with mussels and with fish, particularly turbot and salmon, and it is very easy to make. It can also be used as a salad dressing; it is a really useful sauce. Make it ahead of time if possible, to give the flavours time to mingle, and it keeps very well for at least three days in the refrigerator.

2 egg yolks
1 teaspoon mustard
2 – 3 tablespoons white wine or cider vinegar
200ml (8 fl oz) sunflower oil or light olive oil
1 tablespoon chopped fresh chervil
1 tablespoon chopped fresh tarragon
1 tablespoon chopped chives

1 tablespoon chopped fresh parsley
1 tablespoon chopped capers
1 hard boiled egg
salt, freshly ground pepper

Put the raw egg yolks, mustard, 2 teaspoons of the vinegar and 2 teaspoons of water into a medium bowl or food processor and whisk until foamy. Gradually add the oil slowly and steadily, whisking or blending constantly until the mixture is emulsified and the oil is completely incorporated. Whisk in the remaining vinegar, then gently mix chervil, tarragon, chives, parsley, and capers into the sauce. Grate the hard-boiled egg and stir it into the sauce. Season to taste with pepper, go easy on salt as the capers can be very salty. Cover and refrigerate. (Serves 6)

Gascon Vinaigrette

The word for this vinaigrette is powerful – it is strong and I love its fresh tang. If you want to spice it up still more substitute sherry or cider vinegar for the red wine vinegar.

Bordelaise chef Bruno Loubet adds half a teaspoon of Maggi liquid seasoning to his mix. It sounds odd but it is delicious and worth a try.

The recipe, as all good vinaigrettes are, is utterly simple, and if you whizz it briefly – I use an electric spice and nut grinder, a cheap and natty little tool – it emulsifies beautifully in a few seconds, and comes out looking creamy, with a consistency that clings perfectly to the leaves and other ingredients of the salad. (Serves 4 – 6)

1 tablespoon sherry, cider or red wine vinegar
1 teaspoon Dijon mustard
½ teaspoon of Maggi seasoning
1 tablespoon water
salt and black pepper
3 – 4 tablespoons olive oil

Blend the vinegar, mustard, Maggi seasoning and water in a small blender or spice grinder and add seasoning. Pour in half the olive oil and blend, then add the remaining oil and blend again until creamy – it only takes a few seconds. (Serves 4 – 6)

Walnut Vinaigrette with Roquefort

Walnut trees grow along every little lane in the lovely Dordogne valley, and much of the crop of nuts is made into walnut oil. Use this nut-flavoured dressing on salads of chicory, endive or dandelion, or with little mixed leaves including wild salad leaves such as sorrel and chickweed (*mesclun*).

2 tablespoons olive oil
1 tablespoon walnut oil
1 tablespoon lemon juice
1 teaspoon sherry vinegar
50g (2 oz) Roquefort cheese, crumbled
black pepper, pinch of sugar

Whisk the oils, lemon juice and sherry vinegar together.

Add seasoning – a pinch of sugar and some pepper, the Roquefort is quite salty. Crumble the Roquefort into the dressing and then whizz the mixture in a small blender until emulsified and a lovely silky grey green colour. (Serves 4 – 6)

Sharp Cream
Crème Vinaigrée

I first came across this at La Pipelette in Pau, spooned into the centre of bowls of an unusual, dusky-pink red cabbage soup.

This invigorating mixture can be used to liven up any soup, especially pumpkin, but also watercress, beetroot or leek.

Add chives or capers and it magically becomes a fine companion to cold salmon. It can also give a jolt to a cucumber salad.

150g (5 fl oz) double cream
150g (5 fl oz) single cream

1 heaped teaspoon strong Dijon mustard
1 clove of garlic, peeled (optional)
2 tablespoons cider vinegar
salt and pepper
chopped chives or chopped capers (or both)

Put the two creams into a saucepan with the mustard and, if you want it, garlic, and heat slowly to scalding point, that is when it is just about to simmer. Remove from the heat, cover and allow to cool completely. Remove the garlic. Gradually incorporate the vinegar, a little at a time, and then season with salt and pepper. Whisk well, stir in the chives or capers and then cover and leave to thicken in the refrigerator. Use when needed, it keeps for several days, and gradually gets thicker. (Serves 6)

Apple Aïoli

I have come across quince *aïoli* in Catalonia, and I was pleased to find this easy Basque version using apples, which is delicious with fish soup (see page 110).

It also makes a perfect snack with roasted pork cracklings.

1 green apple, peeled, cored and sliced
1 teaspoon Dijon mustard
4 cloves garlic, crushed to a paste with coarse salt
½ teaspoon *piment d'Espelette* or cayenne
freshly ground black pepper
125ml (5 fl oz) olive oil
salt

Cook the apple, covered, with 2 – 3 tablespoons of water until soft. Allow to cool.

Put the apple, mustard and garlic into a food processor, add two kinds of pepper and little salt, and blend until smooth. Pulsing the blender, slowly add the olive oil in a trickle, until it is all absorbed. Taste for seasoning. (Serves 4 – 6)

Saffron Mayonnaise with Charred Lemon

Serve this golden sauce with asparagus, with fish and with cold chicken

100ml (3½ fl oz) olive oil
½ lemon
2 pinches saffron
2 egg yolks
100ml (3½ fl oz) sunflower oil
salt

Heat a tablespoon of olive oil in a small pan and fry the cut side of the lemon until it is softened and beginning to char.

Put the saffron in a small bowl and just cover with 2 tablespoons hot water; let it infuse like tea.

Put the egg yolks in a blender with the saffron and its liquid and salt. Squeeze in the juice of the charred lemon and blend. Gradually add the olive oil and sunflower oil, pulsing the mixture until all the oil has been added. Taste for seasoning. (Serves 4)

Pesto Aquitaine

The largest watercress beds in Europe are in the Agenais at the heart of Gascony. I was rather intrigued by the highjacking of basil pesto from Genoa, by Agenais chef Michel Dussau, to make this beautiful emerald-coloured watercress sauce. He serves it with his watercress soup, but it is perfect with vegetable soups of all sorts.

60g (2 oz) watercress
35g (1 oz) pine nuts
25g (just under 1 oz) grated parmesan
juice of ½ lime
1 clove garlic, finely chopped
125ml (4 fl oz) virgin olive oil
salt, freshly ground pepper

Prepare a bowl of cold water with some ice cubes in it. Cut the thick stalks off the watercress. Blanch the leaves by plunging them into a large pan of boiling, salted water for 1 minute and draining them immediately. Quickly plunge them into the iced water which fixes the colour.

Drain them again and dry them thoroughly on kitchen paper or spread on a clean tea towel.

Grind the leaves together with the pine nuts with a pestle and mortar or in a small grinder, keep the mixture grainy, add the Parmesan, lime juice, garlic and olive oil and pulse briefly. Season well. (Serves 4)

Wild Garlic Oil

This has a bright, stimulating springtime flavour. Add it to almost anything, but particularly to vegetable soups such as leek.

When picking wild garlic, also known as rampions, pick them early in the season before they start to flower and dig up a bit of the white lower stem with each bunch of leaves, as it helps the leaves to stay fresh. But for this recipe use only the green leaves.

12 leaves of fresh wild garlic
1 clove garlic
125ml (4 fl oz) olive oil
salt

Drop the leaves and garlic into a pan of boiling water for 30 seconds. Drain and put the colander immediately under the cold tap for a further 30 seconds.

Allow to drain, then dry on kitchen paper and chop coarsely. Pulse the garlic leaves and garlic together with the olive oil until smooth. Season with a little salt. (Serves 4)

Guindillos

Also known as *piparra* these long, yellow-green, mildly tingling chillies are picked early, before they turn red. They are eaten, pickled in vinegar, with local charcuterie.

If you see them in a deli or supermarket, these hot pickled peppers are a real find, but if not you can make them yourself. They can be used on many *pinchos* (see Gildas page 67), or to decorate a plate of small pieces (*copeaux*) of *jambon crû* or a wooden board of thinly sliced charcuterie. They can also replace the Northern French pickled gherkins, as an accompaniment to pâté and cold cuts of all kinds, and to garnish a Gascon salad (see page 81).

4 bay leaves
24 long thin green guindillo peppers
600ml (20 fl oz) water
400ml (13 fl oz) cider vinegar or distilled white vinegar (at 5% acetic acid)
salt

Wash a couple of dozen green guindillo peppers or other mild, long yellowy green chillies.

Add two bay leaves to a pan of well-salted water and bring it to the boil.

Blanch the chillies for 1 minute and drain in a colander. Run under cold water for a moment.

Bring a solution of 60% water and 40% cider or white vinegar to the boil with 2 more bay leaves. Allow to cool.

Put the cooled, drained peppers, dried with kitchen paper, into a clean preserving jar. Fill to the top with the prepared liquid and cover the jar. Keep in the fridge for 1 month.

Cherries Pickled in Vinegar

These are perfect with charcuterie, with cold game or cooked ham.

Distilled white vinegar, made by fermenting grains, has a high acetic acid content and therefore is often used in pickling, although it is rather crude in flavour (hence the change of vinegar in this recipe once the cherries are pickled). White vinegar does the job and keeps the colour of the fruit or vegetables to be pickled, whereas cider vinegar, also high in acetic acid, darkens the fruit. White wine vinegar is generally not suitable for stage one or for pickling in general as it usually has a lower acetic acid content.

500g (18 oz) of red cherries with firm flesh (such as *coeur-de pigeon*)
1 litre (34 fl oz) distilled white vinegar
1 litre (34 fl oz) of white wine vinegar
1 sprig of tarragon
1 tablespoon salt
10 black peppercorns

Cut the stalks off the cherries, leaving 1cm (half an inch).

Put them into a preserving jar with the salt, peppercorns, tarragon and the white vinegar.

Leave to pickle for 6 weeks. Pour off the distilled white vinegar and replace it with the white wine vinegar.

Allow to mature for 6 months before opening. (Makes 4 jars.)

Red Onion Confit
Confit d'Oignons au Vinaigre de Cidre

This is served with *foie gras*, for a pre-Christmas feast, and it is also excellent with rare roasted or grilled *magret de canard* (duck breast) and with cold turkey, chicken or goose, with cheese, with everything really.

1kg (2¼ lb) red onions, peeled and cut in half
4 tablespoons olive oil
200g (7 oz) golden granulated sugar
100ml (3½ fl oz) cider vinegar
2 – 3 bay leaves
1 teaspoon coriander seeds
salt

Slice the onions finely.

Heat the olive oil gently in a heavy pan and soften the onions until they are darkening in colour, but not yet brown.

Add the sugar and vinegar, bay leaves, coriander seeds and a little salt.

Cook very gently stirring from time to time. Use a heat diffuser to make sure the onions do not catch and add a little water if necessary.

Cook for half an hour. Taste for seasoning and transfer to clean pots. (Serves 4 – 6)

Basque Cornbread
Taloa

I first came across this bread at a Basque Festival. The *taloa* was in pancake or flat-bread form and was being made on a *plancha* on a street stall; the cook and his helper were extremely busy folding newly griddled *taloa* around a variety of fillings; party goers were ordering black pudding or grilled streaky bacon, but the flavour going the fastest was hazelnut and chocolate spread, *pâte à tartiner chocolat noisettes* (page 300).

375g (13 oz) plain white flour
125g (4 oz) fine cornmeal
300 – 350ml (10 – 12 fl oz) water
½ teaspoon salt

Heat a griddle or thick iron skillet.

Mix the flour, cornmeal and salt in a bowl. Gradually add water to make dough. Let it rest for an hour.

Form the dough into balls with oiled hands and roll them out into 20cm (8in) rounds. They are hard to handle at this point, lift them onto the hot plate by curling one at a time round a rolling pin.

Cook them on a hot griddle, turning them once. (Serves 6)

Savoury Fritter Batter
Pâte à Beignets

Savoury fritters of all kinds are popular throughout the region of Aquitaine. If you can obtain fresh golden courgette or pumpkin flowers, remove the green stalk and the pistil and make fritters with the following batter.

200g (7 oz) plain flour
2g (1 pinch) quick dried yeast
100ml (3½ fl oz) sunflower oil
2 teaspoons Dijon mustard
30g (1oz) grated Parmesan
1 egg white
200ml (6¾ fl oz) water

Sieve the flour into a bowl, add the yeast, oil, mustard and grated cheese. Slowly add water until you have a smooth batter.
Beat the egg white lightly with a fork and mix it into the batter. Allow to sit for 2 hours before use. (Serves 4)

Hot Red Pepper Bread
Pain au Piment d'Espelette

This rather surprising bread can be served alongside delicately sliced Bayonne or Ibaiama ham or *cochonaille* – charcuterie – lightly piled on a slate or wooden board, and scattered with a few topaz-coloured pickled guindillo peppers.

500g (18 oz) white bread flour
1½ teaspoon salt
1 teaspoon quick dried yeast granules
1 teaspoon sugar
2½ teaspoons hot paprika or *piment d'Espelette*
325 ml (11 fl oz) warm water
1 tablespoon chilli-flavoured olive oil (see page 43)
1 handful uncooked polenta meal

Preheat the oven to 220°C (430°F).
Put the flour in a large bowl and mix in the salt, yeast, sugar and paprika. Pour on the water and start to mix it in with a wooden spoon. When it is roughly mixed, pour in the oil and continue to knead with your hands in the bowl, until you have a fairly wet sticky dough; it takes about 10 minutes.

Cover the bowl with cling film. Let the dough rise in a warm kitchen for an hour or more, until it has doubled in size.

Put the dough on a well-floured board and knock it back, that is, knead it briefly. Shape it into a loose oval loaf.

Put it onto a piece of baking paper (sprinkled with polenta) placed on a baking sheet. and cover the loaf loosely with a cloth. Let it prove in a warm place until it is swollen and puffy. If, when you prod it lightly with a finger, the hole fills up again, it is ready. Turn down the oven to 200°C (400°F). Bake for 40 – 50 minutes. Tap the bottom to see if it is cooked; it should sound hollow. Cool on a rack. (Makes 1 loaf.)

Chicken Gravy
Jus de Poule

This is based on a recipe by Michel Guérard, and will give an open-armed, generous, chicken flavour to gravy or any sautéed, braised or stewed chicken dishes.

500g (18 oz) of chicken wings
250g (9 oz) shallots, skinned
4 sprigs thyme
30g (1 oz) butter or 2 – 3 tablespoons olive oil
1 or 2 cloves garlic
1 chicken stock cube
2 teaspoons soy sauce

Heat the oven to 180°C (360°F).

Put the wings and shallots with the butter or oil and thyme into a roasting tin.

Roast until they are well browned and caramelized, turn them over a few times.

Pour on water to cover generously, put in the garlic, crumbled stock cube and soy sauce and simmer, on top of the cooker, scraping up all the juices, for 20 minutes. Strain. Keep the gravy in the refrigerator.

The chicken wings, incidentally, can be boned and given to the dogs. (Makes about 700ml or 23 fl oz.)

Chapter Three

Pinchos, Tapas and Salads

Pinchos and Tapas

Along the Atlantic coast of the Basque Country are fishing towns and villages whose streets are lined with small, intimate and very individual tapas bars. Each one is serving tiny appetising little mouthfuls called pinchos – intense flavours including ham, cured sausage or a simple assembly of such things as ham and cheese or anchovies and peppers, placed on little bits of bread, with toothpicks stuck in to hold them together.

Pinchos, also spelled pintxos, are there to make you linger in the bar, drink more wine, raise your voice, discuss current affairs with animation and enjoy your companions to the full.

They are the big brothers and sisters of tapas, perhaps a little bit larger and a bit more complex. A selection of a myriad pinchos lined up on a bar, like the window of a French patisserie or a jewellery shop, is designed to tempt and seduce you. They are the original small plates to share and can be tiny miracles of flavour, they can look like bouquets made of tripe, tiny fried fish or baby octopus and they can also be rather handy for using up leftover bread, ham and cheese.

In San Sebastian and Bilbao, there are many dark bars that feel as if they have been there for a century or more, but there is, too, a flowering of much-tweeted new tapas bars with glamorous lighting, serving exotic, modern versions of pinchos, which can be very flamboyant or spare and minimalist – two slices of raw cep on toast with parsley, olive oil and salt.

On the Atlantic, just over the border from France, in the fishing port of Hondaribbia, you can find all the traditional dives, originally the meeting places of local fishermen, lined up side by side in a beautiful traditional Basque town square. Sit at one of the tables outside (tourists do). Once you have chosen your selection – perhaps thin slices of chorizo, hot salt cod croquettes, fresh local red prawns, garlicky razor clams cooked on the *plancha*, little fried sardines and grilled mushrooms – the plates come in quick succession.

Pinchos can be hot or cold, some need a fork or even, with such specialities as oxtail or pig's ears, a knife and fork. At my first bar-crawl in San Sebastian some decades ago, pinchos were always eaten standing up, served from a long counter. There were no chairs, just bar stools, and inside and outside, the only tables were upturned wine barrels – very often they still are. The pinchos were downed with a glass of Txakoli, the local slightly sparkling, very dry white wine, or with sherry or cider, a ritual part of a nightly opportunity to gossip with friends in a smoky, shadowy bar, with large, fat-dripping hams dangling everywhere. Dinner comes later.

Now they are sought after by foodies from all over the world – a great way to spend an evening is the *txikiteo*, (pronounced tchikiteo) walking from one bar to another, through the streets of Biarritz, Hondaribbia, San Sebastian or Bilbao with friends, tasting a few of the day's special pinchos, written up in chalk on the blackboard, at each one.

Some bars, reeking of hot olive oil, sell mostly fried fish and bits of salt cod, others are grilling tiny squids and prawns on the *plancha*, while several have practically turned pinchos into an art-form, as can be seen from this list of the sort of thing you will find in the narrow streets of the old town of Saint Sebastian

At Atari, an upmarket, modern pinchos bar, with a view across the little square to the jewel-box rococo church of San Sebastian in Calle Mayor, you may find:

1. Gildas (see page 67)
2. Gambas (prawns) on half an oval toasted bridge roll covered with finely chopped raw shallots in vinegar – like mignonette sauce for oysters, but with white wine vinegar instead of red- and finely diced raw tomato, sprinkled with startling green oil – parsley and garlic flavour.
3. Accras or Urkabitos – also called *croquetas de la morue* – which are little croquettes of salt cod purée. The usual shape is oval, 4 cm (1½ in) long, and the very light coating is fine breadcrumbs.
4. Octopus tentacles boiled and grilled, (see page 75-76) with braised banana shallots, torn roasted peppers and tiny potatoes braised in their skins, plus rouille.
5. Small shot glasses of fresh, chilled broad bean gaspacho (see page 113).
6. Fillet steak tails; small steaks 6cm (2⅓ in) across, grilled *à la plancha* and served with pumpkin purée, the juices from roasted peppers and scattered with black and white sesame seeds.

Different seductive small plates are made on the spot at La Cuchara da St Elmo – a bar well worth seeking out in the old quarter of San Sebastian, at the bottom of the sloping street that runs down from the rococo church of the Saint. Busy and deft behind the bar, the young chefs are producing more and more tempting pinchos, and the barmen are carving, by hand, exquisite charcuterie.

For us, they produced:

1. Pig's cheek braised in red wine.
2. Crispy pig's ear with fine white bean purée.
3. Cheese with pickled mustard seeds on a purée of tiny, fresh broad beans.
4. Smoked and dried ceps with orca (rice-shaped pasta), cooked like risotto.
5. Octopus, grilled, with pickled vegetables.

6. A marquetry board covered in paper thin slices of ruby-red *saucisson sec*, made with Iberico pork.

Don't Try This at Home – Making Pinchos

Pinchos are more demanding to make than they look. Each small dish is just as much work as a large dish would be, and you are expected to make about five or six different things all at once. You have to be very well organised and do all your prepping in advance, ready to assemble them as near the time of serving as possible, or they will go soggy. Many of them start with a bread or toast base.

The bases can just be slices of fresh French stick, *baguette* or *pain longue* or, for a daintier result, *ficelle,* but the toasted ones (*pain grillé*) are less likely to turn soggy. The recipes in this chapter are for simple pinchos that can easily be made at home.

Base for Pinchos

Pain Grillé 1
1 or 2 artisan *ficelles* (thin French sticks) or baguettes; allow 1 baguette to make pinchos for 4 – 6 people.
Slice them diagonally into thin slices (about ½ cm, ¼ inch).
Heat the grill.
Brush the slices of baguette with olive oil on both sides.
Toast on both sides (do not put too close to the grill, about 10 cm or 4 inches away seems to work).
These keep well for at least a day.

Pain Grillé 2
Try to buy the best artisan type of baguette, although the fluffy mass-produced one works too.
Heat the oven to 150°C (300°F).
Brush a baking tray very lightly with oil or line with baking paper.
Slice a baguette, or, for daintier pinchos, a *ficelle*, diagonally into very thin slices. Lay them on the baking tray and bake for 15 – 20 minutes, until pale brown and crisp. Done this way they are quite fragile, but they will keep for a while without going soggy. These keep well for 2 days.

Pain Grillé 3

Again use the best type of baguette you can find.

Heat a ridged grill pan until it is smoking. Grill the thin slices of baguette on both sides until just starting to char. These will be less fragile, and have a smoky taste, but do not keep so well.

Pain Grillé 4 (more refined)

Use little bridge rolls or plain white bread thinly sliced.

Grill under an overhead grill until just crisp – you need an eagle eye to prevent burning the toast.

Ingredients

The simplest ingredients are often the best – cheese of all sorts, ham, top quality white (albacore) tuna preserved in olive oil, top quality salted or marinated anchovies, fresh ripe tomato, all kinds of red and green peppers and chillies – grilled, preserved or pickled – olives, salt cod, garlic and olive oil.

If you are making pinchos for quite a few people, it is worth having a bowl of olive oil and a brush to hand.

Pain à la Tomate

This dish could become a perennial favourite everywhere, but it is a child of the sun, because tomatoes need sun, and it is particularly good if the toast is cooked on an open wood fire and eaten outdoors.

The tomato you use should be red, but can be large, small, round, long or plum-shaped as long as it is sweet, ripe and juicy with plenty of flavour; the larger cherry tomatoes are usually sweet and have more flavour, especially in the winter. The tomato should leave some of its flesh as well as seeds and juices on the toast.

If you like the idea, you can anoint both sides of the toast with tomato and oil, delicious, but it then becomes impossible to eat without dribbling over your clothes.

You will need 6 pieces of toasted rustic bread such as white sourdough, or pain de campagne or *Pain Grillé*.

3 cloves garlic, cut in half
virgin olive oil
1 – 2 tomatoes, Marmande, Coeur de boeuf or other sweet and juicy
tomatoes, cut in half
crystal salt and freshly ground pepper

First rub the toast with the cut side of half a clove of garlic.

Pick up the half tomato in one hand and the garlicky toast in the other. Rub and squash the tomato onto the toast, letting it absorb the juice and bits of flesh. Sprinkle with salt and pepper and anoint with olive oil. Eat. (Serves 3 – 4)

Bilbao Breakfast

This is a Basque *desayuno*, a version of *pain à la tomate*. I came across it at breakfast on a Bilbao roof terrace, looking at the silver arcs of Frank Gehry's Guggenheim Museum. Instead of rubbing the tomato, you pile it onto the warm toast. What could be more simple or as good?

6 slices of toasted or grilled *pain de campagne*
1 – 2 large ripe Marmande or other French style tomatoes (they can weigh about 500g (18 oz) each)
3 cloves garlic (optional)
olive oil
fleur de sel, freshly ground black pepper
slices toasted country bread

Put the tomato in a bowl and pour boiling water over it. Leave for 1 minute then run under the cold tap.

Skin and chop the tomato, put it into a bowl. Let people rub their toast with halved garlic cloves, pile it with chopped tomato, drizzle olive oil over the top, and sprinkle with salt and black pepper. (Serves 3 – 4)

Pain à La Tomate et Jambon Crû

6 pieces of pain grillé
olive oil
1 – 2 cloves garlic (optional)
1 – 2 tomatoes, cut in half
3 thin slices raw ham such as Bayonne, Kintoa, Noir de Bigorre, Ibaiama,
Iberico or prosciutto

If you like, rub the toast with half a clove of garlic before you smother it with ripe tomato.

Rub with the cut side of half a tomato, sprinkle with olive oil and then season with black pepper. Drape half a slice of ham over the top. Or a piece of chorizo or two, or any kind of cured sausage.
(Serves 3)

Anchois en Salaison

6 pieces of toast
2 cloves garlic
1 – 2 tomatoes, cut in half
1 jar or tin best quality salted anchovies
2 red or orange peppers or 6 piquillos peppers preserved in oil
olive oil

If using fresh peppers, peel them with a potato peeler and remove the seeds. Fry the peppers in olive oil, trim them and cut them into wide strips. Trim the anchovies to fit the toast.

If you like, rub the toast with half a clove of garlic. Then rub the toast with the cut side of half a tomato and sprinkle with olive oil.

Place a strip of pepper or piquillo over each piece of *pain à la tomate*, and place two anchovy fillets on top. Sprinkle with more olive oil. (Serves 6)

Piments d'Espelette drying in the sun

Spicy Txistorra sausages braised in cider

Montauger's fine hams hanging in the charcuterie shop in Bayonne

Smoked milk pudding

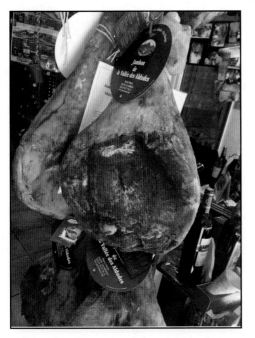

White Asparagus from les Landes

A simple plate of oysters with mignonette sauce

Turbot on the outdoor grill

Salade Biscay

Pinchos at a Biarritz bar

Goat's cheese on sale in Bordeaux

Fongasse, stuffed bread,
on a Bordeaux quayside
market stall

Foie gras pâté in pastry

A Basque baker sells her bread

Gariguette strawberries from Marmande

Sardines with hot ham croquetas at Hondaribbia

Tapas Menu in Biarritz

Gésier salad and olive tortilla

TAPAS

Croquettes Jambon	3
Macaron de Boudin Aizpurua	3,50
Crevettes grillées "Lady Rosé"	5
Toast de Foie-Gras Landais	3,5
Pikillos Morue Daxila Brebis	3,5
Panko de Pieds de Cochon	3,50
Chipiron, risotto à l'encre	5,5
Verrine de Foie Gras Biraben	16
Taloa, cochon fermier, et brebis	4
Xistora, la merguez basque	4
Oeuf de poule, cappucino Jambon	4
Planche de Charcuterie	16
Boîte de Sardinillas de Santoña	9
Artichaut de Saint-Jean	8,50
Tartine d'oreille de cochon	4
St Jacques Rôtie, Jambon Ospi.	4,50

Commande au Bar svp

Crèmerie cheese labels in the St Charles area of Biarritz

Pinchos on display at Bar Jean, Biarritz

Plateau de fruits de mer at Biarritz Halles

Fishing boat in Getaria fishing port

Grazing sheep in les Aldudes

Miramar beach, Biarritz

Red mullet on the grill

Starting the wood fired grill

Piquillos stuffed with salt cod

Anchovy Toast

I had this at Asador Exteberri at Axpe Achondo, one of the most exciting restaurants I have been to, tucked away in the hills behind Bilbao. It was so simple, but it was the fineness of the anchovies and the homemade thin, crusty rolls, grilled lightly to make wood-smoky toast, that made it so special.

12 fillets of best quality salted anchovies (not marinated in vinegar), trimmed
6 long strips of the bottom part of bread rolls or slices of baguette cut lengthwise
1 clove garlic
olive oil
1 large, ripe tomato

Cut the bread the length of one anchovy fillet and the width of two laid side by side. Serve it hot, grilled, preferably on a smoky fire, rub with half a clove of garlic, sprinkle with olive oil and then rub with half a tomato.

Serve with two anchovies neatly laid on top, and drizzled with a few more drops of olive oil. (Serves 6)

Anchovy Toast with Tapenade

Make it exactly the same as anchovy toast but spread the toast with tapenade instead of tomato.

Peppers, Salt Cod and Marinated Anchovies
Pintxo Ainhoa

Marinated anchovies are pickled in a solution containing vinegar and salt, which turns them white; they have a sharper taste than salted anchovies. You could also use smoked anchovies, which are from the Bay of Biscay and are brined rather than salted, before being smoked and packed in olive oil.

12 small pieces of toasted baguette
1 red pepper
1 green pepper
100g (18 oz) brandade of salt cod (see page 152)
6 marinated or smoked anchovies
olive oil

Preheat the oven to 250°C (480°C).

Place the peppers in a roasting tin and sprinkle with olive oil. Cook for 15 – 20 minutes until blackened, with skin coming away. Pick them up with tongs and put them in sauce pan with the lid on or place in a plastic bag, and allow to cool a bit. Remove the skin and seeds and cut the pepper into small strips.

Rub twelve small pieces of toasted baguette with a clove of garlic, spread a spoonful of brandade on each one, then a slice of red pepper placed lengthwise. Arrange a small, neat slice of green pepper across the top of each one, and a trimmed anchovy on top of that. (Serves 6)

L'Assiette Ibérique

A small slate on which are arranged the following, in thin overlapping slices – chorizo, serrano or Ibaiona ham, *fromage à brébis*, (hard sheep's cheese), plus a slice of *pâté Basque* (pâté made with pork, pork fat and hot red pepper).

This is served with grilled *pain de campagne* drizzled with olive oil and a side dish of *piquillos* (long, thin, hot pickled yellowy green peppers) sprinkled with olive oil and a few thin slices of garlic.

Ham and Hot Camembert
Pisao

Pedro Martín is an expert on the food traditionally eaten by pilgrims on their way to Compostella and has won prizes for his book on Basque dining societies. This recipe is based on one in his *Les Meilleures Tapas de Donostia*, (2004). '*Donostia*' is Basque for San Sebastian.

6 pieces very thin *pain grillé*
½ camembert, (or try using Brie or Chaumes)
6 thin slices Iberico, Ibaiama, Bayonne or other raw ham
piment d'Espelette or paprika

Cut the camembert across into thin slices. Place them on the small pieces of toast. Season with *piment d'Espelette* or paprika.

Melt the cheese under the grill.

Drape a slice of ham on top, trickle a little olive oil over them and serve. (Serves 6)

Biarritz Breakfast
Petit Dejeuner

In Les Halles de Biarritz you can buy a box of thin, delicate shavings of ham, called *copeaux* (about ⅓ of a slice); you can choose dark Iberico, Pie Noir or Ibaiama ham or pink Bayonne ham and the lady will slice it for you. To serve, buy a *ficelle* (thin breadstick). Cut it in half and pile the lower half with ham, complete with fat. Put the top back on, cut into four and serve as a heavenly breakfast or lunch or as tapas.

Gildas also known as *Banderillos*

A great pincho with a great story. Sometimes called *banderillos*, these little pinchos look just like the decorated sticks used by picadors to goad the bull at a bullfight.

They have also been called Gildas, (pronounced Hildas), since Blas Vallés, coolest bar owner amongst all the cool bars in the streets of San Sebastian, used to put out a few olives and anchovies and some pickles for his customers, when they gathered at about 6.00 p.m. for the usual glass of wine.

One customer started skewering these items together on a cocktail stick – or was it a toothpick? – and the combination – so vivid – caught on. The taste is described as *verde, picante, salado* which means green, spicy, salty, but these words can also mean 'saucy, witty, smutty', so the snack was name after Rita Hayworth's sassy character in the movie

'Gilda', made in 1946 with Glenn Ford.

1 x 350g (12 oz) jar green anchovy olives
1 x 350g (12 oz) jar guindillas (pickled pepper see page 53)
1 x 100g (3½ oz) jar of salted anchovy fillets,
1 x 350g (12 oz) jar of pickled cocktail onions, pickled aubergines or
gherkins

Wrap a guindilla around an olive and skewer it on to a cocktail stick.
Wrap an anchovy around a pickled onion and skewer it on. Skewer
on a second olive. Brush lightly with olive oil. Repeat (making fresh
skewers) until everything is used up. Alternatives might include red
pepper, a cube of salty cheese or a piece of very expensive albacore
tuna preserved in oil (ordinary tuna will fall to pieces).

Pimientos de Gernika or *Gernikako*

I like the following description of eating Gernika peppers – according
to Estanis Bilbao, member of a wealthy family from Bizkaia, 'It leaves
a sensation of having enjoyed something very good'.

Gernika peppers are small, bright green, mild, triangular in shape,
with bright, glossy, smooth skin. Brought over from Mexico and
Bolivia in the sixteenth century, they are grown in the Basque country
near Guernica, and they are known for their exceptional flavour.

You will get enough for 5 – 6 people in a kilo – one person can eat
20 or more over the course of an evening, with a glass or two of the
light, slightly sparkling Basque white wine *txacoli*.

To prevent the peppers exploding in the frying pan, it is worth
slitting each one before frying them in hot olive oil (deep fry or shallow
fry). Leave the stalks on when you cook them, as it provides a handle
to pick them up.

Eat them with your fingers, hot as they are, sprinkled with sea salt.
They are eaten at breakfast, lunch and before dinner and are good with
shellfish.

Pimentos de Padrón

These are similar to Gernika peppers, but a bit stubby in shape, and are grown in Galicia. They are mild, but have the odd quality of throwing up an occasional fiery one, (about one in ten) and the larger and more mature they are the more likely to be hot – that can mean stingingly hot. Fry them in the same way as the Gernika peppers.

Truite Fumée de Banca

Smoked Trout, Cream Cheese, Mayonnaise, Grated Egg

This smoked trout resembles smoked salmon but is less fatty; the large, pink fleshed Banca trout are delicious; they are reared in the purest of rivers, crystal waters that come straight off the Pyrenees, high up in the Basque territory of les Aldudes.

250g (9 oz) cold-smoked trout or smoked salmon in slices
200g (7 oz) cream cheese
black pepper
125g (4 oz) mayonnaise
1 – 2 hard boiled eggs
slices of toasted baguette

Cut the sliced trout or salmon into pieces, as neat as possible (it can be a messy business) about 5 cm by 10 cm (2 inches by 4 inches).

Put a spoonful of cream cheese in the middle of a slice of salmon, season with freshly ground black pepper.

Roll up the salmon to make small rolls with cream cheese inside.

Grate the hard boiled egg on a plane-type grater.

Put a salmon roll on top of a piece of toast, cut in half if it looks huge, place a blob of mayo on top of each piece and then sprinkle grated egg on the mayo. (Serves 6)

Ham and Cream Cheese with Thyme
Tapas Breuil et Jambon de Bayonne

Breuil is fresh sheep's cheese made from the whey pressed out during the making of such cheeses as the famous Pyrenean *tomme de brébis*, Ossau Iraty. Natural and fresh, it is made by farming families in well kept mountain dairies, from December until July.

12 slices baguette
1 clove garlic, cut in half
200g (7 oz) *breuil* or *brousse* or cream cheese
fresh thyme
trickle of olive oil
6 very thin slices *jambon crû* such as Bayonne
salt, pepper

Rub the slices of baguette with garlic and then grill them.

Mix the cheese with thyme leaves, salt and pepper and a little olive oil.

Put a generous spoonful or two of the cheese on each slice of toast and then half a slice of ham. (Serves 6)

Prawn Pinchos with Rémoulade Sauce

250g (9 oz) small shelled cooked prawns

For the sauce:
125ml (4 fl oz) mayonnaise
dill, parsley, tarragon – chopped
1 tablespoon capers, chopped
1 teaspoon Dijon mustard

4 hardboiled eggs, quartered
slices of toasted baguette

Mix the chopped herbs and capers into the mayonnaise.

At the last moment, mix in the prawns and spoon the mixture onto the toast. Top each with a quarter of a hardboiled egg. (Serves 4)

Garlic Prawn Pinchos

350g (12 oz) medium sized raw prawns
5 cloves garlic, finely chopped
4 tablespoons olive oil
¾ teaspoon *piment d'Espelette* or ½ teaspoon cayenne pepper
2 tablespoons white wine
salt, fresh ground black pepper
slices of *pain grillé*

If they have shells, peel the prawns, leaving their tails on. Heat the olive oil in a frying pan and cook the garlic over a medium heat, stirring until the garlic just starts to turn pale golden, do not let it darken. Stir in the *piment d'Espelette* or cayenne. Turn the heat up to medium and add the prawns to the pan. Let them cook for one or two minutes, turning them over once and then add the white wine and season with salt and pepper. Let everything cook together for a minute until the prawns are just cooked through. Place the prawns on toasted bread, spoon the garlic oil and garlic over the top and serve warm. (Serves 4)

Txistorra (pronounced 'Chistorra')

At the Hotel Restaurant Erreguina in Banca, high up in Les Aldudes, the acorn-fed pig rearing part of the Pyrenees, close to the border with Spain, everything is traditional and everything is home-made, including the pinchos, which consist of sausages, pâtés and black puddings, which they conserve themselves. A speciality of the house are *boudins noirs de sanglier*, splendid small, drum-shaped black puddings of wild boar, flavoured with hot red pepper, cinnamon and nutmeg and served hot with a little Sauce Basquaise, see page 43, (red and green peppers and tomatoes).

Another local favourite are *Txistorra*, hot chipolatas made of lean and fat minced pork, flavoured with sweet and hot smoked paprika and garlic and packed into sheep's casings, which are narrower than pig's and give a slightly different taste. I have made these in a modified form without casings and they tasted pretty authentic.

500g (1lb 2 oz) minced very fatty pork such as shoulder, at least 30-40% fat
4 dried choricera peppers (on line from Lunya.co.uk)
2 cloves garlic, crushed to a paste
2 – 3 teaspoons hot paprika (or more – sometimes *txistorra* are very spicy – for this effect use plenty of hot paprika)
a generous amount of salt

Put the choricera peppers in a bowl and pour boiling water over them. Let them soak for 5 – 8 minutes; when they are limp, lift them out and remove the stalk and seeds. Scrape the thin dark red flesh off the inside of the skins with a teaspoon, chop it and mix it into the pork, together with the garlic, paprika and a little salt. With floured hands, roll the mixture into golf ball sized balls of 50g (1¾ oz) and then form into slim sausage shapes. (Makes 12 chipolata sized sausages.)

To serve as tapas:
1. Form into short sausages with floured hands and fry in olive oil, then serve on a piece of toasted baguette; trickle some of the cooking oil over the toast and then skewer the sausage on top with a vertical cocktail stick.
2. Fry the sausages or grill them and finish by braising briefly in a *cazuela* (a small round terracotta dish) with a little cider and serve in the *cazuela*, skewered with cocktail sticks to pick them up.

Salt Cod Croquettes
Urkabitos

These mini *croquetas*, served hot from the pan, are one of the most popular pinchos – you can make them with potatoes or with bechamel sauce. (See recipe for ham *croquetas*).

500g (1lb 2 oz) salt cod, soaked for 24 hours, see page 151
500g (1lb 2 oz) potatoes, peeled and quartered
1 leek finely chopped
2 tablespoons olive oil
1 – 2 tablespoons chopped parsley
1 teaspoon hot red pepper
1 egg
oil for frying

Place the cod in a pan of simmering, unsalted water and bring back to simmering point. Remove the pan from the heat.

Allow the cod to sit in the water for 8 minutes, then drain, keeping the cooking water. When cool enough, remove the skin and bones. Flake the cod into tiny pieces.

Cook the potatoes in the cooking water from the cod until tender.

Soften the chopped leek in olive oil with a tablespoon of water over a low heat, until the water has evaporated and the leek is translucent and tender.

Mix the cod with the potato (do not use a food processor).

Add the leek, parsley, red pepper and egg, but no salt and mix them in. Taste for seasoning.

Bring a pan of oil up to 170°C (340°F) – at this point bubbles will sizzle round the handle of a wooden spoon dipped into the oil. Keep the oil at between 170°C (340°F) and 177°C (350°F).

With two dessert spoons, form small croquettes about 4cm (1½ inches long. At this point you can cook them as they are or you can dip them in flour, beaten egg and breadcrumbs, as explained in the recipe for *Croquetas*, for a very crunchy finish.

Fry until crisp and golden. Drain, place briefly on a plate on top of several sheets of kitchen paper to remove some of the oil and serve at once. (Makes around 30)

Ham Croquettes
Croquetas (Jamon)

I am grateful to food writer Felicity Cloake for finding the best way of making *croquetas*. This is a slightly simplified version of her recipe as she uses Japanese panko crumbs and mixes them with grated *manchego* cheese for the coating. Spanish and Italian delis always have good crispy crumbs.

A deep fryer would be ideal for making these crisp and succulent, hot croquettes, probably one the favourite things in the whole Northern Spanish pinchos repertoire. If you don't have one, you can deep fry them in 2cm (¾ inch) of oil in a saucepan, turning them over a few times.

Once you have made the mixture and shaped it into ovals you can freeze it, ready for frying.

150g (5 oz) cured, sliced Serrano ham with fat
2 tablespoons olive oil
60g (2 oz) unsalted butter
60g (2 oz) plain flour
750ml (25 fl oz) whole milk
freshly grated nutmeg
freshly grated black pepper
2 free-range eggs, beaten
150g (5 oz) breadcrumbs
1 litre (34 fl oz) sunflower or peanut oil, to fry

Dice your ham as finely as possible. Heat the oil in a medium, heavy-bottomed saucepan over a medium heat, add half the ham, including the fatty bits and cook until the ham fat has begun to melt. Add the butter and let it melt.

Turn the heat down, gradually stir in the flour and cook gently, stirring regularly, until it loses its raw flavour – this should take about 5 minutes.

Gradually add the milk, stirring it in well, until it is all incorporated. Put the pan on a heat diffuser and cook very gently for another 10 –

15 minutes, stirring frequently, until it has the consistency of smooth mashed potato, then fold in the rest of the ham and season to taste with a grating of nutmeg and some black pepper (you probably won't need any salt).

Put the béchamel in a bowl and allow to cool, then cover, pressing the cling film on to the surface of the sauce to prevent a skin from forming, and refrigerate for at least 2 hours, preferably overnight.

Put the beaten eggs in a bowl, and the breadcrumbs on a plate. With floured hands, roll tablespoons of the mixture into rounds, shape into ovals and roll these in the egg, drain off the excess egg, then roll the *croquettes* in the breadcrumbs until well coated.

Heat the oil in a large pan to 170°C (340°F), or until it begins to shimmer. Prepare a plate lined with absorbent paper.

Fry the *croquettes* in batches for 2 – 3 minutes until golden all over, then lift up the basket and shake it (use a slotted spoon if you are not using a basket), and quickly drain off the excess oil by tipping the *croquettes* onto the paper towels. Pat lightly with more paper towels and serve at once. (Makes about 30 small *croquettes*.)

Warm Octopus Galicia Style
Pulpo a la Gallega

This is one of the best ways to eat octopus. If the potatoes are waxy, firm and freshly cooked, the flavours together become magically enhanced.

1kg (approx. 2¼ lbs) fresh octopus
250g (9 oz) potatoes
½ teaspoon sweet paprika
½ teaspoon hot paprika
1 tablespoon parsley, chopped
2 cloves garlic, chopped
3 – 4 tablespoons virgin olive oil
250 ml (8½ fl oz) water
salt, coarsely ground black pepper

To cook the octopus:
Heat a pan and put the clean octopus into the hot pan, put the lid on and simmer gently for 1 hour in its own juices. Add 250 ml (8½ fl oz) of water and the sliced potatoes and cook a further 15 minutes. Remove the potato slices and continue to cook the octopus for another 15 – 30 minutes, until tender. Allow to cool, then cut the large tentacles into slanted, diagonal slices.

Put the sliced potatoes on a hot platter, season with salt and sprinkle with a little *persillade,* chopped parsley and garlic.

Put the hot, slices of octopus on top. Sprinkle everything copiously with olive oil. Season with salt and pepper and scatter generously with paprika, and the remaining chopped parsley and chopped garlic. (Serves 6)

Grilled Octopus with Piquillo Sauce and Marcona Almonds

4 large cooked octopus tentacles
50g (2 oz) Marcona almonds or pine nuts
4 tablespoons olive oil
100g (3½ oz) piquillo sauce (page 44)

Toast the almonds or pine nuts and if you are using almonds, cut them into pieces. Stir them into the sauce. Put a tentacle on a plate and serve it sprinkled with olive oil and with a spoonful of the bright orange sauce. (Serves 4)

Tortilla of Mushrooms and Shrimps

For tapas, cut a large tortilla into cubes and stick each cube with a cocktail stick. Alternatively, it is possible to find tiny omelette pans to make several little individual tortillas instead of one large one, in which case cut the mushrooms and prawns into small pieces. (Serves 3 – 4)

3 – 4 large, firm open cap Portobello mushrooms, cut into large dice sized pieces
150g (5 oz) small raw prawns, shelled
1 banana shallot, finely chopped
1 clove garlic, finely chopped
3 – 4 tablespoons olive oil
5 eggs
salt, *piment d'Espelette* or ground black pepper

Heat 2 tablespoons of olive oil in a frying pan, add the mushrooms and shallots, and season with salt and pepper. Sauté them over a gentle heat until soft and cooked through, adding more oil if needed. The mushroom juices may come out, in which case keep cooking them until the liquid has evaporated. Set aside to cool somewhat.

Wipe out the pan and heat a tablespoon of olive oil, fry the prawns with the garlic until barely cooked. Allow to cool.

Break the eggs into a bowl, season and whisk with a fork. Stir the cooled mushroom mixture and the shrimps into the beaten eggs.

Heat the remaining oil in a 20cm (8 inch), reliably non-stick frying pan.

Tip the egg mixture into the pan when it is hot, and cook over a medium heat, shaking it to prevent it sticking. Cook until almost set but take care not to burn it underneath.

Turn the tortilla by holding a saucepan lid, which must be just larger than the omelette pan, by the handle with a cloth and placing it over the pan. Holding the pan firmly in your other hand, reverse it quickly so that the tortilla sits, cooked side up, on the lid. Slide it back into the pan, cooked side up, and continue to cook it for a minute or two. It should be firm but juicy. Slide it out onto a plate and let it set for at least 10 minutes or more before attempting to cut it.

Cut into cubes and spear each cube with a cocktail stick. Eat at room temperature.

SALADS

This is the Midi, and although it is on the Atlantic, Biarritz is actually quite far South, and it gets hot. Salads are the big thing, and they can be very big, giant in fact, and definitely the right choice for a summer main course or even a whole meal. Every restaurant has salads, from the most delicate to robust to stupendous to utterly limp and depressing.

For a typical Gascon salad, take a large bowl for each person. Pile it to the brim with ingredients and dress with the traditional creamy, mustardy vinaigrette (which has recently been eclipsed by plates doused with thick, sweet and sticky Balsamic vinegar, now a great favourite in the South West).

There really are no rules and making salad can be a creative thing; in Lot et Garonne there are locally made walnut oils, hazelnut oils and truffle oils to experiment with, and excellent wine vinegars, sometimes flavoured with tarragon or spiced up with chillies. Further South, cider vinegar is popular and so is well made sherry vinegar (look for *vinagre de Jerez Reserva)*, this is gentler when mixed half and half with lemon juice, I find.

Giant Salads such as those on the menu of Le Relais Gascon, a restaurant with a taste of the South West in Paris, where they go under the name of *Salades Géantes*, often have hot golden discs of potato fried in goose fat on top of the enormous bowful.

Bitter salads such as all kinds of dandelion, chicory and endive, rocket, sorrel and raw spinach are seen as healthy and very refreshing. They are accompanied with chopped hard-boiled egg to mitigate the bitterness. Raw onions often feature, as do every kind of asparagus – pink, green, purple and white – palm hearts, purple artichoke hearts, red and green peppers, green beans, pickled peppers, horrid bits of sweetcorn and delicious potatoes, boiled or fried.

Mountain salads may have wild leaves mixed in and sheep's cheese in triangular slices or little whole creamy goat's cheeses on top, softened a bit under the grill. Sometimes fresh or toasted walnuts or hazelnuts are included, or a slice of toast covered in melted Roquefort.

By the Atlantic coast, salads may contain prawns and mussels, lobster, octopus, squid, salted or marinated anchovies or preserved tuna fish.

Many of the large Gascon salads are vehicles for charcuterie, slices of ham or saucisson, (in Bordeaux it may be the gamey, peppery *Grenier Médoquin* sausage, made of pig's small intestines, which we call chitterlings), hot lardons of smoked pork belly, slices of stuffed goose neck pâté and they are especially fond of duck – sliced smoked duck breast, confit duck gizzards, confit duck hearts, confit duck legs, shredded and fried and of course *foie gras de canard*. You can sometimes find luscious Agen prunes or quartered figs amongst the leaves; both go along extremely well with the duck.

Gascon Vinaigrette

This is the vinaigrette to go with your Gascon salad – the strong flavours are ideal with the rich *foie gras*, lovely charcuterie, and eggs that you may wish to use. As mentioned earlier, you can spice it up further by adding the ingredient that Hélène Darroze uses. She is from les Landes and adds chicken roasting-juices to her salads, while Bordelaise chef Bruno Loubet adds half a teaspoon of Maggi liquid seasoning to the mix.

The recipe, as all good vinaigrettes are, is simple, and if you whizz it briefly – I use an electric spice and nut grinder, a cheap and natty little tool – it emulsifies beautifully in a few seconds, and comes out looking creamy, with a consistency that clings perfectly to the leaves and other salad ingredients.

I tablespoon red wine, cider or sherry vinegar
I tablespoon Dijon mustard
I tablespoon water
I teaspoon roasting juices from a chicken or ½ teaspoon Maggi seasoning
3 tablespoons olive oil
salt and black pepper

Place all the ingredients except the olive oil in a food processor and whizz briefly, then add the olive oil in three parts, whizzing in between each addition, until emulsified.

Gascon Vinaigrette Light Version

1 teaspoon Dijon mustard
1 tablespoon white wine vinegar
1 tablespoon water
75 ml (3 fl oz) olive oil or ½ rapeseed ½ olive oil
salt, black pepper.

Place all the ingredients except the olive oil in a food processor and
whizz briefly, then add the olive oil in three parts, whizzing in between
each addition, until emulsified.

Salade du Sud-Ouest

2 confit duck legs
1 *frisée* (frizzy endive) lettuce
450g (1lb) *gésiers confits* – duck gizzards – preserved in duck fat
200g (7 oz) *lardons*
2 tablespoons duck or goose fat
750g (1lb 10 oz) medium potatoes, peeled and sliced into rounds, not
too thick
3 cloves garlic
1 small banana shallot, finely chopped

For the dressing:
2 teaspoons Dijon mustard
1 tablespoon good quality red wine vinegar
1 tablespoon water
3 tablespoons olive oil
1 teaspoon sugar (optional)
salt, freshly ground pepper

Make an emulsified dressing by whisking the mustard with salt and
pepper and stirring in the wine vinegar and the water. Slowly add the
olive oil, beating with a whisk as if you were making mayonnaise. Or
whizz the ingredients in a spice grinder. Taste for seasoning, add sugar
if you like at this point.

Remove the meat from the confit duck wings or legs and shred into manageable pieces.

Put the *frisée* salad in a bowl.

Cut the *gésiers* in half or if large, slice them into four.

Sauté the lardons and shredded duck in a little duck or goose fat until they are starting to brown and the duck is getting crisp. Keep hot.

Sauté the gésiers in their own fat until browned, drain off the fat. Keep the *gésiers* hot.

Dry the sliced potatoes; heat the remaining duck or goose fat in a wide frying pan and sauté the potatoes until starting to brown. Stir in the garlic, cover the pan and continue to cook for 15 – 18 minutes, turning the potatoes to distribute the garlic evenly. They should be just cooked but still firm.

Toss the salad with the dressing, the confit duck, the *lardons* and the shallots. Scatter on the hot *gésiers* and top the whole bowlful with fried potatoes. (Serves 6)

Salade Gascon

50g (2 oz) mature goat's cheese log
8 slices smoked duck breast
1 red oak leaf lettuce
2 tomatoes (if possible use Marmande or Black Russian or other well flavoured tomatoes) sliced crossways
1 shallot, thinly sliced
Gascon Vinaigrette (page 79)

Prepare the salad; put the oak leaf lettuce leaves on a plate, arrange the tomatoes and shallots on top. Have the vinaigrette ready

Slice the cheese 1cm (½ inch) thick. Grill the slices until melted and turning brown and lacy round the edges. Sprinkle the salad with the dressing and toss it lightly, lay the duck breast on the salad and lift the melting goat's cheese on top. Serve fast. (Serves 4)

Salade Géante du Béarnais

Fill a bowl with *salade frisée*, (frizzy endive), throw on hot lardons, dress with robust garlic and mustard dressing, top with rounds of goat's cheese, lightly browned under the grill, and finish with thinly sliced garlicky potatoes fried in goose fat.

Salade de Manège

A *manège* is a circular horse - or mule-driven threshing mill, so perhaps at harvest time this was the salad served to the peasants doing the threshing – circular threshing floors are still to be seen, outside some of the older Pyrenean farmsteads.

The idea for this salad comes from the mountain inn of Etchebarne in Mendionde.

It consists of two or three different cheeses – all *brébis* – sheep's cheeses – hearts of lettuce with dressing, and, for each person, a slice of toasted baguette with Roquefort or other blue sheep's cheese melted on top. A bowl of olive oil and fresh bread is ready on the table.

Salade Biscay

One of the best Bayonne hams is the Ibaiama from Maison Montauzer, whose pigs are reared in Guiche near St Jean Pied de Port. M. Montauzer is one of three producers who produce Ibaiama hams from pigs reared in the traditional slow way.

Black and white Basque pigs – only the best – are fed outside, where they can be seen trotting along with sheep and horses, on the mountain slopes. In the autumn they forage in the woods of the Pyrenees, and they will reach at least one year old, before being made into ham and charcuterie.

The large hams, cushioned with a thick layer of fat, sweet and nutty, are cured for 18 to 22 months and have a deep ruby colour and intense flavour. The Bar François, on the quay of Bayonne, serves this ham. You can also buy Montauzer's ham in their charcuteries in Biarritz and Bayonne, or order on-line.

1 oak leaf lettuce
Gascon Vinaigrette (page 79)
12 spears asparagus, lightly cooked
½ large white onion, sliced into small pieces
2 hard boiled eggs, cut in quarters
12 green olives
8 thin slices Bayonne or Ibaiama ham or Spanish ham such as Serrano or
Iberico
8 thin slices of mountain ewe's milk cheese such as *Ossau Iraty, Abbaye de Belloc* or other *tomme de brébis*
4 - 8 Guindilla pickled peppers

Dress the lettuce leaves with vinaigrette. Place all the other ingredients except the cheese and ham, on top and lightly sprinkle them with a teaspoon or two of dressing. Lastly arrange the ham and cheese on top of the salad. Top with a guindilla or two for each person. (Serves 4)

Salade Gourmande

I originally tried this recipe when I translated Michel Guérard's *Cuisine Gourmande,* (I still consider it a cookbook of genius). This Gascon classic is one of a whole genre of massive local *salades composées*, but made fresher and prettier; it is a real treat. This recipe departs from Guérard and adds smoked duck breasts to the foie gras.

2 very good, fresh eggs
1 dozen asparagus spears
1 *frisée* (frizzy endive)
1 oak leave lettuce, inside leaves only
200g (7 oz) smoked duck breast
100g (3½ oz) fresh foie gras
1 shallot, finely chopped
Gascon Vinaigrette (see page 79)

Boil the eggs for 8 minutes, cool them under cold water and shell carefully when cold.

Trim the asparagus and steam for 6 minutes. Drain well.

Wash the frizzy endive cutting off all the dark green parts and keeping only the fresh, pale yellow leaves. Mix these with the young lettuce leaves in a bowl.

Slice the duck breast, allowing three or four slices per plate.

With a hot knife, (dipped in a jug of hot water), slice the foie gras, allowing two slices per plate.

Dress the salad and share between 6 plates, piling it up a bit. Sprinkle with chopped shallot. Place 3 slices of duck breast on one side and the foie gras nearby, put half an egg opposite and lay 3 asparagus spears alongside. Serve as a first course with hot, toasted *pain de campagne*. (Serves 4)

Nasturtium Salad
Salade des Fleurs

The best, says Jean Suhas, Basque writer, wine lover and gourmet, is a salad of nasturtiums.

Fill a bowl with as many golden, red and orange nasturtium flowers as you need, using just the petals; add small sprigs of flat parsley, and if you can, a few blue borage flowers. Make a light dressing with walnut or hazelnut oil and balsamic vinegar; do not dress the flowers until the last moment. Sprinkle with *fleur de sel*, toss briefly and serve.

Tuna Fish Salad
Salade de Thon Blanc

This salad is made with bottled or canned tuna fish, but not the ordinary tin. Find, if you can, Albacore tuna belly fillets, called *Filets de Thon Blanc*.

These small tuna (*thunnus alalunga*), called *germon* in France, are fished in the Gulf of Gascony from July to October. Their flesh is white and tender. They are not cheap, but they are superb in a simple salad, one which makes the perfect summer lunch in a few minutes. If you like to add herbs, chives, parsley and chervil are the ones to choose.

150g (5¼ oz) tinned white tuna fillets.
4 hard-boiled eggs (boiled 8 minutes only)
1 fresh white onion
1 red cos lettuce or other tasty lettuce

For the dressing:
juice ½ lemon
1 dessertspoon red wine vinegar
1 teaspoon French mustard
3 – 4 tablespoons olive oil, to taste
salt, black pepper

Remove the tuna from its olive oil, and you can use a bit of this oil in the dressing. Peel and quarter the eggs.

Cut the onion in half and slice from top to bottom, cutting it thinly into crescents.

Make the dressing in the usual way, emulsify it by long whisking or make it with a blender.

Fill a bowl with fresh lettuce leaves and dress them with the dressing, enough to lightly coat the leaves. Divide the lettuce between 4 plates. Put a quartered egg and the tuna fillets on each pile of lettuce, top with small crescents of onion. Sprinkle lightly with herbs if you like. That is it. (Serves 4)

Octopus Salad

Freezing the octopus tenderises it, but it still, in this recipe, needs cooking three times over. It ends up looking somewhat gnarled and dark, but it tastes authentic.

1 large octopus weighing 750g (1lb 10 oz), cleaned, frozen overnight
2 green peppers, grilled, skinned and deseeded
2 yellow peppers, grilled, skinned and deseeded
6 asparagus spears, lightly cooked
3 tomatoes, skinned and deseeded
½ red onion, thinly sliced
4 handfuls of rocket

For the dressing:
1 tablespoon white wine vinegar
squeeze of lemon juice
3 tablespoons olive oil
salt, freshly ground pepper

First deal with the octopus. Defrost at room temperature.

Preheat the oven to 120°C (250°F) and put the octopus, well washed, in a covered dish or casserole, without salt, and leave it for one hour if it is small, an hour and a half if large. All its liquid will run out. This can be discarded.

Put it into a saucepan, cover it with red wine and add a tablespoon of olive oil, a couple of bay leaves and a splash of water. Cover the pan and simmer for one to one and a half hours. Remove it with tongs and, if you prefer, strip off the tentacles.

For added flavour, heat a grill or *plancha*, brush the octopus with olive oil and grill the legs and body on both sides. Cut it up, leaving the legs whole. They will be nicely curled.

Cut or tear each of the cooked peppers into 4 or 6 nice pieces and lay them out on a platter to form a circle. Place the asparagus spears around like wheel spokes. On top, arrange the tomatoes, cut into thin slices, then the red onion. Scatter the rocket over the top and place the octopus pieces on top with the legs spiralling round. Dress with copious amounts of dressing made with oil, lemon and vinegar, seasoned with salt and pepper. (Serves 6)

Marinated Octopus Salad

A large octopus is a good choice to achieve a soft, non-rubbery texture.

For the marinated octopus:
1 raw octopus, cleaned (approx 750g or 1lb 10 oz)
1 tablespoon vinegar
¼ cup light olive oil
2 tablespoons lemon juice
freshly ground black pepper to taste

To prepare the octopus:

Bring a pan of water to the boil, with the vinegar. Drop in the octopus.

Turn down the heat and simmer for from one hour to an hour and a half until tender. Remove it from the pan and plunge into cold water.

Drain the octopus well, cut it into nice pieces, leaving the tentacles whole and toss with fresh lemon juice and olive oil. It will keep for 2 days in the refrigerator.

To serve as Octopus Salad:

marinated octopus, prepared as above

1 bunch watercress

3 spring onions, chopped

1 dill pickle, diced

1 teaspoon capers

1 – 2 tablespoons chopped parsley

4 salted and 4 white anchovies (see note), optional

juice of ½ lemon

2 tablespoons olive oil

salt and freshly ground pepper

Make a salad with the watercress, spring onions, diced pickled cucumber, capers, parsley and anchovies and arrange the octopus in curls on top. Or serve as *tapas* – a tentacle with a bit of the salad and some capers on top of a piece of *pain grillé*. (Serves 2 – 4)

Salt Cod and New Potato Salad
Salade de Morue

You can put a generous handful of capers into the salad if you like them.

500g (1lb 2 oz) salt cod, previously soaked for 24 – 48 hours

2 bay leaves

300g (10½ oz) waxy new potatoes

2 – 3 shallots, finely chopped

1 clove garlic, finely chopped

I tablespoon cider vinegar
3 tablespoons olive oil
piment d'Espelette or chilli flakes
I tablespoon chopped parsley
I tablespoon chopped chervil
freshly ground black pepper

Bring a large pan of water to the boil with the bay leaves, when it
reaches simmering point put in the cod and remove it from the heat.
Leave the cod in the water for 5 minutes. Take it out of the water which
you will need for cooking the potatoes.

Remove the skin and any bones from the barely cooked cod and
flake it into a bowl; set on one side.

Break the potatoes into small chunks with a small sharp tool such
as an oyster knife. Use the cod cooking water to cook the potatoes for
20 minutes. Drain them well.

Mix the hot potatoes with the flaked cod; ideally they should still
be on the warm side when you mix in the shallots and garlic. Make the
dressing – whisk the vinegar with the olive oil and season with black
pepper (no salt as the cod may be salty). Coat the cod and potatoes with
the dressing, sprinkle with hot red pepper, chopped parsley and chervil.
Serve at room temperature. (Serves 4 – 6)

Asparagus Salad with Bayonne Ham

In spring, asparagus is one of the very best things to eat in and around
les Landes, where the sandy soil produces the most exquisite white and
green asparagus. This recipe is adapted from one by Bertrand Auboyneau
of Bistrot Paul Bert in the Rue Paul Bert in Paris.

400g (14 oz) white or green asparagus, trimmed
4 thin slices Bayonne or other *jambon crû*, cut into shavings
4 eggs
I tablespoon white wine vinegar

Vinaigrette:
juice of ½ lemon
1 dessertspoon red wine vinegar
1 teaspoon French mustard
3 – 4 tablespoons olive oil, to taste
salt, black pepper

First make the vinaigrette, whisking the lemon, vinegar, mustard and seasoning together and then adding olive oil a little at a time.

Boil or steam the asparagus for 5 minutes or longer if it is very fat. Poach the eggs in the water, gently simmering, with the vinegar added to the water. Lift them out with a slotted spoon and let them drain well.

Dress the asparagus with vinaigrette, divide between four plates and top with shavings of thinly sliced Bayonne or other raw ham and a poached egg on each plate. (Serves 4)

Grilled Red Pepper Salad with Marinated Fresh Anchovies

Grilled red peppers make a very simple, luscious salad combined with tomatoes and onions or with goat's cheese or, simply but splendidly, with fresh anchovies, as in this one originally from the Paris restaurateur Bertrand Auboyneau, mentioned above.

500g (1lb 2 oz) very fresh anchovies
5 red peppers
piment d'Espelette, chilli flakes or cayenne
200 ml olive oil (6¾ fl oz)
Salt and freshly ground pepper
a drizzle of olive oil, for serving
country bread and black olive tapenade, for serving

Prepare the red peppers and anchovies a day ahead.

Preheat the oven to 180°C (360°F).

Place the red peppers on an oiled roasting tin and roast for about 20 minutes. Remove them from the oven and put them in a saucepan with a lid or a plastic bag until they have cooled enough for you to remove the skin easily. Skin the peppers and remove the seeds and cores.

Cut them into strips just under 1 inch (2cm) wide. Season them with salt and pepper and marinate them in 2 tablespoons of olive oil overnight in the refrigerator.

To prepare the anchovy fillets: remove the fillets from the central bone with a sharp knife. Season with salt and pepper and sprinkle with the *piment d'Espelette*. Cover and leave to marinate overnight in the refrigerator.

To serve, alternate slices of red pepper with the anchovy fillets on the plates. Drizzle with the very best olive oil. (Serves 4 – 6)

Duck Confit, Sautéed Ceps and Walnut Salad

To make this into a Salade Royale, add slices of foie gras, thin slices of green apple and a few spears of asparagus to the Duck Confit and Cep Salad.

2 legs of duck confit
1 – 2 tablespoons duck fat
400g (14 oz) fresh ceps, cut in pieces
2 cloves garlic, chopped
12 walnut halves
1 curly endive, *frisée* yellow part only
1 – 2 handfuls lamb's lettuce (*salade mâche*)

For the dressing:
1 tablespoon Dijon mustard
2 tablespoons good red wine vinegar
4 tablespoons walnut oil
salt, freshly ground black pepper

Preheat the oven to 180°C (360°F). Place the duck confit skin-side up in a roasting tin with a glass of water. Put in the top of a preheated oven for 10 minutes or until hot and crispy.

Remove the meat and shred it. Discard the bones. Keep the meat warm.

To make the dressing, mix the mustard, vinegar and salt and pepper in a bowl. Whisk well and pour in the walnut oil in a thin stream, still whisking.

In a frying pan, heat the duck fat and fry the ceps. Season with salt and pepper. It is important to get them golden brown. Then add the chopped garlic and stir it in. Place the curly endive and the *mâche* in a large bowl, add the dressing, the walnuts and the ceps. Mix well then place in a large deep dish and place the confit on the salad and serve. (Serves 4)

Chapter Four

Soups

Soup twice a day? Yes, in fact in the South West, until recently country families often ate soup three or four times a day and soup was what made the world go round.

For several summers we stayed *en pension* at a château-cum-Post Office, perched above the Dordogne river. Soup is what the postmistress and her sister cooked for us every single lunchtime and evening, without fail.

Ducks and geese wandered between the kitchen and the outdoor dining terrace. At noon, wearing a sprigged dress and black apron, granny sat by the kitchen door and prepared the green beans from the vegetable garden. In the evening, the brother brought in the wild boar and rabbits for the pâtes, which the ladies canned at home themselves, and a local friend came by with pike and trout and lots of very small fish from the river, which ended up as *friture de la Dordogne*. Greengages and figs came off their trees. And, if it was your birthday, Baked Alaska (*Île Flottante)* was made from their own eggs.

But first you had soup and this is how the guests at our small pension were fed, with an unknowing and timeless self-sufficiency. It all cost nearly nothing, and there were often tiny glasses of free locally-made digestifs, *Vieux Prune* (greengage) or *Vieux Noix* (walnut) liqueur or an eerie purple thing called *l'Inconnu*, at the end.

By the Atlantic, rich fish soups are the thing. But away from the sea there are a handful of earthy, mainstay soups made with vegetables and often a bit of confit duck or ham, which change with the seasons.

In the winter, it is bean soup or *Garbure* – put in lots of root vegetables, leeks, confit duck or ham and cabbage; it will keep you fortified. In spring, soups freshen up, with sorrel, garlic shoots, wild garlic and other green leaves to cleanse the blood, and in summer there is chilled *gaspacho* or a tomato soup with tiny vermicelli, and garlic soup, while autumn brings wild mushrooms or splendid pumpkins to the *soupière*. So the rule is always the same – make soup out of whatever is plentiful, in season and cheap – you will not go wrong.

Tourin à la Tomate

The tomato version of *tourin* is a friendly summer dish; it can be eaten at the start of a relaxed meal with friends – or it can be the only dish. You can add as much garlic as you like (one recipe advises you to add 3 heads of garlic) and plenty of pepper, either black or red, probably both. The large *croûtons* topped with cheese are traditional too, but not always on offer.

2 medium onions, finely chopped
1 – 2 tablespoons olive oil or duck or goose fat
2 cloves of garlic finely mashed
600g (1lb 5 oz) large, ripe tomatoes, skinned
800ml (27 fl oz) water or light chicken stock
½ teaspoon sugar
bouquet garni, including thyme
2 small handfuls vermicelli
4 slices of day-old country bread
4 tablespoons grated Gruyère cheese
salt, *piment d'Espelette* or cayenne pepper

Soften the onions in the olive oil or duck or goose fat until tender and transparent, but not brown, stir in the garlic and cook for a minute or two.

Chop the tomatoes and add them to the pan with all their juice, season well adding the sugar and plenty of pepper and cook for 5 minutes, then stir in the stock or water and add the herbs.

Simmer for 30 minutes then purée in a blender. Add the vermicelli and continue to cook until it is tender, for 3 – 4 minutes. Serve with small slices of French bread, grilled or baked in the oven and sprinkled with grated Gruyère. The cheese can then be melted under the grill or not, either way works well. (Serves 4)

Tourin à l'Aillet

Everyone eats these young garlic shoots in the South West; tender green garlic shoots the size of a pencil are gathered from March to May, and must not be confused with spring onions, which they resemble. To tell them apart, *aillet* or *l'ail jeune d'Aquitaine*, has flat leaves, while a spring onion has hollow leaves. The taste and smell are completely different; these are mild and sweet, but definitely garlic.

Considered very health-giving, *aillets* are eaten *croque-au-sel* (raw with coarse salt), made into a fine Easter omelette or a delicate garlic soup.

This version is a variation on one from Chef Aurélian Crosato of the Soléna Restaurant in Bordeaux, who prides himself on headlining fresh local produce. He also likes this soup made with new garlic bulbs, early in the season, while they are still fresh, mild and juicy.

2 bunches spring garlic shoots, or two heads of new season's garlic
2 potatoes, peeled and diced
2 eggs
30g (1 oz) of duck or goose fat
2 litres (34 fl oz) stock, see below or use stock cube
30ml (1 fl oz) white wine vinegar
salt, freshly ground pepper

For the stock:
1 ham hock or 1 leg of confit duck
1 onion
1 leek
1 stick celery
bunch thyme

To make the stock:
Put the stock ingredients into a pan with 2 litres of water and simmer, covered, for 2 hours, adding more liquid if needed. Leave to infuse for 2 hours. Remove the meat and thyme. Skin the ham or duck and remove the bone. Pull the meat into little pieces.

To make the soup:
Cut the aillets into short lengths, discarding the top of the green leaves.

Peel the garlic cloves if using new season's garlic and chop coarsely. Melt the duck fat and soften the garlic shoots or chopped garlic without browning. Add the stock and the potatoes and cook gently, covered, for an hour.

Separate the eggs and whisk the yolks together with the vinegar.

Remove the soup from the heat, let it cool a little, add the yolks and purée in a blender. Season with salt and plenty of pepper and ladle into bowls. Put a tablespoon of shredded ham or duck in the middle of each bowl and serve hot. (Serves 4)

Chilled Red Pepper Soup
Soupe aux Légumes Grillés

This very original idea for the perfect, rich, red soup with a smoky flavour comes from Basque writer Catherine Pinaguirre; it can be served hot, but in summer it is refreshing chilled.

It is important to use the more robust, bell peppers for this dish as the long, pointed ones have thin flesh and will burn easily.

3 red peppers
2 yellow peppers
2 onions

4 – 6 cloves garlic
500g (18 oz) tomatoes
juice of ½ orange
4 – 6 teaspoons sherry vinegar, to taste
500 ml (17 fl oz) chicken stock or water
3 tablespoons olive oil
salt, cayenne pepper, hot paprika or *piment d'Espelette*

Preheat the oven to 220°C (430°F).

Skin the tomatoes and cut them in half, keeping their juices.

Heat the grill, or better still light up the barbecue or a wood fire. Grill the peppers until the skins are starting to blacken, turning them over so they are evenly blistered on all sides and place them in a covered saucepan or a plastic bag to steam until cool. Skin them, remove the seeds and cut the flesh into quarters.

Put them with their reserved juice in a roasting tin with the quartered onions, the tomatoes and the unpeeled garlic. Sprinkle with olive oil and roast for 25 – 30 minutes turning the vegetables from time to time. They should be soft.

Peel the cloves of garlic. Place them with the roasted vegetables in the food processor and whizz to a purée. Add the orange juice and the vinegar and whizz. Add enough stock or water to make a light but thickish soup, season with salt and cayenne pepper and serve chilled or at room temperature with a drizzle of olive oil. (Serves 4)

Wild Mushroom Soup

Mushrooms, known as *Camparos*, and mushroom-hunting, known as *la ceuillette* or *chasse aux champignons*, are in the blood in the South West, and their oak, chestnut and pine forests provide vast, hunting grounds for the sport.

Fortunately people no longer shoot each other for getting there first, but your tyres may be let down, if you encroach on someone else's favourite secret mushroom patch.

And watch out for your eyes, which will get poked with twigs as you forage through the under-brush. The main prizes are *cèpes de Bordeaux* (*boletus edulis*) and *cèpes des pins* (*boletus pinophilus*). The older ones are

Oysters from Arcachon with Hot Sausage

Anchovy toast   Local red prawns from Geteria

Magnificient Garbure soup

Razor clams in Biarritz

Razor clam with broad beans

By the Atlantic in Biarritz

The promenade by the sea at San Sebastian

Duckburger and frites   Salade Gourmande

Ham from Gascon pork waiting to be sliced

Clams to eat with beans

Pumpkin slices for sale in the market at Biarritz

Gracious Rice

Sausages in the dryer being cured

made into soup, giving a velvety texture. Dried ceps give an excellent flavour too.

100g (3½ oz) of fresh or frozen ceps or 30g (1 oz) dried ceps
250g (9 oz) medium chestnut mushrooms
1 leek, white part only, sliced
1 onion, finely chopped
30g (1 oz) butter
1 teaspoon olive oil
400ml (13½ fl oz) chicken stock, home made or stock cube
300ml (10 fl oz) creamy milk
salt, freshly ground pepper
sprigs of fresh chervil

Clean the ceps with damp kitchen paper towels and cut them into large pieces. Frozen ceps should be defrosted. Dried ceps should be soaked in 200 ml (7 fl oz) warm water for 30 minutes and cut into small pieces. Keep this water and use it in the soup.

Wash the button mushrooms briefly under the tap and cut them into 8 pieces.

Cut the leek in half lengthways, wash it well, shake it dry and slice into 1cm (⅓ in) pieces. Soften the onions in butter and olive oil in a large saucepan, add the leeks and mushrooms and stir, let them cook for 5 minutes.

Season with salt and pepper and add the chicken stock. Bring to the boil and then simmer gently, covered, for 30 minutes. Bring the milk to simmering point and pour it into the soup.

Let it cool a bit, then purée half of it in a blender until the texture is very smooth. Return it to the pan. Taste for seasoning.

You could carefully place a thin slice or two of fried mushroom on top of each bowl and perhaps a few sprigs of chervil. (Serves 4)

La Cousinette or Soupe Verte à la Mauve

This is an ancient soup from the wilds of Béarn and the Pays Basque – some say it may even be prehistoric. But *mauve* or *cousine*, the hedgerow plant mallow (*malva sylvestris*), with its pink flowers, is still enjoyed here as a vegetable and has been eaten by humans for thousands of years; mallow is considered to be health giving, and does in fact have properties that help boost the immune system. Our ancestors would have eaten the plant before it flowered, and might have included in the *Cousinette*, if not a ham knuckle, perhaps a pig's ear or tail, probably salted, or even a handful of snails. Serve the soup as it is or poured over thin slices of toast.

1 ham or gammon hock (*crosse* or *trébuc*)
150g (5 oz) spinach
150g (5 oz) *blette* (green part of chard)
150g (5 oz) lettuce
1 large leek, sliced
1 stick celery, sliced
10 – 20 cloves of new season's garlic, sliced
1 large potato, sliced thinly
2 tablespoons olive oil
1 handful of young shoots and leaves of wild mallow (mauve) - *malva sylvestris* (optional)
1 handful leaves, flowers and buds of *bourache* (borage) *borago officinalis* (optional)
salt, *piment d'Espelette*
toasted *pain de campagne*

Place the ham knuckle in a large pan with 2 litres of water, bring to the boil, and let it cook for 90 minutes or more.

Slice the garlic thinly. Soften the leeks, celery, potato and garlic in olive oil.

Chop the well-washed and drained spinach, chard and lettuce and add to the pan with the softened vegetables. Add one litre of ham stock. Season if necessary and simmer for 10 minutes.

Add the chopped mallow and borage if they are available, and cook for a further 10 minutes. Serve with very thin slices of toast – these can be placed in the soup bowl. (Serves 4)

La Cousinette Maigre

This version of *cousinette* is like a tonic after a heavy winter diet, a Spring soup from Béarn, fresh and healthy and full of all and any of the young and old green plants that can be picked in hedgerows and gardens, early in the year in the South West.

You can include spinach, chard, spinach-beet, lettuce, potato and leek as the base vegetables.

It can then be made slightly acidic with sorrel, and given bitter notes with chicory or dandelions, while the texture can be made velvety and gloopy if you include mallow (*mauve*) and the effect can be blood-cleansing if you add a handful of nettles. Some people add cream or *crème fraiche,* others add large slices of toasted rye bread. I add peas, because this looks and tastes good and you could also add asparagus.

I vegetable stock cube
I onion, cut in quarters
2 leeks, cut in half lengthwise and sliced across
150g (5 oz) spinach
150g (5 oz) *blette* (chard) or spinach beet
150g (5 oz) lettuce
50g (2 oz) sorrel
50g (2 oz) nettles (optional)
50g (2 oz) mallow (if you can find it)
If possible add chickweed, wild asparagus, wild sorrel, wild garlic, etc.
I large potato
125g (4 oz) peas

Make a vegetable broth; put the onions and leeks in 1½ litres of water with the stock cube and simmer for an hour.

Cook the peas in boiling salted water for 4 minutes, then drain them and add their cooking water to the broth. Set them on one side; they will be added at the end.

Wash and chop all the green vegetables. Dice the potato. Add all the chopped vegetables and potato to the pot, and cook gently for 30 minutes.

Then add the peas and simmer for a minute or two. Serve with toast;
I like to put a sprinkling of grated Cantal or Gruyère cheese on the toast
and quickly melt it under the grill. (Serves 4 - 6)

Split Pea Soup with Oeufs Mollets
Soupe de Pois Cassés, Oeuf Mollet

On a fresh, squally Atlantic day, this warming soup was on the April
menu at La Tupina, Bordeaux's finest traditional restaurant. It was a
homely dish, but the split peas were delicious and made exciting by
the soft egg poised, ready to be broken into, in the middle of the bowl.

250g (9 oz) split green or yellow dried peas
1 onion, chopped
1 leek, sliced
1 carrot, diced
25g (just under 1 oz) butter
1½ litres ham or chicken stock (see recipe for *Cousinette*)
1 potato, diced
2 sprigs of thyme
2 sprigs of rosemary
1 bay leaf
4 eggs
salt, freshly ground pepper

Rinse the peas in cold water.

Melt the butter in a large saucepan and soften the onion, leek and
carrot over a gentle heat for 10 minutes, stirring. Do not allow them
to brown.

Add the stock, potato, and herbs, stir in the peas, cover the pan and
simmer for 40 – 50 minutes until the peas are well cooked. Add more
stock if it gets too thick.

Pour off the liquid and reserve it, remove the herbs and bay leaves
and purée the peas and vegetables briefly in a food processor, adding
some of the liquid back until you have the right consistency. Taste for
seasoning, and keep hot.

Boil the eggs for 6 - 7 minutes, remove and quickly dip into cold water. Crack gently and peel very carefully, taking care to cup the egg in one hand while you peel with the other.

Ladle the soup into heated bowls and place a soft boiled egg in the middle of each bowl. Serve with fingers of toast. (Serves 4 – 6)

Winter Green Pea Soup with Cheese Toast

Dried whole green peas are an almost forgotten vegetable, but their comforting flavour and old-fashioned rough texture, partly given by the skins of the peas, are uniquely restoring on a cold winter day.

200g (7 oz) dried whole green peas
2 litres chicken stock or water
1 onion, coarsely chopped
1 stick celery, coarsely chopped
4 bay leaves
4 sprigs fresh marjoram or a teaspoon of dried marjoram
4 sprigs parsley
2 thick slices of ham, cooked or raw, complete with fat
4 tablespoons single or double cream
salt, plenty of freshly ground pepper

Soak the peas in cold water for 24 hours. Drain well. Put them in a saucepan with all the ingredients except the salt and the cream.

Bring to the boil and cook, covered over a low heat for an hour or more, until very tender. Allow to cool a bit.

Remove the bay leaves and ham, and purée the soup in batches in the food processor. Reheat, stirring, and season well with salt and pepper. Shred the ham and stir it into the soup. Ladle into bowls and put a tablespoon of cream into each bowl. Serve with toast topped with slices of cheese and melted under the grill. (Serves 4)

Lentil Soup with Greens

If possible, make this earthy soup the day before you want to eat it, but do not add the spinach. Keep the soup in a cold place and let the flavour develop. Basque cooks sometimes stir some fresh greens into their soups at the last minute; instead of spinach you could use greens such as kale or purple sprouting broccoli, sorrel, watercress or chard leaves or even nettles or dandelions; add a dash of olive oil and a squeeze of lemon when the greens are tender.

200g (7 oz) dark green lentils
bunch of parsley and 2 bay leaves
2 onions, finely chopped
1 carrot, finely diced
2 cloves of garlic, chopped
2 litres water or stock
2 – 3 tablespoons olive oil
100g (3 ½ oz) lardons
1 teaspoon smoked hot paprika
1 teaspoon ground coriander
1 tablespoon red wine vinegar
1 potato, finely diced
salt, freshly ground pepper

To finish:
3 handfuls fresh, young spinach, or greens sliced into manageable pieces
quarters of lemon to squeeze
drizzle of olive oil

Put one chopped onion, the carrot and garlic in a large pot together with the lentils. Cover generously with water or stock and bring to the boil. Simmer for 30 minutes.

In a small pan soften the second onion, with the lardons, in olive oil over a low heat, stir in the spices, and then the red wine vinegar. Add this mixture to the lentils together with the diced potato, taste for salt, add more water or stock if necessary and simmer until the potato is tender, for 15 minutes. If possible keep overnight.

Heat the soup, and 5 minutes before serving, remove the herbs, stir in the spinach or greens and let it barely cook, it should be a nice bright colour.

Serve with a dash of olive oil and a squeeze of lemon. (Serves 4)

Lenten Soup

In the lean days before Easter there is always abundant wild sorrel, called *sarrous*, sprouting in the banks and hedgerows of the Pyrenean meadows, which country cooks make into a delicious Lenten soup with chickpeas. Soups relying solely on vegetables can be rather unsatisfying, but this one has a very warm, full flavour. The same soup could of course be made with ham or chicken stock.

100g (3½ oz) dried chickpeas, soaked overnight
2 litres (68 fl oz) vegetable stock or water
2 bay leaves
1 tablespoon coriander seeds
1 dried chilli, ancho, choricera or guindilla, or ½ teaspoon chilli flakes
2 onions, chopped
6 cloves of garlic, chopped
1 stick celery, chopped
1 large potato, cut in small pieces
1 packet paëlla seasoning such as Spigol or Dalia or 2 big pinches of
saffron
2 large handfuls sorrel leaves (wild sorrel could be used) or spinach,
greens or chard (blanched in boiling water if the leaves are tough)
sea salt

Put the drained chickpeas in a large pan and add the stock, bay leaves, coriander and chillies. Bring to the boil, simmer for one and a half hours, then add the onions, garlic, celery, potato, paëlla spice or saffron and salt. Simmer for a further half hour, then remove the chilli. Take a third of the soup and blitz it roughly, return it to the pan and heat through, stirring it in well. Lastly add the sorrel, greens or chard and cook until tender.

For a deeper flavour:
Toast a slice of bread, then fry it in olive oil with one clove of garlic, until the bread is crisp and golden.

Break it into pieces and pound it with the garlic in a pestle and mortar, adding a cup of the chickpea cooking liquid, or do it with a hand held blender. Add this and the frying oil to the soup.

Stir it in well to emulsify it. (Serves 4 – 6)

Leek Soup
Soupe de Poireaux

This is a rather comforting, thickish soup, eaten in the colder months, when leeks are one of the few seasonal vegetables. The Bar de la Poste in Oloron, high in the Pyrenees, serves it in glazed earthen bowls with lion's head handles; it is more beige than green and full of rather large chunks of potato cooked until they are almost melting into the soup – a real restorative.

1½ litres (53 fl oz) well-flavoured chicken stock
4 leeks
6 medium potatoes
salt, plenty of freshly ground black pepper
2 thin cut slices of ham such as Bayonne or Serrano, cut into little strips
50g (2 oz) duck fat or pork dripping
100g (3½ oz) piece of ham knuckle (*huesos de jamon*)
6 medium potatoes

Cut the leeks in half lengthwise and wash them well, then slice them across into 1cm (⅓ in) slices. Discard the tougher parts of the green tops. Dice four of the potatoes.

Heat the duck fat gently and soften the leeks together with the sliced ham, over a low heat, until well wilted, but not coloured. Add the diced potato and the piece of ham knuckle. Pour on the stock, bring to the boil, cover and simmer until the leeks are very tender and the potatoes falling to pieces. Stir vigorously to release the potato starch and thicken the soup a bit.

Add the remaining potatoes broken into small chunks. (Do this by sticking a short stout blade into the peeled potato and breaking it into small chunks. This way it will release its starch better.) Taste for seasoning, adding plenty of pepper, cook gently for a further 30 minutes, stir well. Eat as it is, or with Watercress Sauce (see page 51). (Serves 4 – 6)

Lenten Leek and Salt Cod Soup
Porrusalda

This satisfying version of the traditional Lenten leek and cod soup is the colour of yellow amber and has a slight kick to it. If it isn't Lent, you can add chicken stock to give even more flavour.

300g (10 ½ oz) salt cod, soaked for 24 – 48 hours, depending on how thick it is
2 tablespoons olive oil
1 large Spanish onion, finely chopped
2 leeks, cut in half lengthwise and sliced
2 cloves of garlic
2 potatoes, cut into small chunks
1 litre (34 fl oz) water
2 bay leaves
½ teaspoon *piment d'Espelette* or ½ teaspoon chilli flakes
2 large pinches saffron or 2 packets saffron powder such as Spigol or Dalia
salt if needed
slices of *pain de campagne*

Cook the cod according to instructions (page 151), lift out the fish and reserve 750 ml (25 fl oz) of the cooking water. Remove the skin and bones, flake the fish and break into manageable pieces.

Heat the oil and soften the onions, leeks and garlic a little, then add the potatoes and pour on the salty cod cooking water. Add the bay leaves and hot red pepper.

Make up to the required amount with water or chicken stock, and add the saffron or Spigol. Simmer for 15 - 20 minutes, covered. Add the flaked cod and bring to the boil. Remove from the heat, taste for seasoning and serve with slices of toasted *pain de campagne*. (Serves 4)

Pumpkin Soup

Pumpkin is everywhere in January, the market stalls are piled with whole giant pumpkins alongside multi coloured and strangely shaped squash and ready-sliced wedges of bright golden flesh. Probably the most popular thing to do with it is to make it into soup.

Roasting the pumpkin beforehand, rather than simply boiling it, gives a slightly caramelized flavour. This soup should be rather thick, sumptuous and satisfying. You could make it with butternut squash.

In spring, a spoonful of Wild Garlic Oil (page 52), swirled in at the last minute, will liven up the flavour.

900g (2lb) pumpkin, peeled and cut into chunks
1 tablespoon olive oil
2 cloves of garlic, peeled and crushed
2 leeks, white part only, halved lengthwise, washed and shredded
1 tablespoon butter or goose or duck fat
1¼ litres (42 fl oz) chicken stock or use a stock cube
100g (3½ oz) sheep's cheese or manchego, grated
4 slices toasted *pain de campagne*
salt
½ to 1 teaspoon hot red pepper, to taste

Preheat the oven to 200°C (400°F).

Put the pumpkin in a roasting tin, coat it with the olive oil and add the garlic. Roast for 30 minutes, until soft and beginning to brown around the edges.

Heat the butter or duck fat gently in a large pot and soften the leeks stirring over a low heat until they have wilted down.

Add the pumpkin and chicken stock, season with salt and hot red pepper and simmer for 15 - 20 minutes. Allow to cool.

Blend until smooth, add more stock if it is too thick, reheat and serve with slices of toast covered in grated sheep's cheese or manchego. (Serves 4)

Bean and Olive Soup
Soupe à St-Jean-de-Luz

Some versions of this soup, rustic and hearty, use dried broad beans and black olives, this one is lighter and is made with white beans and green olives – if you choose olives flavoured with anchovy this gives and added depth to the flavour.

Any white haricot or butter beans will do, but the best are the *haricots-maïs Béarnais,* these climbing beans, in season in the Autumn, are cultivated alongside maize plants which they use as a climbing pole;[1] they are sought after for their flavour and their thin skins, which make them very digestible.

As with the pumpkin soup, you can liven up the flavour at the last moment with Wild Garlic Oil (see page 52).

200g (7 oz) potatoes, peeled and cut in cubes
150g (5 oz) white haricot or butter beans, soaked overnight
60g (2 oz) stoned green olives
3 leeks, pale parts only, sliced
2 shallots chopped
4 cloves garlic, chopped
salt, freshly ground pepper

Put all the ingredients in a large pan with 1½ litres (50 fl oz) of water.

Bring to the boil and simmer gently, covered, for 1½ – 2 hours. Allow to cool.

Purée in a food processor in batches, until the soup is very, very smooth with not a trace of the husks of the beans. Sieve if the husks are still palpable.

Season well and if you like, serve with Wild Garlic Oil, which is a beautiful, violent green. You can also make this oil with parsley instead of garlic leaves. (Serves 4 – 6)

[1]
The farm hands planting the seeds in spring wore blue aprons with two pockets, one for maize and the other for beans.

Basque Red Bean Soup

I had this soup in a very unspoiled country restaurant in the village of Mendionde, deep in the country lanes of the Pays Basque, where a hospitable mother and son cooked and served entirely local food, as well as running the village bar, café and post office. The warming red bean soup was perfect on a bright cold day in early spring.

It is important to buy kidney beans that have not dried out too much. If they are nearing their sell-by date, they will already be rock hard and will not soften.

150g (5 oz) dried red beans, soaked overnight
2 litres (70 fl oz) chicken stock
2 leeks, white part only, finely sliced
2 small onions, finely chopped
3 tablespoons olive oil
1 red pepper, peeled, deseeded and diced
1 clove of garlic
1 tablespoon sweet paprika
1 teaspoon *piment d'Espelette* or hot paprika
2 large tomatoes, skinned, deseeded and chopped or ½ tin tomatoes, chopped
salt, freshly ground pepper

Put the beans in a saucepan with the stock, add the leeks and one chopped onion and boil for 2 hours, or until the beans are soft.

Heat the olive oil in a frying pan and soften the remaining onion and the chopped pepper, without letting them brown, for 15 minutes. When they are tender add the garlic, then the paprika and red pepper and finally the tomatoes. Season with salt and continue to cook, stirring often, for 10 minutes.

Add the mixture to the beans, taste for seasoning and cook for a further 15 minutes. You can purée the soup or leave the beans whole. This soup reheats very well. (Serves 4 – 6)

Marmitako

Apparently this soup-stew began life on the Basque fishing boats; onions, potatoes and dried peppers will all last a month or two on board a boat, so all that needed to be done was to catch the tuna. Instead of potatoes, you could try adding the sweetness and golden colour of pumpkin or squash.

500g (1 lb 2 oz) fresh tuna
2 dried choricero or ancho chillies
250g (9 oz) small red potatoes or 1 acorn squash, peeled, deseeded and cubed
6 tablespoons olive oil
1 large red onion, finely chopped
2 cloves of garlic, chopped
1 red pepper, grilled as on page 96
2 teaspoons paprika
250ml (8½ fl oz) white wine
2 tablespoons chopped parsley
salt

Cut the fish, skin removed, into chunks and salt it for 30 minutes. Pour boiling water over the chillies and let them soak until soft.

The potatoes are not cut, but broken into chunks the size of a chestnut, by inserting a knife or an oyster shucker and levering bits off. The rough surfaces will release their starch to thicken the soup.

Open the softened dried peppers, remove the seeds, and scrape up the inner pulp from the skins with a knife. Chop the pulp a bit, as it can be stringy.

Heat the olive oil and add the onion; let it soften then add the garlic and choricero or ancho pepper pulp, stir well and cook for 5 more minutes.

Add the red pepper cut in small pieces, the paprika, the potatoes or squash, and the white wine. Let it bubble for a few minutes. Add 1 litre (35 fl oz) of water to cover well and season with salt. Simmer for 30 minutes over a low heat.

Add the fish and chopped parsley and bring to a quick simmer. Turn off the heat and allow to stand, covered, for 10 minutes. Flake the pieces of tuna carefully, Spoon potatoes and soup into bowls and place the flaked tuna on top, then serve with bread. (Serves 4)

Basque Fish Soup
Ttoro

You can serve the stew with a light, fresh, zingy apple *aïoli*; this idea is from Arzak, one of the world's most fabulous restaurants, and they understand what is perfect to serve with a simple fish soup.

One of the traditional fish to include here is conger eel, essential to any *Ttoro*. Conger tail has a multitude of fine bones, so choose the thick part immediately behind the head.

800g (1¾ lbs) fish fillets such as cod, monk fish, conger eel, red mullet and gurnard
500g (1lb 2 oz) mussels, washed and scraped
250g (9 oz) raw prawns
3 tablespoons olive oil
1 onion, finely chopped
1 leek, sliced lengthwise, washed and chopped
1 stick celery, chopped
200ml (7 fl oz) white wine
100ml (3½ fl oz) fish stock or water
4 tomatoes, skinned and chopped
1 bay leaf
5 sprigs of thyme
1 teaspoon *piment d'Espelette* or 1 teaspoon sweet paprika plus plenty of cayenne pepper
4 slices toasted *pain de campagne*

To serve:
apple *aïoli* (page 50)
4 slices toasted *pain de campagne*

Cut the fish into 4cm (2 inch) chunks, removing the skin. Clean the mussels.

Heat the olive oil in a large, deep pot, and cook the onions, leeks and celery for 10 – 15 minutes, until soft. Add the white wine, let it bubble for 2 or 3 minutes, add the tomatoes, herbs and red pepper or paprika and cayenne, and cook gently for a further 10 minutes or until the tomatoes lose their wateriness. This base can now be kept in the refrigerator until you need to finish the *Ttoro*.

Reheat the tomato base adding the fish stock and 250ml (8½ fl oz) of water. When it reaches simmering point, add the fish and mussels, stir carefully, cover the pan and let it boil fast for 3 minutes. Lower the heat, add the prawns and simmer, covered until they are just cooked, it will take about 2 minutes. Serve very hot in big bowls, accompanied with apple *aïoli* spread on toast. (Serves 6)

Ham and Cabbage Soup
Garbure

This rustic soup is practically a national dish in the Béarn, but what makes a good *garbure*? Traditionally, it should be simmered over a wood fire, in a great big black pot, for ages, it must be thick enough for a spoon to stand up in it, and it must contain cabbage and goose or duck fat.

Chef Pierre Kauffman's Gascon grandmother and her neighbours kept hams and sausages hanging up in their kitchens and a cellar or cool room full of big jars of confit duck or goose, made in the autumn. A well-kept vegetable garden stood outside; all the essential ingredients were, after much labour, there to hand.

For an every day *garbure* a piece of goose or duck confit, skin or giblets would provide the meat element, while a bigger feast could include ham, pork knuckle, salt pork, sausage, or pork throat, for the basic broth; vegetables can include turnips, carrots, onions, leeks, garlic, dried chillies, pumpkin, broad beans, green beans, chestnuts, nettles, borage – and don't forget the cabbage – and white haricot beans, potatoes and bread for the comforting part.

You will also need hot red pepper – chillies, hot paprika and *piment d'Espelette* – and grated Cantal cheese. All the ingredients are cooked into a *'soupe-plat'* – a one-pot meal. If you want the vegetables to be comparatively fresh, then make it as follows and do not cook it all day long.

Two days before: (48 hours) ahead:
150g (5 oz)) white *haricot* beans or *haricots maïs* *
Start soaking the beans. Put them in a large bowl of cold water and leave them.

24 hours ahead:
750g (1lb 10 oz) smoked gammon or ham knuckle, soaked for 1 – 2 hours in cold water
1 head of garlic
1 dried red chilli or 2 fresh ones
1 bunch thyme, parsley and bay leaves
3 litres (100 fl oz) water
4 carrots sliced
400g (14 oz) potatoes, cut into large dice
3 small turnips, quartered
200g (7 oz) pumpkin or butternut squash, cut into large dice
1 green cabbage or spring greens, shredded
200g (7 oz) green beans cut into short lengths
6 slices country-style bread
150g (5 oz)) Cantal or Gruyère cheese, grated
piment d'Espelette or chilli flakes

Put the ham or gammon in a large casserole with, the pre-soaked, drained beans, the garlic, the chilli, and the bouquet garni. Add 3 litres of water.

Bring to the boil, skim, turn down the heat, cover the pan and simmer for 2 hours.

Add the carrots, potatoes, turnips and pumpkin. Simmer for 45 minutes. Leave to stand in a cool place overnight. Spoon off most of the layer of fat from the top. Remove the garlic, chilli and bouquet garni.

Remove the ham knuckle and cut off the rind; cut the meat into lardon-shaped pieces and return it to the soup. Bring back to simmering point.

Add the green beans and cabbage to the soup, and simmer for 10 minutes, or, for a fresh element, cook them separately for 7 minutes in a pan of boiling, salted water, drain well in a colander and add them to the soup.

Heat the grill.

Toast slices of bread – preferably *pain de campagne* – and cover them with grated Cantal or Gruyère. Put them under the grill until the cheese is melted. Serve each person with soup, vegetables, pieces of ham and some hot, melting cheese toast. Sprinkle *piment d'Espelette* or a few chilli flakes on top. (Serves 6 – 8)

Broad Bean Gaspacho

The most delicate, beautiful and uplifting chilled green soup, but making it is labour intensive and so it's preferably served in tiny amounts in a coffee cup or a little shot glass, with a teaspoon.

1kg (2¼ lbs) fresh broad beans
100g (3½ oz) blanched almonds
100ml (3½ fl oz) best olive oil
½ to 1 tablespoon cider or sherry vinegar
water
salt

Pod the beans and plunge them into boiling salted water for a minute if very young, two if larger. Drain and run them under the cold tap. You can now remove the outer skin, leaving a little bright green jewel of a bean.

Pulse the beans and almonds together in a food processor, add the olive oil a little at a time. Chill overnight – the next day sieve the soup and then add salt, a little cider vinegar to freshen the taste and a little water. Chill before serving. (Serves 2 – 4)

Basque Gaspacho

This has a real punch to it and is utterly refreshing. It is really easy to make as it does not have diced raw vegetables added, has a rustic texture and relies solely on croûtons for the necessary crunch.

4 large very ripe tomatoes
5 slices stale bread, crusts removed
1 red pepper
1 cucumber
6 spring onions
3 cloves garlic
4 tablespoons olive oil
100ml (3½ fl oz) sherry vinegar
large pinch cayenne pepper
½ teaspoon *piment d'Espelette* or hot paprika
sea salt, freshly ground black pepper

Skin the tomatoes and chop in large pieces; put them into a bowl with their juice and three slices of the bread, cut in cubes.

Deseed the peppers and cut in pieces, peel the cucumber and cut in pieces. Chop the onions and garlic. Put all the vegetables together in the bowl with the olive oil, sherry vinegar and seasoning. Chill in the refrigerator for an hour to blend the flavours.

Put everything in a blender with 125ml (4 fl oz) water and blend until you have a fine textured soup. Sieve at this point if you like a really smooth texture, and return the soup to the refrigerator to chill for a few hours or overnight.

Cut the remaining bread into small cubes and toast in the oven at 180°C (360°F) until crisp and golden. Serve the soup very chilled with croûtons to scatter on top. (Serves 4)

Chapter Five

Rice, Eggs and Corn

RICE

When the Moors stormed across Spain and into les Landes and the Garonne Valley in the eighth century, they brought with them a cornucopia of trees, plants, horses, chickens and new foods, including rice, together with the vital skill of irrigation, which made growing rice possible.

Now some of the most exquisite varieties of rice are grown in Spain, although little is known of them elsewhere. It is almost impossible to find the fantastic Bomba rice across the border in France. Strange, since paëlla is ubiquitous in South West France, on restaurant menus and as take home food, cooked in giant pans, fragrant and fresh, at every market.

Spanish-grown rice is quite important in the Basque diet. The flavour and quality of the rice cultivated are equal to anything grown in Italy, and I find the Spanish varieties are more tolerant and easier to cook with than risotto rice and they reheat better, remaining juicy but not soggy.

Although Gascon and Basque cooks are comfortable serving plain rice as a vegetable with fish, chicken or meat, I find that this seldom seems to work very well. But not to be missed is carefully prepared, succulent *riz,* when bathed in olive oil and the rich juices of shellfish, squid, pigeon, chicken, rabbit or quails, and combined with tomato, peppers, chillies and artichokes or mushrooms.

Rice Varieties

For cooks at home there are several interesting varieties of Spanish rice – these are the main contenders. You can substitute cheaper round grain rice and still get a good result, but it does not have the same magical qualities of expansion and absorption; it tends to go soft and stick together.

Bomba – also called Valencia Rice, is a short grain, almost round rice, with a pearly colour. It absorbs three times its volume in liquid (as opposed to the average rice grain, which absorbs only twice its volume), and instead of opening up like a book along the length of the grain, it breaks open crosswise as it cooks, expanding like a concertina to three times its original length during cooking. This means it absorbs more flavour, and does not stick.

For these reasons, *bomba* rice is highly prized by cooks particularly for making paëlla.

Senia and Bahia – short grain rice varieties of Japanese origin, similar to *bomba*. Senia, which is cheaper than Bomba, can absorb more than the average amount of liquid, retaining a creamy texture after cooking. These are the two most widely grown varieties of rice in Spain.

Calasparra – high quality short grain rice, with all the best qualities of Bomba rice, grown in the area around the town of Calasparra in Murcia which has an ideal climate for rice cultivation.

Balilla X Sollana – is also cultivated in Calasparra; arroz Sollana is suitable for paëlla.

Other Varieties of Rice Suitable for Paella

Rice varieties like *Bomba* and *Calasparra* are often available. However, if buying these varieties is a problem, try the internet, and gourmet and ethnic grocery stores. Or, at a pinch, you can use an ordinary medium or short grain rice. In the USA, a variety called Calrose rice is reputed to be a fair substitute.

Cooking Times

These rices take various different times to cook.

Arroz Bomba, very good for paëlla, takes 18 minutes, as does Arrroz Sollana, whereas Arroz Calasparra takes 20 minutes.

Arroz Bahia and Arroz Senia take only 16 minutes – use this as a rule of thumb, what it really means is take care with your timing, because some rice varieties cook faster than others.

Paëlla and it's Pans

The very finest paëlla is cooked outside in a terracotta rice *cazuela* – a wide round, shallow dish with two small handles – over an open fire of fragrant wood or on a little gas tripod.

The cook tends the fire and adds the prepared ingredients in the right order; the rice is not stirred during cooking. The skill is to temper the fire so the rice is cooked through without being burned on the bottom. The telltale sign is the smell – experienced cooks can tell when it is just right by inhaling the warm scents rising from the pot, scooping the air with a cupped hand to bring a handful of this aroma to their noses.

If you cook on gas, you can still buy and use these lovely terracotta pans which are flameproof. They cook evenly and retain the heat, and they look beautiful.

Seasoning Your Earthenware Pan:

New terracottta *cazuelas* need seasoning. To do this. soak them in water for 24 hours. Dry well, then coat the inside with olive oil and place in the oven at 150°C (300°F) for 40 minutes.

When cooking on a gas flame or over charcoal, never put an empty pot on the heat, use medium heat and remember that terracotta retains the heat and goes on cooking after it comes off, so remove it a bit early.

To clean the pot after use, fill with warm water while it is still hot.

Frequent use is the best method to keep a well-seasoned *cazuela*.

Paula Wolfert, a great fan of the traditional *cazuela,* recommended using a heat diffuser with this type of dish.

Copper paëlla pans, tinned inside, are beautiful too, but mainly used in restaurants or wealthy households and they are high maintenance. It is hard work to keep them shining on the outside, as copper should be, and they need frequent retinning inside, so most are now hanging on the wall.

Seasoning your Metal Pan:
Today the majority of cooks have stainless steel pans. Look after your metal pan, season it before its first use by coating the inside with olive oil and placing it in the oven at 150°C (300°F) for 40 minutes. It will soon develop a patina – never use metal utensils, only wood, and never clean it with a metal scritcher – disastrous! I have seen a grown man (a newsreader at that) cry over his spoiled paëlla pan!

There are so many different ways of making paëlla that it almost seems presumptuous to offer recipes. But these combinations are favourites in the South West.

Octopus Paëlla

This succulent rice dish was ideal for rustic life as it could encompass almost anything that came off a boat, grew in the garden, came out of a hunter's bag or hung in the larder at the time – maybe a net bag of snails, or a bit of chorizo sausage, a bucket of squid, an octopus, a scrawny chicken, a wild rabbit or some peas. It does not have to have mussels or pork, or decoration on the top, or it can have them all.

Spigol and Dalia are inexpensive yellow paëlla seasonings that can be used to replace saffron. They also add a characteristic warmth to the flavour (see page 32).

350g (12 oz) baby octopus
200g (7 oz) squid
250g (9 oz) mussels, cleaned
12 small prawns in their shells
2 red peppers
6 tablespoons olive oil

1 onion, finely chopped
4 cloves garlic finely chopped
500ml (½ pint or 10 fl oz) fish stock
4 large pinches saffron or 1 packet Spigol or Dalia
1 teaspoon fresh or ½ teaspoon dried thyme
2 tablespoons chopped parsley
½ teaspoon smoked paprika
1 large tomato, peeled and chopped
200g (7 oz) Bomba rice
1 sliced lemon
salt

Grill, deseed and skin the peppers (see page 96). Cut them into strips.

Wash the squid and octopus and drain them well, cut them into small pieces. Keep a few baby octopus or octopus legs whole to decorate the top.

Place the mussels in a pan with a tablespoon of water and steam them open. Set them aside, straining their liquid into the fish stock.

Heat a tablespoon or two of olive oil in a paëlla pan and fry the prawns, sprinkling them with a little salt. Remove them to one side and add more olive oil to the pan. Fry the chopped onion for 5 minutes, then add the garlic and fry gently for a further 5 minutes, stirring; do not brown.

Heat the fish stock and stir in the saffron or paëlla seasoning.

Add the squid and the whole and sliced up octopus to the pan and cook them in the oil for 10 minutes; they will give out some liquid, which is fine. Add the herbs, paprika and tomato, and half the sliced peppers, and stir them in; simmer for a few minutes.

Stir in the rice and pour on enough stock just to cover everything. Stir once or twice gently, simmer uncovered, without stirring, for 18 minutes. Add a little more stock if it seems to be getting too dry. After 16 minutes bring the whole octopus or legs up to the surface, place the mussels, prawns and extra strips of pepper around and cook 2 minutes more. Remove from the heat, taste the rice, decorate the top with slices of lemon, cover the pan and leave to rest for five minutes before serving. (Serves 6)

Soupy Rice with Cockles
Arroz Caldoso de Berberechos

Berberechos are cockles (*cerastoderma edule*) but you can also use clams, *amandes de mer* (*glycymeris glycymeris*) known as bittersweet clams or dog cockles.which are not, strictly speaking, cockles.

You will use the water they are cooked in, so scrub them and wash them well in several waters to make sure they are clean.

1kg (2lb 3 oz) cockles or clams, well cleaned
60ml (2 fl oz) dry white wine
250g (9oz) Calasparra rice
1 red pepper, roasted and skinned
2 dried choricero or ancho peppers, seeds removed, or 2 dried chillies
100ml (3½ fl oz) olive oil
3 large cloves garlic, chopped
juice of half blood orange (or lemon)
extra olive oil
1 litre (35 fl oz) water
salt

Rinse and scrub the clams. Bring the wine and 4 tablespoons of water to a boil, throw in the clams, cover and cook over a high heat until the clams open. Remove the clams from pan and reserve the clam cooking liquid for later. Cut the roasted red pepper into strips. Heat a few tablespoons of olive oil in a large heavy bottom frying pan. Sauté garlic and both red bell peppers and dried peppers or chillies, stirring. When the garlic starts to colour, remove the pan from the heat. Transfer the peppers to a blender, adding 250ml (9 fl oz) of the reserved clam broth, and blend until smooth.

Return the mixture to the pan and add any remaining broth, 500ml (18 fl oz) water and salt and bring to the boil. Add the rice and stir. Reduce the heat to a simmer for approximately 18 – 20 minutes, or until the rice is cooked. Add additional liquid if needed, so that the rice is soupy.

When the rice is cooked, add the clams. Cover the pan and let it rest for 5 minutes. Adjust the salt to taste, sprinkle with orange juice and olive oil and serve. (Serves 4)

Salt Cod with Rice
Riz à la Morue

Use the thick part of the salt cod, which will give nice big, white flakes.

When preparing the tomatoes, collect all the juices and seeds in a bowl, and use this as part of the cooking liquid for the rice, to add flavour and richness.

400g (14 oz) salt cod, soaked for 24 – 48 hours and prepared as page 87 in the recipe for Salt Cod and New Potato Salad
2 red peppers and 2 yellow peppers
4 – 5 tablespoons olive oil
I large onion chopped
2 cloves garlic, chopped
700g (1½ lb) tomatoes, skinned, deseeded and chopped
I or 2 teaspoons *piment d'Espelette* or chilli flakes
250g (9oz) Bomba or Calasparra Rice
I lemon, cut into 8 slices
salt, freshly ground pepper

Skin, debone and flake the cooked cod into large flakes.
Grill, deseed and skin the peppers and cut them into strips. Heat most of the oil in a paëlla pan and soften the onion for 10 minutes. Add the garlic and let it soften for a minute or two, then add the tomatoes, peppers and chilli.

Stir everything together and cook for 5 minutes, then add the rice and the remaining olive oil and cook, stirring until the rice has absorbed the oil and juices for 2 – 3 minutes.

Add salt and pepper and 500ml (18 fl oz) water, you can use the water from cooking the cod if it is not too salty; cover the pan and cook for 18 – 20 minutes. Scatter the flaked cod over the top. Remove the pan from the heat, arrange the lemon slices on top, cover the pan and let it stand for 5 minutes, to heat the cod and let the rice mellow before serving. (Serves 4 – 6)

Black Rice
Arroz Negro (also known as *Paëlla Negro*)

Dramatic Black Rice, coloured and flavoured with squid or cuttlefish ink, usually contains squid, but can also include clams, mussels, miniature cuttlefish (*Sepiola rondoletti* or *Rossia macrocosoma*) (*sépiole* in French or *chipiron* in Spanish), prawns, lobster and pieces of lemon. There can hardly be a more striking dish than a glistening plate of black rice with a fat piece of pink lobster on top.

200g (7 oz) mussels, scrubbed
500g (1lb 2oz) fresh squid, cleaned
100g (3½ oz) prawns in their shells or the meat of a small lobster
100ml (3½ fl oz) olive oil
1 large red pepper
2 large, ripe tomatoes, skinned and deseeded
2 cloves garlic, chopped
1 onion, finely chopped
2 tablespoons chopped flat parsley
250g (9 oz) Calasparra rice
100ml (3½ oz) white wine
1 or 2 x 6g (¼ oz) packets squid ink
juice ½ lemon
1 lemon, roughly cut into small pieces
1 teaspoon *Espelette* pepper, ¼ teaspoon cayenne pepper or ½ teaspoon chilli flakes
salt

Roast or grill the pepper (see page 96), skin and deseed it and chop it into small pieces.

Chop the tomatoes.

Put the cleaned mussels in a pan with a few tablespoons of water, cover the pan and steam them open. Save the liquid for cooking the rice.

Heat the prawns or lobster briefly in a tablespoon of olive oil. Keep warm but do not allow it to dry out.

Put the squid in cold water and bring to simmering point, simmer for 10 minutes and drain them. Again save the liquid. When cool, cut them into thin rings.

Mix the garlic with the peppers and tomatoes.

Heat the remaining olive oil in a wide pan such as a paëlla pan, and soften the onion without letting it brown too much. Add the garlic, tomatoes, peppers and parsley and cook for 5 minutes, stirring. This is the basic *sofrito* and can be made ahead.

Stir in the rice, cook for 2 – 3 minutes. Pour on 400ml (14 oz) liquid using the mussel and squid cooking juices and making up the volume with boiling water.

Mix the ink with the white wine and strain into the paëlla pan. Add the lemon juice, stir in the squid and season with salt and *Espelette* pepper, cayenne or chilli.

Cover the pan and cook gently. Add more liquid if needed. After 15 minutes decorate the top with prawns or lobster and mussels and slices of lemon. Cover and cook for a further 3 – 5 minutes, then allow to cool down, off the heat for 5 minutes, still covered. (Serves 4 – 6)

Basque Rice
Riz Basquaise

This is a sofa and slippers type of dish – even more so if you make little depressions in the rice at the end of cooking and break eggs into these holes. Cover the pan again and cook on until eggs start to set, then turn off the heat and let them finish cooking.

Soft, fresh chorizo is best for cooking; mature cured chorizo which is harder, is better for slicing and eating as tapas

250g (9 oz) Bomba or Calasparra rice
1 large onion, finely chopped
2 red peppers, grilled and skinned, see page 66
1 clove garlic, thinly sliced
500g (1lb 2 oz) soft chorizo, cut in 1cm (¼ inch) pieces
2 large, ripe tomatoes cut across into slices
1 teaspoon chilli flakes or *piment d'Espelette*
4 tablespoons olive oil
500ml (18 fl oz) chicken stock or water
salt

Cut the deseeded peppers into strips.

Heat the olive oil in a terracotta *cazuela*, a frying pan or paëlla pan and soften the onions for 10 minutes over a low heat, without browning. Add the peppers and garlic and chorizo and cook, stirring once or twice, for 5 minutes. Stir in the rice and combine it with the sautéed peppers and chorizo in the pan.

Add the chilli flakes or piment d'Espelette and 500ml (18 fl oz) stock or water. Cover the pan and leave to cook 10 minutes. Arrange the slices of tomato on top and cook, covered, for a further 8 – 10 minutes. Remove from the heat and, still covered, allow to rest for 5 – 10 minutes before serving. (Serves 4 – 6)

Bayonnaise Rice
Riz à la Bayonnaise

Based on a recipe from Maïté Etchegoyen, a stall holder in Bayonne covered market, who recorded her recipes in her little book *Manuel de Cuisine Basque*. Unsurprisingly, it features Bayonne ham. According to a Gault et Millau *Guide Gourmande de France*, Bayonne ham, usually eaten raw, was sometimes cooked whole and then cut in slices as almost as thick as a beef steak; even raw ham was traditionally cut into thick slices resembling the leather sole of a shoe, and you needed at least a few really good teeth to chew it. Currently it is cut very thin and takes seconds to cook.

125g (4 oz) Bomba or Calasparra rice
1 tablespoon olive oil
1 tablespoon goose or duck fat
1 large onion, finely chopped
250ml (9 fl oz) chicken stock or water
4 thin slices of Bayonne or Serrano ham, cut into little strips
100g (3 oz) Gruyère cheese, grated
25g (1 oz) butter
4 eggs
salt, *Espelette* pepper or freshly ground black pepper

Heat the oil and goose fat in a wide pan such as a paëlla pan and soften the onion until it is tender and a pale gold colour. Pour in the rice and stir it round until well coated with the oil.

Add the water or chicken stock. Cover the pan and cook for 18-20 minutes.

Stir in the strips of ham and half the grated cheese.

Butter a gratin dish and transfer the rice to it, Smooth it out and make 4 depressions in the surface. Break an egg into each. Scatter the remaining cheese on top dot with nuts of butter and brown lightly under the grill, without overcooking the eggs, the yolks should still be runny. (Serves 2 – 4)

Gracious Rice
Riz à la Gachucha

Gachucha is the translation of the forename Gracieuse, but I think this dish can be called 'gracious' because it is such an easy going dish. You can keep it hot, you can reheat it, you can add things – green peas or skinned, chopped tomatoes – and it always comes good – perfect comfort food. Serve it with a green salad, scattered with chopped parsley and basil.

8 chicken legs and thighs
5 – 6 tablespoons olive oil
2 red onions, finely chopped
150g (5 oz) lardons, smoked if possible
4 cloves garlic, chopped
150g (5 oz) soft cooking chorizo, thickly sliced
2 red peppers, grilled skinned and cut into strips
1 teaspoon chilli flakes, *piment d'Espelette* or hot paprika
250g (9 oz) Calasparra or other Spanish rice
500ml (18 fl oz) chicken stock
20 stoned black or green olives, or a mixture of the two
salt and freshly ground black pepper

Heat 3 tablespoons of olive oil in a large flattish pan such as a paëlla pan. Brown the pieces of chicken all over in batches; transfer them to a dish when they are well-browned.

Add more oil when necessary. Lower the heat a little and soften the onions in the same oil, together with the lardons, until melting and pale golden. If you don't like it too rich, pour some of the oil off at this point. I personally love the olive oil, chicken fat and bacon fat, as they add flavour and succulence, but it does come out somewhat rich with oil.

Stir in the garlic, the chorizo, the strips of red pepper and the chilli flakes, piment or paprika and pour in the rice. Stir it so that it is well coated with oil.

Put in the pieces of chicken. Pour on the stock, season well and cover the pan. Simmer gently until the rice has absorbed the stock, about 18-20 minutes. Remove from the heat, scatter the olives on top, cover and allow to sit for 5-10 minutes or longer if you like. (Serves 4)

Eggs

The rearing of domesticated hens both for eating and for eggs has burgeoned in les Landes along with the growing of maize. Rearing poultry for the table and egg-farming are serious occupations here and many people in the business choose *la poule Rousse* (little red hen) as a laying hen, since she is a sensible, friendly, hard working chicken that lays lots of eggs.

But there is a breed of Landaise chicken with a great reputation of its own.

La poulet Landaise, according to a tome written by Abbé Dubourdieu in 1922, is "Ferocious, suspicious and flighty; she will never become completely tame. She likes to live in the woods and perch in the trees. She is made to live in liberty".

It seems she perches in all weathers in a pine or plum tree, rather than in the barn and she is secretive about where she makes her nest. Because of her freedom to scratch everywhere, she has an interesting diet. An ideal chicken for a second home, apparently, as, like some cats, she is happy to look after herself while you are not there.

Black or grey with dainty yellow legs, she is a prodigious layer, but of course her freedom makes finding her eggs extremely difficult. But so rewarding!

Lots of Landaise dishes are based on eggs, but perhaps the most famous is Piperade; here are two variations.

Espelette Pepper Piperade
Piperade Biperra

This is not like any piperade I have ever had – it is more like a thin omelette, piled with delicious, colourful things. It makes a fine lunch dish and would be perfect after a morning outside.

You can add rounds of fried morcilla – black pudding – to the dish.

I large red or green bell pepper
3 tablespoons olive oil
I small onion, chopped
I clove garlic, sliced
I teaspoon *Espelette* pepper, hot paprika or I fresh red chilli, sliced
10 cherry tomatoes, cut in half
2 bay leaves
2 – 3 sprigs of thyme
I tablespoon goose or duck fat or butter
3 eggs, beaten
I small soft chorizo sausage, sliced into 3cm (I inch) rounds
6 – 8 small slices (shavings) of coppa or ham
2 pork sausages, cut into short pieces
salt

Peel the bell pepper, with a swivelling potato peeler. Remove the seeds and cut it into thin strips.

Fry gently in olive oil for 15 minutes until thoroughly cooked. Set aside and soften the onions, garlic and chilli if you are using it, in the same olive oil, then add the hot pepper, the tomatoes and herbs and cook gently for 10 minutes; mix in the fried strips of red or green pepper. Next fry the chorizo, coppa or ham and sausage in a separate pan.

Keep them warm.

Season the beaten eggs, go easy on the salt.

In a non stick pan heat the goose or duck fat until it is quite hot. Pour in the eggs, swirl them round once, then spoon the vegetables on top and put the ham and sausage on top of that. Remove from the heat when lightly set and serve in the pan – share with gusto. (Serves 2)

Piperade Souletine

You can buy sweet long pale green peppers in specialist greengrocers and Turkish shops. (Make sure that you are not buying hot peppers for this dish by mistake, as I did.)

Otherwise use green bell peppers.

500g (1lb 2 oz) long green sweet peppers or green bell peppers
2 – 3 tablespoons pork fat or olive oil
3 onions, finely sliced
500g (1lb 2 oz) large ripe tomatoes, skinned, seeds removed and chopped
2 eggs
1 thin slice of Bayonne or Serrano ham per person
salt and pepper or *piment d'Espelette*

Cut the long green peppers in half lengthwise and remove all the seeds. Cut them into lengths of 2 cm (¾ in). If using bell peppers peel them with a swivelling potato peeler or roast them and skin them. Cut them into small strips.

Heat the pork fat or oil in a large frying pan and add the peppers and sliced onions. Cover the pan and let them cook gently for 10 minutes.

Add the tomatoes, season well and simmer uncovered for 20 minutes, without stirring too much, until the excess water is gone and you have a fragrant vegetable stew.

Add the beaten eggs and stir them in. Immediately remove the pan from the heat.

Put the soft piperade into a warm dish and place the slices of ham on top. (Serves 2)

Morcilla, Serrano and Fried Quail Eggs

45g (1¼ oz) morcilla de Burgos, boudin noir or other soft black pudding, sliced
2 slices Serrano ham
6 quail eggs
2 tablespoons olive oil
pinch of *Espelette* pepper or cayenne

Heat the olive oil and fry the slices of morcilla for one minute on each side until a bit crisp. Tear the ham into small pieces. Gently fry the quail eggs.

Place a piece of ham or two on each slice of morcilla then a fried egg on top, sprinkle with red pepper. Serve hot, as a snack. (Serves 2)

Scrambled Eggs with Morcilla

This is a cross between scrambled eggs and omelette, very tender and light.

50g (2 oz) morcilla de Burgos, boudin noir or other soft black pudding
olive oil
20g (1 oz) butter
2 eggs
100ml (3 fl oz) double cream
salt, freshly ground black pepper

Remove the skin from the morcilla and crumble it into large chunks. Heat a little butter in a non stick pan and fry the sausage over a moderate heat until it is crisp. Remove it and keep it warm. Beat the eggs with the cream and season with salt and pepper. Have two warm plates ready.

Heat the butter in a small non-stick pan over a gentle heat until it starts to foam. Add the morcilla and the egg mixture to the pan. When bubbles start to lift the egg slightly from underneath, make an anticlockwise circular movement with a wooden spatula, to pull the lightly cooked egg round into a pleated fan. Tilt the pan to allow the uncooked egg to run out onto the bare part of the pan.

Immediately, when the egg is barely cooked, fold it over and cut it roughly in half with a spatula

Lift half onto a plate and pile the second half on top.

Share. (Serves 2)

Fresh Cheese Croustade with Artichokes
Croustade au Cailladou

You could make this with fresh sheep's whey cheese*(breuil or faiselle)* or with soft fresh goat's cheese or with ricotta. You can in fact make it with any light creamy sheep or goat's cheese and possibly use asparagus, cut into small pieces, instead of artichoke hearts.

300g (10 oz) puff pastry
6 baby artichoke hearts, preferably fresh
slice of lemon
3 eggs
375g (13 oz) fresh, soft creamy cheese
100ml (3½ oz) double cream
2 tablespoons finely chopped parsley
tender green tops of 2 spring onions, very finely sliced
salt, freshly ground black pepper
butter for the tart tin
egg for glazing

Preheat the oven to 200°C (400°F).

If you are using fresh artichokes, prepare them and cook them briefly until just tender in boiling salted water with a slice of lemon and drain well. Allow to cool.

Beat the eggs in a bowl. Work in the fresh cheese, crushing it with a fork and beat until smooth, then gently whisk in the cream.

Add salt, pepper and chopped parsley and onion tops and stir in the artichoke hearts.

Butter a tart tin, preferably with a removeable base, and line the base with baking paper. Roll out two thirds of the pastry into a disc, and line the tart tin, so that it comes right up the sides and hangs over the rim.

Fill with the cheese and artichoke mixture.

Roll the remaining pastry into a disc and brush one side with half the beaten egg. Place it on top of the tart, egg side down, and press the lower and upper pastry edges together. Trim off the excess pastry with a sharp knife.

Brush the top with the remaining beaten egg.

Place on a baking sheet and bake for 40 minutes. Allow to rest for at least 10 minutes before removing from the tin. (Serves 4 – 6)

Salt Cod and Potato Omelette
l'Omelette à la Morue Béglaise

Bégles, on the outskirts of Bordeaux was once filled with great cod-salting sheds, in fact it was called Stink-town because of the pungent smell of the curing cod. In summer they still hold a Fête de Morue, with giant salt cod omelettes, still a favourite, served in the street and every restaurant featuring salt cod on the menu.

You can add *piment d'Espelette* to the omelette.

Start by soaking the cod for 24 hours or more, changing the water three times.

150g (5 oz) salt cod, soaked for 24 – 48 hours
4 eggs
2 tablespoons olive oil
2 small or 1 large new potato
1 tablespoon olive oil
1 teaspoon leaves of fresh thyme
1 tablespoon chopped parsley
plenty of freshly ground pepper or *piment d'Espelette*

Bring a pot of water to the boil. Remove it from the heat, put in the salt cod and leave it, uncovered, off the heat, for 8 minutes. Drain it and allow to cool. Remove the skin and bones and flake the fish into fairly small pieces.

Cook the potatoes in boiling salted water. Drain well and crush them lightly with a fork

Beat the eggs lightly in a bowl with the chopped herbs and plenty of pepper.

Gently fork together the flaked cod, potato flesh and 1 tablespoon of olive oil. Add the eggs, carefully mixing everything together.

You will be making two omelettes.

Heat ½ tablespoon of olive oil oil in a small omelette pan. Pour in half the egg and salt cod mixture. Let it cook until it starts to bubble round the edge, then sweep it all to one side of the pan with a wooden spatula. Let the uncooked egg run out over the bottom of the pan again and remove immediately from the heat.

Fold it and turn it onto a plate and repeat with the second omelette. Serve the omelettes with a glass or two of cider. (Makes 2 omelettes.)

l'Omelette aux Truffes

1 black truffle, allow at least 15g (½ oz) per person
6 eggs
30g (1oz) butter, plus butter for glazing
salt and freshly ground black pepper

Carefully clean the truffle of mud, or better still buy a clean one, and then you need not pare it, just scrub it lightly with a dry brush and then wipe it with a damp cloth.

Make a fine julienne out of half the truffle.

Beat the eggs with salt and pepper and stir in the julienne. Let it sit for half an hour to develop the flavour.

Now slice the remainder and keep back a few nice slices to decorate the omelette. Stir the rest of the slices and any crumbly bits of truffle into the eggs at the last minute. Heat half the butter and when it starts to brown, make an omelette out of half the mixture (see recipe for salt cod omelette).

Repeat with the remaining eggs.

Rub a piece of butter over the top of the omelettes and decorate with a slice or two of truffle; the heat of the omelette will release their delicious perfume. Serve with a green salad dressed with walnut oil dressing. (Serves 2)

l'Omelette Périgourdine

This is a truffle omelette, as above, but it also includes sliced potatoes fried in butter and a few slivers of foie gras, which are slipped in just before you fold the omelette.

Omelette of Elvers
l'Omelette aux Pibales

This is an interesting recipe, and a great delicacy, but not a practical one, as *Pibales* are tiny, baby elvers, so small that en masse they look almost like transaprent spaghettini. Disastrously, eels have become extremely scarce, so it seems rather criminal to eat them so small. However I once stopped in a very small restaurant while walking near Condom on the Pilgrim's Way to Santiago. It only had about two things on the menu and this was one; it was memorably good and was livened up with garlic and lots of hot red pepper.

You can get still get *pibales* in tins and also false cooked *pibales* (called *Surimi en Forma de Angulas* which are made of fish and are similar to crabsticks in flavour, but which look like elvers. They need no cooking).

This is the recipe of Françoise Pardies, author of Manuel de Cuisine Landaise.

Wash the elvers several times. Take brown tobacco from a cigarette and put it in a pan of boiling water. Put the elvers in a sieve and dip them into this water until they are very white. Drain them.

Heat oil in a terracotta cooking dish together with peeled cloves of garlic and a little red chilli.

Fry the elvers in this, then pour off most of the oil and pour the beaten eggs over the fried elvers. Make the omelette in the usual way.

Scrambled Eggs with Ham and Fried Potatoes
Oeufs Brouillés aux Jambon et Pommes de Terres

This is family supper dish, made with things you are likely to have in the fridge or larder.

2 slices thinly cut Bayonne or Serrano ham
I tablespoon olive oil
3 eggs
2 tablespoons double cream
2 large potatoes, peeled and cut into small dice
salt, freshly ground black pepper

Tear the ham into small pieces with your fingers.

Break the potatoes into small pieces with a small, sharp implement such as an oyster knife, or dice them.

Heat the oil in a non-stick pan and fry the ham very lightly.

Remove it to a plate and, in the same oil, fry the potatoes, covered with a lid, for about 15 – 20 minutes, until they are just cooked, turning them over to brown a little on all sides.

Beat the eggs with the cream.

Pour the beaten eggs over the potatoes and swirl them around, then turn them once with a wooden spatula. Swirl and fold over lightly one more time, and remove the pan when the eggs are just cooked, creamy and light. Scatter the ham over the top at the last minute.

Lobster with Eggs Mimosa
Oeufs Mimosa à l'Homard

Beautiful golden Oeufs Mimosa is not really a South Western dish but a classic of French cooking. However I keep coming across it around the Bassin d'Arcachon and in les Landes and again in Pau. This is partly because the South West is famous for poultry and eggs are very popular, but could it also be because mimosas grow abundantly there and are part of a beautiful rite of spring, when people go picking branches of the fluffy yellow flowers. On the shores of the Bassin, cooks cannot resist putting shellfish into the eggs, which does bring them up a notch or two, particularly if the shellfish happens to be lobster.

1 small cooked lobster, cut in half
12 large free range eggs

For the mayonnaise:
2 raw egg yolks
2 teaspoons Dijon mustard
200ml (7 fl oz) sunflower oil
1 teaspoon warm water
salt, freshly ground pepper

Boil 12 very fresh eggs for 10 minutes. Cool under the tap and shell them.

Make the mayonnaise; put the raw egg yolks into a bowl and blend in the mustard and salt. Gradually add the oil a little at a time. Season and add a little warm water if it seems too stiff, it should be light.

Remove the lobster flesh from the claws and body and cut it into little pieces. Combine it and any coral with the mayonnaise.

Cut the hard boiled eggs in half lengthwise and remove the yolks.

Pile the mayonnaise neatly into the halved eggs with a teaspoon.

With a wooden spoon, push the yolks through a sieve onto a plate, where it will make a bright yellow fluff. With a teaspoon, pile it as neatly as possible on top of the mayonnaise, where it will stick. It looks like mimosa flowers and tastes like paradise on a plate. Serve with lengthwise quarters of Little Gem lettuce sprinkled with salt and olive oil. (Serves 4 – 6)

Oeufs Sur le Plat

chorizo sauce (page 40)
4 eggs
2 – 3 tablespoons double cream
50g (2 oz) *tomme de brébis*, sheep's cheese
butter

Preheat oven to 200°C (400°F).

Put a layer of sauce in a gratin dish. Break four eggs on top. Pour on 2 – 3 tablespoons of cream, and season. Add a few little slices of cheese. Bake for 6 – 8 minutes, the yolks must stay soft and runny. (Serves 2)

Baked Eggs
Oeufs en Cocottes

A lovely little dish to make if you have some leftover chorizo sauce

chorizo sauce (page 40)
butter
4 eggs
100ml (3½ fl oz) single cream
50g (1¾ oz) *tomme de brébis*, sheep's cheese

Preheat oven to 200°C (400°F). Butter 4 cocottes.

Put a tablespoon or two of sauce in the bottom of each cocotte, then break an egg on top – the yolk must stay whole. Pour on a tablespoon of cream and season. Add a few little slices of cheese. Bake for 8 minutes, the yolks should be soft and runny. (Serves 2-4)

Sheep Herder's Tortilla
Omelette du Berger

This is another comfortable, homey weekend lunch dish. Most fresh sausages (*saucisses*) in the South West are made of pure pork and resemble Toulouse sausages which are flavoured with garlic, a bit of white wine and plenty of black pepper.

Originally this omelette would have been made with all sorts of young wild greens such as dandelions, sorrel and milk thistles etc. If you have a good hedgerow near you, early spring is the time to go foraging for the wild greens, before they get tough and start to flower.

150g (5¼ oz) greens such as dandelions or turnip tops (*grelos*) or pick young nettles, wild leeks, chickweed
(*mouron des oiseaux, stellaria media*), wild asparagus, wild garlic and milk thistles
100g (3½ oz) pure pork sausages such as Toulouse, or fresh chorizo or other spicy sausage
4 eggs
1 clove garlic, sliced
½ teaspoon coarse black pepper
4 tablespoons olive oil
1 small onion, sliced
2 potatoes, thinly sliced
salt

Cook the greens in boiling salted water for 10 minutes, drain thoroughly, pressing gently. If they seem to be in long strings, cut them into smaller pieces.

Remove the skins from the sausage or chorizo and break up the sausagemeat into small pieces.

Beat the eggs with salt and pepper.

Heat a tablespoon of olive oil in a large non-stick omelette pan and fry the crumbled sausage or chorizo and onions until lightly browned.

Remove the sausage and onions and put in a bowl, leaving the oil behind. Add 2 tablespoons of olive oil and the sliced potatoes and cook gently, covered, for 15 – 20 minutes or until they are just tender. Drain off the oil and transfer the potatoes to the bowl with the sausage and stir in the cooked greens, and then the eggs.

Wipe out the pan and heat it again with 1 – 2 tablespoons of oil. When it is medium hot, add the egg mixture and cook over a low heat, shaking the pan a bit to prevent the tortilla from sticking. When it is almost set, get ready to turn it over. I do this with a large, flat saucepan lid. (If you are not happy with doing this flip, you can finish cooking the tortilla under the grill.)

With rubber gloves or a cloth, grasp a lid, large enough to more than cover the frying pan, with one hand and the frying pan with the other hand. Place the lid on top of the frying pan and quickly flip the whole thing over, keeping the lid tight on the frying pan – the tortilla will now be on the saucepan lid, so keep it level or it will slide off. Lift off the frying pan, now empty, and turn it the right way up. Return the omelette to the pan, cooked side up.

Cook for a few more minutes until set. Allow the tortilla to sit for at least 10 minutes before cutting. (Serves 4)

Cake with Walnuts and Two Cheeses
Cake aux Deux Fromages et Noix

You can buy these savoury little '*cakes sâlés*' in the markets, they come in many flavours, and are usually loaf-shaped, individual size and cooked, like cupcakes, in a paper case rather than a tin. They have the texture, almost, of a batter, as they contain a lot of eggs and a lot of olive oil.

On the market you will see '*Cake au Saumon et Légumes*', '*Cake aux Olives et Lard*', '*Cake au Jambon*' and more.

100g (3½ oz) plain flour
1 teaspoon baking powder
3 eggs, beaten
100ml (3½ fl oz) milk

4 tablespoons olive oil
100g (3½ oz) goat's cheese
100g (3½ oz) grated Gruyère
handful of walnuts, cut in half
black pepper, little salt

Butter a 450g (1 lb) loaf pan or four small pans; line the bottom of the pans with baking paper.

Heat the oven to 180°C (360°F).

Mix the baking powder into the flour and gradually incorporate the eggs, beating the mixture with a wooden spoon until it is smooth. Add the olive oil, mix it in thoroughly and then add the milk. Stir in the two cheeses. Add the walnuts and some black pepper and very little salt, as the cheeses are salty.

Fill the prepared loaf pan or pans with the mixture, leaving 1cm (⅓ inch) at the top, and bake for 45 – 50 minutes for a large loaf or 25 – 30 minutes for smaller ones.

Remove and cool on a rack, but eat while still fresh. (Serves 4 – 6)

Green Olive Cake
Cake aux Olives Vertes

This is one of the most popular versions of 'cake', it also comes with black olives.

200g (7 oz) stoned, anchovy-stuffed green olives
100g (3½ oz) plain white flour
1 teaspoon baking powder
3 eggs, beaten
4 tablespoons olive oil
100ml (3½ fl oz) milk
100g (3½ oz) grated cheese
pinch salt, black pepper

Heat the oven to 180°C (360°F).

Slice the olives across into four pieces, making little rings. Butter a 450g (1 lb) loaf pan or 4 smaller ones and line the bottom with baking paper.

Mix the baking powder into the flour in a bowl. Pour the eggs into the middle and gradually stir in the flour, mixing it well with a wooden spoon. When you have a smooth mixture, add the oil, working it in well. Season with a little salt and plenty of pepper. Gradually add the milk and then the cheese and olives.

Spoon into the baking tins and bake for 45 minutes for a large loaf, 25 – 30 minutes for small ones.

Cool on a rack. (Serves 4 – 6)

Oeufs Frits à la Landaise

You could place an escalope of fried foie gras on the eggs instead of the confit. Foie gras, fried from raw, is very popular in the region.

½ Savoy cabbage
I tablespoon fat from confit or roast duck, or butter
I leg of confit duck
I shallot, finely chopped
4 eggs
piment d'Espelette or hot paprika
little salt

Shred the cabbage and wash it. Drop it into a pan of boiling salted water for 6 minutes, then drain well and while it is hot stir in a tablespoon of duck fat or butter. Keep it hot.

Fry the leg of confit duck in some of its own fat in a non stick frying pan, until the skin is crisp and the meat heated through. Lift it out and shred it roughly, removing the bone. Slice the crispy skin into pieces. Keep the duck meat hot.

Fry the chopped shallot for 1 – 2 minutes in the same pan. Drain them on kitchen paper.

Fry the eggs in the same fat, adding a bit more if necessary. Arrange the cabbage on two plates. Sprinkle it with fried shallots. Place the confit on top and then the eggs on top of that. Sprinkle with red pepper. (Serves 2-4)

Maize

Escatoun, Broy, Armotes, Milhas Rimotes, las Pous or

Bouillie de Maïs Polenta

To the poorest families of Périgueux, les Landes and the Béarn, maize porage, *bouillie de maïs*, which is essentially the same as Italian polenta, was the daily food throughout the eighteenth and nineteenth centuries. Millet polenta, in some form, goes back to earliest times, but millet and sorghum were replaced as crops by the newly introduced corn on the cob in the sixteenth and seventeenth centuries.

Brought over from the West Indies in the late fifteenth century by Columbus, who, it is said, thought it tasted of chestnuts, corn was also transported by other Portuguese, Basque and Spanish conquistadors.

One hundred years later, it had become a well-established and valuable crop, and one that flourished very well in the hot, rain-sprinkled Atlantic summers of the South West. The strains with smaller, sweeter cobs became popular with humans, while the larger field corn was perfect for fattening poultry, which became and remains one of the great specialities of the region.

Once people became used to the taste, this, together with rye bread and if they were lucky, a bit of cheese or a cabbage, some sardines, pork scratchings or some scraps of ham, was the staple diet. If someone was killing a pig or making confit, some of the fat or the liquid from boiling the sausages and black puddings or from the confit pot could be added to the bouillie before or after cooking.

The maize meal was boiled over the fire in a cauldron, stirred with a long wooden baton and when it thickened, it could be eaten with a spoon like porridge, or poured out on a floured cloth.

When it was cold, it was cut into slabs or slices with a wire and grilled on the fire, to eat with savoury food, while farm workers would put a piece in the pocket of their blue work clothes, *bleu de travaille*,[1]

---

1. *Bleu de travaille* has been the classic colour for work clothes in France since the nineteenth century. Blue was worn only by the poor in fourteenth century until Saint Louis, to do penance, adopted the humble colour, from which time it was immensely fashionable and worn with pride by rich and poor alike. It also made fortunes for the woad merchants of Toulouse, and later for the indigo shippers of Bordeaux.

to take out to the fields.

Bouillie de maïs featured in the daily menus of prosperous families too; people liked it and had a taste for it when it was made with milk, cut thin, fried in little squares or triangles and sprinkled with sugar or eaten with jam, marmalade or prunes.

When times became more prosperous, *bouillie,* which was not particularly rich in nutrients, was mainly replaced by nourishing soup and bread, but you can still buy it on the occasional market stall. They tend to use white maize, but yellow is fine too.

Bouillie de Maïs Polenta

130g (4 oz) instant polenta
70g (2 oz) yellow maize flour
1 litre (34 fl oz) water, stock or the bouillon from a Garbure
1 tablespoon fat from a confit duck or duck dripping from a roast duck or buttter
1 teaspoon salt

Oil a rectangular gratin dish 25cm by 20cm (10 inches x 8 inches).

Mix the maize flour to a smooth consistency with 100ml (3½ fl oz) of the measured water.

Bring the remaining water to the boil in a heavy pan, add salt and scatter the polenta into the water, whisking with a wire whisk until it is all incorporated. Now add the maize flour mixture and keep whisking continuously. Add more hot water if the mixture is too thick.

At this point, swap to a wooden spoon and stir for about five minutes, until it starts to reveal the bottom of the pan and has become a smooth porridge. Away from the heat, add duck fat and juices and work them in thoroughly.

Transfer to an oiled gratin dish, flatten it out and allow to cool. Cover the dish with cling film to prevent a crust forming.

Cut into small square or triangular pieces when cool and fry in goose or duck fat or butter in a non-stick pan. Serve with a dish of wild mushrooms, with melted cheese, with a beef cheek daube, with tomato sauce or with game – traditionally braised pigeon but equally good with any civet or braised game. (Serves 4 – 6)

Gratin of Polenta and Ham
Gâteau de Maïs au Jambon

This is a light version of polenta, it rises a bit like a soufflé, but it does not keep well. Eat it all in one go if possible.

200g (7 oz) instant polenta
100g (3½ oz) raw ham cut into small strips, or small lardons
1 tablespoon of duck fat from confit
6 eggs, separated
1 tablespoon chopped parsley
little salt

Preheat the oven to 180°C (360°F). Butter a gratin dish 20cm by 25cm (8 inches x 10 inches).

Briefly sauté the ham or lardons in a little of the duck fat.

Make the polenta as above but add 250ml (9 fl oz) more liquid, so that it is very soft; when it is cooked stir in the strips of ham or lardons and the remaining duck fat. Allow to cool for 5 minutes.

Meanwhile separate the eggs and whisk the whites to a soft foam.

Stir the egg yolks and parsley into the polenta until they are thoroughly incorporated and then fold in the whites very gently with a metal spoon.

Transfer to the buttered gratin dish and bake for 50 minutes. (Serves 4)

Broye

Broye is polenta made into a sort of dumpling for serving in broth.

Make the polenta as before, but use milk instead of water or stock. When it is cooked, stir in some butter, seasoning and grated cheese if you like. Pour it into a large flat dish, so that it is about 1 cm thick.

Let it get cold, then cut it into small rounds with a small circular biscuit cutter. Heat in bowls of clear broth – *bouillon*.

Mique Blanche

This particular dumpling is from the Pyrenees, other versions can be found all over the South West. In Périgueux they may put salt pork, *fritons* of duck, eggs and garlic into one large round Mique de Maïs, which is then wrapped in a muslin cloth and poached in stock for an hour. It is served with duck or pork confit or with braised game.

Make the polenta as before, when it is cooked, add some chopped ham. When it is cool enough to handle, form it into small round balls with your hands.

Blanch some cabbage leaves in boiling salted water and wrap each ball in a cabbage leaf. Place on top of a simmering *garbure*, cover the pan and steam for 30 minutes.

Chapter Six

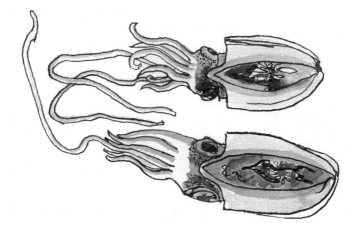

Fish and Seafood

A walk along the beaches of Biarritz, St Jean de Luz or Cap Ferret will give you a view of the holiday maker's Atlantic, wide sands, cleaned and groomed, steady breakers – a surfer's dream. But the coast of Aquitaine and the Pays Basque is also famous for its skilled and fearless fishermen, the best in the Western hemisphere, who were paid undreamed-of rewards to join the voyages of the conquistadors in the fifteenth and sixteenth centuries.

Basque fishermen have to be both brave and skilful to navigate those Atlantic breakers. Count Henry Russel wrote in 1873:

"Near the lighthouse of Biarritz, you are sure to see, in autumn and winter, even in the calmest and loveliest weather, such a stupendous swell as is never witnessed even on the West coast of Ireland. The mass, height and length of these enormous waves is scarcely credible; they are hills of water, and their deafening roar is heard inland most distinctively at more than twenty miles."

The Basques and Médocains know all about fishing and the markets of Bordeaux, Cap Ferret, Bayonne, Biarritz and St Jean de Luz are brilliant with shiny bright-coloured fish, gastropods and shellfish from the Bay of Biscay and the Bassin d'Arcachon. Caught fresh locally, you will see tuna, bass, hake, sardines, anchovies and bream, but you will no longer see what was once their most prized catch, whale.

Whale fishing was in full swing along the Biscayan coast and beyond, throughout the twelfth century; with its rocky headlands, Biarritz offered the best sites for spotting the distant black humps of the North Atlantic right whales, *Eubalaena glacialis,* their prize, and was for three centuries one of the great whaling ports. Over many centuries, meat of any kind was extremely scarce in the South West, so it is easy to imagine how exciting it was when a whale was sighted.

One whale could provide vast amounts of meat and up to twelve tons of oil for lamps, while the best bits, the gigantic tongues each weighing a ton, were cut up and salted like bacon, ready to be eaten during Easter celebrations, with fresh green peas, by the well-fed clergy and their friends, for whom the tongues were reserved.

When the whales moved north to colder waters, the Basques went after them, staying at sea for months on end – whaling and cod-fishing are probably responsible for early Basque contact with both the North Sea and Newfoundland.

Basques, although they wish to be autonomous, have always wanted to learn from the outside world – they had found out from the Vikings how to build stronger ships, and they needed to be strong, to survive those perilous transatlantic journeys; they also learned the Nordic method of air-drying the North Sea cod to make stockfish – which they improved by salting the catch, having ready access to the salt of Saliés-de-Béarn. Thus the salt-cod could be transported home, a voyage of 4,000 kilometres (2,480 miles).

Basqueland and Bordeaux were at the centre of a huge international salt-cod trade. Not only was it the main food throughout France, during Lent and fast-days, but the lower quality pieces of fish also provided the cotton growers of the Southern States of America and the sugarcane growers and tobacco farmers of the West Indies with cheap food for their slaves.

In return, the cargoes that came back to the UK included cotton, sugar, tobacco and rum.

The Bay of Biscay itself is known for its oily fish called 'blue fish' which include tuna, sardines, anchovies and mackerel.

Ciboure, Guéthary-Bidart and Biarritz are still tuna fishing ports; the Basques fish for tuna with lines, several to each boat, traditionally using bait of salted eel or false sardines made of blue cloth.

Each summer, since Roman times, their boats have set out after the red tuna (bluefin tuna, *Thunnus thynnus*), beautiful creatures that can weigh 400 kilos (nearly 900 lbs) and also the smaller more delicate *germon*, albacore tuna (*Thunnus alalunga*), which as the sea warms up, head for the bay of Biscay from the North Atlantic.

Tuna is on sale today in the covered fish markets of St Jean de Luz, Biarritz and Bayonne, but is madly expensive; reduced quotas have raised prices but also allowed the shoals of these glorious fish to rebuild and things are slowly improving after long years of over-fishing.

There are five high quality fish canneries along the Basque coast, making the highest quality tinned tuna, as well as canned sardines and anchovies, and the *germon* is still fished from St Jean de Luz, being a less transient catch than their other love, the sardine.

Sardines started arriving off the shores of the Biscayan coast in winter months in unprecedented numbers in the nineteenth century, to the joy of the local fishermen – at night the phosphorescent shoals could be seen, shimmering just below the surface of the water. By day, thrashing porpoises, ravaging the schools of fish, gave the boats their bearings. Alongside the silver sardines were reddish shoals of anchovies. They are eaten as fresh anchovies which are called *bocartes*, or tinned and salted when they become *anchoas* and when made into tapas, by pickling them in vinegar with garlic and parsley, they are *boquerones*.

Once landed in St Jean de Luz, sardines and anchovies were loaded into round willow baskets and onto the heads of *sardineras* or *kaskarots*, young women with skirts bundled up, who would then run barefoot, flying along the sandy roads to nearby Biarritz and Bayonne to sell the fish – they covered 20 miles or more in a day.

Sardines are still fished here, eaten in large quantities and there are shops specializing in the excellent locally canned fish. Basque fishermen also catch plenty of gilt-head bream and silky, grey hake, Spain's favourite fish, in the Bay of Gascony, (also known as the Bay of Biscay and Côte d'Argent); their lines are baited with hundreds of sardines and the fish are proudly labelled 'Pêché à la ligne – St Jean de Luz'.

Fishing is also an essential activity in the Gironde and the Bassin d'Arcachon, where the best oysters are reared, and every local man has his own fishing boat or, along the estuary and the river Gironde, fishing platform, with cantilevered nets that dip down into the estuary and cosy huts for hanging out in. Where the Atlantic salt water pulses up the Gironde river, the catch is likely to be smelts, shad, lampreys, shrimps and, importantly, *maigre,* a large, silvery sea bass-like estuary fish, (*Argyrosimus regius*), which, unlike the smart and clear eyed bass, 'has the sad look of the defeated'.[1] A *maigre* can reach over 100kg (220 lb) but the youngsters taste better.

Shad is another great favourite in Bordeaux, while pickled baby shads called *gates,* and fried shad roe are both local specialities.

At one time there was a steady catch of *créa,* the wild sturgeon (*Acipenser sturio),* in the Gironde and Dordogne rivers, and I have seen it on menus recently, served with fennel, but by the 1980s, overfishing and gravel extraction had put paid to the wild native fish. However, there are several fish farms rearing sturgeon for caviare and this industry has become very big bucks – it is estimated that French caviare accounts for a sixth of the world's farmed caviare. The species they favour is from the Baeri sturgeon (*Acipenser baerii);* Prunier's sell nothing else.

Trout of all sizes from tiny tiddlers to the size of full grown salmon are also farmed, in the clear rivers of the High Pyrenees at Banca.

Les Saumons de l'Adour are wild salmon who have spent a couple of years high in the tributaries of the Adour river, up in the Pyrenees. In spring, when the rivers are in full spate, they descend to the sea and are netted by fishermen – they are highly prized.

You will find smoked salmon trout or salmon tartare on every menu – there is a taste for raw fish and raw shellfish of all kinds along the Atlantic coast. Fortunately spanking fresh fish and seafood are plentiful,

1. Says Michel Doussy, author of *la Cuisine du Bassin d'Arcachon* who calls these fish maigrot.

and the fishing industry is surviving, fish and oyster farming are huge and the seaports still smell of drying fishnets and of frying fish.

Cod in a Black Ink Sauce

The squid ink sauce is a real staple in Basque restaurants, and it is like sorcery – you can make an ordinary tomato sauce and at the last minute transform it into something darkly dramatic, especially when it is served with pearly white cod or red peppers.

This recipe, based on one from La Taverne Basque in St Jean de Luz is served with *Pommes Écrasées* (page 264).

For the cod:
4 cod steaks, each weighing 150g or 5 oz
3 bay leaves
1 tablespoon white wine vinegar
12 peppercorns
salt

For the sauce:
1 onion, chopped
2 cloves garlic, chopped
3 tablespoons olive oil
1kg (2¼ lbs) peeled tomatoes, deseeded and chopped or 2 x 400g (14 oz) tins
3 x 6g (1 oz) packets squid ink
salt, freshly ground pepper, *piment d'Espelette* or paprika
½ teaspoon sugar

Soften the onion in the olive oil until tender, add the garlic and cook for 5 minutes more. Add the chopped tomatoes and seasoning. Cook, covered for 20 minutes. Add the squid ink and a tablespoon of water and blend the sauce with a hand held blender until smooth and shiny.

Bring a pan of water to a simmer with the bay leaves, white wine vinegar and peppercorns, plus a teaspoon of salt.

Slip in the cod and let it poach very gently for 5 minutes. Remove from the heat and leave to sit in the water a further 5 minutes. Remove it from the water, drain and allow to stand for 5 minutes (8 if on the bone). Serve the pearly white fish on top of a pool of black sauce. (Serves 4)

Fresh Cod with Spinach, Asparagus and Garlic Vinaigrette

I sometimes wonder if all this sliced garlic and olive oil sounds a bit too much, but in this recipe the gentle, mellow cooking in olive oil softens the harsh flavours. Ideally, the garlic never goes beyond a pale blonde colour (or slightly greenish if the olive oil is very green, French olive oil tends to be golden).

This dish is wonderfully fresh and healthy.

For poaching the cod:
4 cod steaks each weighing 150g (5 oz)
2 tablespoons white wine vinegar
12 peppercorns
3 bay leaves
salt

6 cloves fresh garlic, peeled and sliced
5 – 6 tablespoons olive oil
1 tablespoon red wine or cider vinegar
200g (7 oz) spinach
200g (7 oz) asparagus
salt

In a small pan, soften the sliced garlic in the olive oil for 10 minutes over the lowest possible heat. Pour into a bowl (keep the oily pan for heating the vegetables). Add the red wine or cider vinegar and the salt to the bowl, whisk well.

Bring a pan of water to a simmer with the bay leaves, white wine vinegar and peppercorns, plus a teaspoon of salt.

Slip in the cod and let it poach very gently for 4 minutes. Remove from the heat and allow to sit in the water a further 4 minutes. Remove it from the water, drain and allow to stand for 5 minutes (8 if on the bone).

Meanwhile, gently cook and wilt the asparagus and spinach in the pan with the remains of the garlic flavoured oil until the asparagus is barely tender.

Serve the cod warm with the vegetables alongside or underneath, or artfully arranged here and there, and the warm garlic vinaigrette poured over everything. (Serves 4)

Cod with Gaspacho Sauce

The idea for this refreshing summer sauce comes from Kate Hill who runs a beautiful and inspiring cookery school teaching Gascon cooking and the art of making charcuterie at Camont, near Nérac in Lot-et-Garonne.

4 steaks of fresh cod each weighing 150g (5 oz)
2 tablespoons white wine vinegar
12 peppercorns
3 bay leaves
salt

For the sauce:
½ red onion chopped
1 clove garlic, finely chopped
1 red pepper, finely diced
3 firm tomatoes, skinned, seeded and diced
1 cucumber, peeled, seeded and diced
125ml (4¼ fl oz) olive oil
2 tablespoons cider vinegar
½ teaspoon smoked sweet paprika
½ teaspoon salt
good pinch *piment d'Espelette* or cayenne

Make the sauce by combining all the ingredients in a bowl, dressing the finely diced vegetables with the oil, vinegar and seasonings; it is as simple as that.

Bring a pan of water to a simmer with the bay leaves, white wine vinegar and peppercorns, plus a teaspoon of salt.

Slip in the cod and let it poach very gently for 5 minutes. Remove from the heat and allow the fish to sit in the water a further 5 minutes. Remove it from the water, drain and allow to stand for 5 minutes (8 if on the bone). Serve the cod with the sauce, and have plenty of fresh bread to mop up the juices. (Serves 4)

Salt Cod at Bégles

Once sniffily called the '*Fauborg des Odeurs*' by the Bordelaise, Bégles, a suburb of Bordeaux, is a river port on the Gironde, and was once a thriving hub of the French salt cod trade. From the mid nineteenth century, the quays were teeming with ships and people, landing and processing cod catches – the characteristic smell must have been intense.

The green cod, brined but not dried, came off the fishing boats on the shoulders of the '*sangdious*' and was then transported to the drying sheds in wooden carts. There it was washed, coated in *Saliés* or other local salt and dried, to become '*morue*' also known as '*boeuf du pauvre*' the beef of the poor. At the peak of its industry, thirty salting works in Bégles provided over 70% of French demands, but after a steep rise in the price of cod, thanks to over fishing, trade declined rapidly in the 1950s. Today there remains one *sécherie,* Sar Océan.

To make Salt Cod at home:
1kg (2¼ lbs) fresh cod fillets
250g (9 oz) coarse or kosher salt

Bury the cod in the salt in an earthenware dish and leave for 24 hours.

Remove, pour off the liquid, shake off excess salt, place two fillets face to face, skin sides out, wrap lightly in cling film and place between two boards. Leave it in a cold place or in the fridge for 7 days. It will become hard and stiff. Remove cling film and wrap in a cloth to store it.

When using home made lightly salted fish, an overnight soak followed by a rinse should be enough to desalt it.

Red Peppers Stuffed with Salt Cod
Poivrons Rouge à la Brandade

A Basque classic, often made with small, pointed, *piquillo* peppers, the sort that come in a jar or a tin, but it can also be made with fresh peppers. The first time I had it, in Hendaye, the brilliant red of the peppers and white cod were dramatized with a black, squid ink sauce.

300g (10½ oz) salt cod, soaked for 36 hours
6 fresh red peppers
250g (9 oz) potatoes
4 tablespoons olive oil
150ml (5 fl oz) milk
1 clove garlic, crushed
3 tablespoons fresh breadcrumbs
a sprinkling of olive oil
1 lemon cut into 6 slices
salt, freshly ground pepper

Preheat the oven to 200°C (400°F). Cook the salt cod (see page 151).

Cook the potatoes in plenty of boiling, lightly salted water for 25 minutes, until very soft.

When the cod is cool enough, remove the skin and bones and any brown parts, pull the cod roughly into shreds and mix in a food processor until fairly finely shredded.

Drain and mash the potatoes, working in the olive oil, milk, parsley, garlic, seasoning (except salt) and the shredded cod. Add more milk if needed. Taste to see if salt is needed.

Cut the peppers in half horizontally and remove the seeds and internal membranes. Stuff with the cod purée, place a couple of pinches of bread crumbs on top. Sprinkle with olive oil and cook in an oiled roasting tin for 40 minutes. Serve these as a starter or a lunch dish, with salad.

If you want to make the dramatic, black squid ink sauce, find it on page 178. Put it on warmed plates with the peppers and lemon. (Serves 6)

Brandade de Morue aux Senteurs de Pin

Brandade is a comfort dish of the Midi, a friendly mash of salt cod, potatoes, garlic and olive oil – and probably the best way forward for those who are not yet sure if they like the pungency and saltiness of salt cod.

This one, from les Landes, is romantically flavoured with pine, the prevailing scent of the region (with pine nuts, not from local forest pines, but from the beautiful, spreading umbrella pines, *pinus pinea,* of Southern Spain). Serve it with toast.

500g (1lb 2 oz) salt cod, soaked for 36 hours
1 large potato, peeled
100ml (3½ fl oz) milk
3 cloves garlic, crushed
3 tablespoons olive oil
3 tablespoons pine nuts

Cook the salt cod (see page 151), drain the fish and remove the skin and bones. Shred it loosely with two forks.

Boil the potato until it is completely tender. Mash it to a purée.

Heat the oil. When it is quite hot, add the cod and the mashed garlic and stir it round.

Remove it from the heat and crush the cod and garlic together in the oil with a fork, keeping a rough texture.

Toast the pine nuts in a dry frying pan over a medium heat until lightly browned. Chop them coarsely and add them to the cod, together with the potato, and also gradually add the milk, stirring it in a little at a time. Do not make it too smooth. Transfer to an earthenware bowl or a glass jar. Serve with fingers of toasted *pain de campagne.* (Serves 4)

Gratin of Salt Cod and Spicy Tomato
Bacalao con Salsa de Tomate Picante

This is a typical Basque dish, which makes a humble ingredient into a very well-flavoured dish with good textures. Sometimes honey is used instead of sugar.

300g (10½ oz) thin fillet of salt cod, soaked for 24 hours
2 green peppers or one red and one green
2 medium potatoes
2 tablespoons olive oil
1 large onion, chopped
2 cloves garlic, mashed
500g (1lb 2 oz) ripe tomatoes, peeled and chopped or 1 x 400g (14 oz)
tin of tomatoes
1 tablespoon tomato purée
1 teaspoon sugar
½ teaspoon thyme leaves
juice of ½ lemon
75g (2¾ oz) fresh breadcrumbs
2 tablespoons chopped parsley
salt and freshly ground black pepper

Preheat the oven to 200°C (400°F).

Bake the peppers for 20 minutes, until the skin is bubbled and blackening in places. Remove them with tongs and put in a plastic bag to cool. The steam in the bag will make it easier to peel off the skin. Remove the seeds and cut the peppers into strips.

Peel the potatoes and cut into slices, simmer them in salted water for 8 minutes until barely tender.

Put the soaked cod in a pan with plenty of cold water and bring to simmering point. As soon as it bubbles remove the pan from the heat and set aside for 5 minutes, then drain the cod, keeping the cooking liquid. Remove the skin and bones and flake the cod.

Heat the oil in a medium frying pan and fry the onions until soft and transparent, it takes about 10 – 15 minutes. Add the garlic and the peppers and cook a further 10 minutes, then add the tomatoes and cook over a gentle heat to make a sauce. Stir in the tomato purée, sugar and thyme and the hot pepper. Add a squeeze of lemon.

Put a layer of half the sauce in a gratin dish and cover with the potato slices, followed by the flaked fish. Cover with the remaining sauce. Mix the breadcrumbs and parsley and spread them over the top. Sprinkle with olive oil and place under the grill until heated through and golden. Serve with a green salad. (Serves 4)

Ragoût de Morue Gascon

This is a real comfort dish, a bit like an upside down fish pie with the potatoes underneath and the salt cod, prawns and eggs on top.

400g (14 oz) thick salt cod, soaked for 48 hours
400g (14 oz) small new potatoes, thickly sliced
4 – 5 tablespoons olive oil
I tablespoon plain flour
2 cloves garlic, chopped
2 tablespoons chopped parsley
150ml (5 fl oz) milk
150ml (5 fl oz) salt cod cooking water
100g (3½ oz) raw shelled prawns
2 soft boiled eggs (7 minutes)

Cook the soaked cod. Put it into a pan of cold water, bring it to simmering point and turn off the heat. Let it sit in the water for 5 minutes and then remove it. If it is not too salty, keep the cod cooking water to cook the potatoes.

Flake the cod into large pieces.

Heat half the olive oil in a paëlla pan and brown the potatoes. When they are nicely browned, sprinkle them with flour and stir them round thoroughly.

Add the garlic and half the parsley, stir it in well and cover with the milk and water. Let them simmer while you dry the pieces of cod and brown them lightly for barely a minute in the remaining olive oil, over cooking the cod will toughen it.

Spread the cod over the potatoes, and decorate the top with prawns. Cover the pan and simmer for 5 minutes, decorate with the shelled and halved eggs, sprinkle with parsley and serve. (Serves 6)

Morue à la Bizkaïna

This has a typically strong, earthy flavour – soak the salt cod well, as the ham is also salty.

400g (14 oz) best very thick salt cod, soaked for 48 hours (see page 151)
4 dried red ancho or choricero peppers
4 tablespoons olive oil
3 red onions, chopped
3 large cloves garlic, chopped
100g (3½ oz) slices of raw ham cut into strips (or use lardons)
1 teaspoon paprika
½ teaspoon cayenne pepper or *piment d'Espelette*
2 tablespoons chopped parsley
250ml (9 fl oz) chicken stock or fish stock

Pour boiling water over the dried peppers and when they have softened, scrape the pulp off the skins, throwing away the skin and seeds (or you can just chop them up).

Cook the cod by bringing it to simmering point in a large pan of water. As soon as it starts to bubble remove it from the heat and let it rest, covered for 4 minutes. Remove it from the pan, drain well, pat it dry and flake it carefully, keeping the flakes as large as possible.

Heat the olive oil in a frying pan and cook the cod gently for 3 minutes on each side, without browning. Remove the pieces to a dish and in the same oil, soften the onions for 15 minutes stirring occasionally. When the onions are tender and starting to brown, stir in the garlic, the ham, the pimento pulp, and the piment d'Espelette or cayenne and paprika. Add the chicken stock and cook for 15 – 20 minutes. Stir in the parsley.

Put the sauce in a gratin dish and place the pieces of cod on top. Serve with bread. (Serves 4 – 6)

Gilthead Bream
Daurade, Dorade, Bixigu – Besugo

The gilthead bream (*Sparus aurata*) is held in very high esteem by the Basques, and was for centuries one of the main fish found in the Bay of Biscay. Worshipful cave dwellers of Basqueland drew pictures of this fish 12,000 years ago, and it is carried in effigy in a procession up Mount Igueldo on Christmas Eve – to ward off an evil spirit that comes down chimneys and harms people in their sleep. Bream is also a popular Christmas dish. Unsurprisingly, it has been overfished and most *daurade* is now farmed; luckily, unlike sea bass, it lends itself well to farming.

Here are two Basque recipes for gilthead bream one with potatoes and one without. The third recipe is from Arachon.

Bream, Basque Style
Daurade Pil Pil

A really simple recipe that packs quite a smack of garlic, but manages to be sweet, with a mellow flavour, as the garlic is more confit than fried. It was a favourite 100 years ago with a gastronomic society formed by Basques who lived in Madrid. They preferred the long fiery red peppers called *guindillas*, but ordinary red chillies or chilli flakes can be used.

2 gilthead bream weighing 600g (1lb 5 oz) each
6 tablespoons olive oil
4 tablespoons vinegar
1 sliced medium hot chilli pepper or ½ teaspoon chilli flakes
4 cloves garlic, peeled and thinly sliced
salt

Preheat the oven to 200°C (400°F).

Line a roasting tin with baking paper. Season the bream inside and out with salt and place in the roasting tin, sprinkle them with half the olive oil and cover with foil. Roast for 20 minutes, until just cooked.

Put the vinegar in a frying pan and reduce by half. Away from the heat add the juices from the cooked bream and simmer for a minute or two. Cover the fish to keep it warm (try foil and then oven gloves on top).

In another frying pan, heat 3 tablespoons olive oil and fry the garlic until barely turning golden, add the chilli or red pepper flakes and turn down the heat.

Add the reduced vinegar and fish juices to the garlic and cook for one minute, shake the pan to and fro for as long as it takes to amalgamate the sauce.

Put the fish on a nice dish and spoon the sauce over it. (Serves 4)

Dorade Basquaise

1kg (2¼ lbs) gilthead bream (2 medium fish)
1kg (2¼ lbs) waxy potatoes, peeled and sliced
1 onion, chopped
1 teaspoon chilli flakes or *piment d'Espelette*
1 bunch parsley, coarsely chopped
3 cloves garlic, chopped
2 – 3 sprigs thyme, chopped
leaves from 2 sprigs rosemary, finely chopped
5 tablespoons olive oil
juice of ½ lemon
salt, freshly ground pepper

Heat the oven to 220°C (430°F).

Put the sliced potatoes, chopped onions and half the parsley and all of the other herbs in a bowl with the garlic, season well, mix everything together and transfer the mixture to a roasting tin or gratin dish large enough to take the fish.

Add the lemon juice, 3 tablespoons of olive oil and 150ml (5 fl oz) of water, cover the dish with foil and bake for 40 minutes, or until the potatoes are almost tender.

Place the fish on top, season it, sprinkle with the remaining olive oil and bake, uncovered, a further 15 - 20 minutes or until cooked.

Serve sprinkled with the remaining parsley and add a chopped clove of garlic if you like. (Serves 6)

Bream with Chorizo

In this recipe, the fish is stuffed with crumbled chorizo and peppercorns and served on top of mashed potato with red piquillo purée heightened with verjus or vinegar.

If possible, have the backbones removed but keep the fish joined at the tail.

4 filleted gilt-head bream weighing about 300g (10 oz) each, or 2 filleted bream of 600g (1lb 5oz)
100g (3½ oz) soft chorizo skinned and diced
12 peppercorns, smashed in a pestle and mortar
2 tablespoons pine nuts, smashed coarsely
1 tablespoon olive oil

For the sauce:
2 fresh red peppers
6 piquillo peppers from a jar, washed
2 dessertspoons verjuice or white wine vinegar
2 tablespoons olive oil
squeeze of fresh lemon juice
salt

Preheat the oven to 200°C (400°F). Roast the red peppers for 25 minutes, or until the skins look loose and wrinkled – if there are blackish patches here and there, it will add to the flavour. Remove them with tongs and put them into a plastic bag. Let them get cool.

Skin them and remove stalks and seeds. Dice the flesh.

Blitz the chorizo briefly until it is crumbled. Mix with the peppercorns and pine nuts, fry it briefly in olive oil and add a tablespoon of water. Reduce the liquid and put a layer of this stuffing between two fillets of bream like sandwiches.

Make the sauce. Blend the piquillos peppers, the roasted bell peppers, the verjuice and salt and gradually add the oil, blending it in to make a smooth mixture – you can serve it as it is or blend in 2 tablespoons of cream.

Line a roasting pan with oiled baking paper. Put the stuffed bream on top, sprinkle with salt, lemon juice and a little olive oil and cover with foil. Bake for 20 minutes. Allow to rest, covered, for 5 minutes. Serve with the brilliant reddish-gold sauce on the side. (Serves 4)

Sardines de Santurce Grillé

Santurce is a port near Bilbao, well known for its great sardines.

Traditionally in the South West, sardines are grilled over dried vine prunings, which can be bought in rolls at the garden centre, to add a special aroma, but any wood-fire or even proper charcoal (not charcoal bricks) will do; serve them prettily on fresh, or even preserved, vine leaves.

24 small sardines, 12 if they are very large
handful of *gros sel*
24 fresh or preserved vine leaves or several small slices of bread or toast
juice of 1 freshly squeezed lemon
1 lemon cut in slices

Light the barbecue with charcoal or wood.

Wash the scaled, gutted sardines in plenty of water and dry them on kitchen paper.

Sprinkle them with *gros sel* and let them absorb it for 15 minutes. At this point throw the dried vine prunings on the barbecue if you have them.

Oil the sardines lightly with olive oil and place them in a sandwich grill.

When all the flames from the prunings have died down, cook the sardines fairly briefly – small sardines take about 4 minutes. Turn them after one minute, sprinkle the cooked side with lemon juice, turn again after one minute and sprinkle with lemon again. Repeat the turning and sprinkling giving each side one minute more. The time they take to cook will vary considerably according to their size and the amount of

heat in the fire. Use tongs to move them onto plates covered with fresh
vine leaves, put slices of lemon on each plate, and serve with slices of
toast cooked on the grill. (Serves 4)

Sea Bass with Herbs
Louvine aux Herbes

A recipe adapted from one offered by Jean Coussau at his beach-front
restaurant, Jean des Sables, in Hossegor; he offers spanking fresh
seafood and a wave-side seat for swimmers, surfers and fishermen.

In his area sea bass is called *louvine*, elsewhere *loubine*.

2 fresh sea bass each about 600g (1lb 5 oz))
chives, tarragon, flat parsley, coriander and wild garlic
coarse ground black pepper
100g (3½ oz) butter, at room temperature
piment d'Espelette or chilli pepper
1 lemon, sliced very thin
3 – 4 tablespoons olive oil
salt

Preheat the oven to 200°C (400°F).

Cut the slices of lemon in half, slash the fish across at 4cm intervals
and insert the lemon into the cuts. Put the bass in an oiled baking dish
and sprinkle liberally with oil and salt.

Chop all the herbs and work them into the butter, add salt and
coarse black pepper and *piment d'Espelette* or hot chilli pepper. Use this
mixture to stuff the fish.

Cook for 22 minutes, basting every 5 minutes with the hot juices.
Let the fish rest for 5 to 8 minutes before taking it off the bone in pieces,
allowing 2 and a slice of lemon for each person – the cuts will make
this easier to do. Then turn it over and do the same with the other
side. Serve it very simply, sprinkled with the herbs from the interior,
the cooking juices, and with a dish of Crushed Potatoes (see page 264).
(Serves 4)

Roasted Lemon Sea Bass with Garlic and Parsley Oil

The flavour of this particular sauce I associated first with snails – it tastes similar to snail butter, only it is made with olive oil and in South West France you will find it on grilled squid, with steamed lobster and with whole, roasted fish. It's definitely good with sea bass.

2 fresh sea bass 600g (1lb 5 oz) each
2 preserved lemons, flesh removed, rinds sliced into quarters

For the garlic and parsley oil:
1 bunch parsley, stalks removed
2 cloves garlic
5 tablespoons olive oil
juice of ¼ lemon
salt

Preheat the oven to 200°C (400°F).

Salt the insides of the bass generously with *fleur de sel* or Maldon salt. Make deep diagonal slashes in the sides of the fish, sprinkling the cuts with salt. Push the slices of preserved lemon rinds into the cuts. Bake at 200°C for 22 minutes, let the fish rest for 5 to 8 minutes.

For the garlic and parsley oil:
Blanch the parsley leaves – put them in a sieve and pour boiling water over them. Run them briefly under the cold tap, then drain them, pat them very dry and chop finely, together with the chopped garlic. Put the garlic mixture into a pan with 5 tablespoons olive oil and heat on low heat for 5 minutes. Serve the fish with their own juices and the garlic and parsley oil poured over. (Serves 4)

Sea Bass or Sea Bream Rillettes

I first encountered this dish at the fabulous Café du Commerce, opposite the covered market in Biarritz. It came with toast and butter and was served it in a little glass preserving jar. The fish can be cooked as above or left over cooked fish can be used.

120g (5 oz) cooked sea bass or bream
100g (4 oz) sliced smoked trout or smoked salmon, cut into little dice
1 teaspoon grated lemon zest
1 spring onion, very finely chopped
½ teaspoon *piment d'Espelette*
Salt and coarse ground pepper
2 tablespoons softened butter
juice of ½ lemon
salt

Remove the skin and bones of the fish and shred the flesh with two forks, taking care to remove any remaining bones. Put it in a bowl and add the diced smoked trout or salmon, grated lemon zest, spring onion, red pepper and salt and pepper. Mix them into the fish lightly.

Taste and add more of any of these ingredients to heighten to the flavour, then stir in the lemon juice and finally the softened butter working it in with a fork. Put into a small bowl or a jar (a little Kilner jar looks good on the table) and flatten the top with a fork. Sprinkle with cayenne pepper or *piment d' Espelette.*

Pour melted butter or place cling film over the top if you wish to keep it for 2 or 3 days.

Leave in the refrigerator for 2 hours or overnight. Serve at room temperature with toast. (Serves 4 – 6)

Braised Turbot à la Marinera

Good turbot comes from the *Bassin d'Arcachon,* but this dish, often made with bream has a Spanish flavour which comes from the addition of paprika. You can use hot or sweet smoked paprika, whichever you prefer.

600g (1lb 5 oz) skinned fillets of turbot or brill
1 medium onion, sliced
3 tablespoons olive oil
250ml (9 fl oz) white wine
3 cloves garlic, thinly sliced
2 large tomatoes, skinned, deseeded and chopped

1 teaspoon sweet smoked paprika
1 tablespoon chopped parsley
1 tablespoon olive oil
salt, freshly ground pepper

Scatter the onion over the bottom of a generously oiled wide pan, large enough to hold the fish fillets. Place the fish on top. Pour half the wine over it and sprinkle with salt.

Cover with a piece of foil and simmer gently, on top of the stove, for 20 minutes, or until just cooked through.

Heat the remaining olive oil in a saucepan, soften the garlic without browning it, then add the tomatoes and paprika. After 2 minutes, add the parsley, salt and the remaining white wine and simmer for 5 minutes.

When the fish is cooked, transfer it carefully to a hot serving dish. Pour the juices from the cooking dish into the sauce; season if necessary and let it reduce to a good consistency.

Add a final spoonful of olive oil and the fish. (Serves 4)

Poached Turbot with a Garlic Hollandaise
Le Carrelet Printemps

Printemps, meaning spring, is the surname of a family of fishermen, long-established at Teste-du-Buch on the Arcachon bay. M. Printemps loves turbot, which he catches at night. He knows exactly the right place to go, wading into the shallows, with a lantern and a pronged spear. The smaller fish are crisply fried. The larger ones are soaked in cold, salted water for 2 – 3 hours, and then poached. Cod is also superb cooked this way.

1 kg (2¼ lbs) turbot fillets or 1½ kg (3 lbs) whole turbot
2 tablespoons white wine vinegar
3 bay leaves
salt, 12 peppercorns

Soak the fish in salted water for 2 – 3 hours. Drain it.

Heat a wide pan of salted water flavoured with 1 or 2 tablespoons of white wine vinegar and 3 bay leaves. Add a few peppercorns. When the water is simmering, slip in the fish and poach gently for 5 minutes (3 for fillets). Remove from the heat and after 5 more minutes, carefully lift the fish out of the water; let it rest for 8 minutes, if the fish is on the bone.

Garlic Hollandaise

100g (3½ oz) unsalted butter
2 egg yolks
1 clove garlic, finely mashed with a little coarse salt
salt, pepper, pinch nutmeg
juice of ½ lemon
salt, freshly ground pepper

Melt the butter. Whisk the egg yolks with a pinch of salt, gradually stir in the warm melted butter. Add the mashed garlic, season carefully and add lemon juice to taste. Keep warm over a pan of hot (not too hot, and never boiling) water, stirring occasionally, until it thickens.

Remove the skin from the fish and serve a fillet per person with the Garlic Hollandaise. (Serves 4)

Monkfish with Clams

This version, described to me by my part Basque friend Iraïda Iscaza, comes from a lively and popular Basque Restaurant in Panama City.

The fish for this dish is usually hake, but I also find that monk fish or cod work superbly; cooked deep in its olive oil bath, the fish almost melts but not quite.

Authentically the fish is cooked in a *cazuela*, a wide, shallow, terracotta cooking pan, over a fire or a gas flame, but any wide pan will do.

You can add cooked asparagus instead of or as well as peas at the end as a garnish.

500g (1lb 2 oz) monk fish, cut into steaks
500g (1lb 2 oz) mussels (or clams), well cleaned
4 cloves garlic, finely sliced
5 – 6 tablespoons olive oil
1 teaspoon *Espelette* pepper or chilli flakes
3 – 4 tablespoons chopped parsley
125ml (4¼ fl oz) white wine
2 eggs, hard boiled
12 spears of cooked asparagus or
4 tablespoons cooked peas or both
salt

Season the fish lightly with salt.

Steam the mussels or clams open by putting in a pan with 4 tablespoons of water, then clamp the lid shut, and briskly heat. Shake the pan over the heat for a minute or two, until they open. Save the cooking liquid as you will need 125ml (4 fl oz) of it later.

Cook the garlic in the oil very, very gently in a wide pan. Add the red pepper or chilli flakes and parsley, simmer for a minute or two. Add the fish to the olive oil, add the liquids – the wine and mussel or clam juice – and cook gently for 8 minutes.

Carefully remove the fish, which should be pearly, and just cooked through, to a terracotta dish, heat the mussels or clams in their shells, and asparagus or peas in the cooking juices and pour them over the fish; decorate with halves of hardboiled egg. Serve with bread and eat with spoons and forks. (Serves 4 – 6)

Fried Red Mullet
Rougets, Barbarins or Vendangeurs Frits

These little red mullet, in their iridescent pinky-vermilion skins, appear in the Bassin d'Arcachon in the autumn, at the time of the vendange, and are so delicate that it is best to eat them in the simplest possible way – it is usual, if they are very fresh, to eat the livers, which are especially good. Gut them as usual, leaving the livers inside – or you could use the livers by spreading them on little squares of toast.

The only elaboration recommended is anchovy butter.

24 little or 12 larger red mullet
flour
60ml (2 fl oz) olive oil or
100ml (3½ fl oz) sunflower oil
For the anchovy butter:
100g (3½ oz) butter at room temperature
4 anchovy fillets
plenty of freshly ground black pepper
½ to 1 teaspoon of the warm oil from frying the fish

Wash the gutted mullets and, if necessary, remove the scales carefully and delicately with your fingernails. Pat them dry, slash the larger ones 2 or 3 times on each side. Dip the fish in seasoned flour.
Heat the oil to 180°C (360°F).

When it is very hot, fry the fish for about 5 minutes on each side for the large ones, 2 - 3 minutes for the smaller, until they are golden. Remove and drain them on absorbent paper, sprinkle with a little *fleur de sel* or Maldon salt. Serve with lemon quarters or with anchovy butter.

To make the anchovy butter:
Mash the anchovies with a fork, mix them into the butter together with about half a teaspoon of warm oil, season with pepper, the texture should be unctuous. Do not chill the butter but keep it at room temperature. (Serves 4)

Fried Anchovies with Parsley Sauce

Very fresh anchovies (*Engaulis encrasicolus*) from the Bay of Biscay are one of the great summer treats. The anchovies from this coast are known to have an especially good flavour.

500g (1lb 2oz) very fresh anchovies, boned and opened out, kipper-style.

For frying:
100g (3½ oz) yellow cornflour or fine polenta
250ml (9 fl oz) corn oil
For the sauce:
juice of 2 lemons
4 tablespoons olive oil
2 cloves garlic, finely chopped
2 tablespoons parsley, finely chopped
½ – 1 teaspoon dried chilli flakes
pinch salt

Make the sauce first; simply combine the lemon juice, olive oil, garlic, parsley and chilli flakes in a bowl.

Put the corn oil in a saucepan or a deep fryer (not a frying pan as the hot oil will spit too much), heat until very hot. Dip the anchovies in the cornflour and tap them to shake off the excess. Drop them into the hot oil in batches and fry until brown. Remove to a plate covered in 2 layers of absorbent paper.

To eat them, use your fingers and simply dip the fish into the sauce. (Serves 4)

Céteaux, Langue d'Avocat or Wedge Sole

This small flat fish (*Dicologlossa cueata*), brown above and cream below, is plentiful in the Gulf of Gascony, and in summer is fished in the Bassin d'Arcachon. It looks like sole, but is a different species altogether. It is very popular and is eaten fried *en persillade*, with garlic and parsley (see the previous recipe). Allow at least three per person, maybe more, and begin by scraping off the scales, which are easy to remove, unlike Dover sole, which has embedded scales.

SHELLFISH

If you can find Gambas du Médoc, in season from July to November, they are extremely delicate, sweet flavoured prawns, reared organically in the shellfish farm, Eau-Médoc, hidden at the top of Médoc's watery isthmus, at the port of St Vivien de Médoc. This distant, secret and marginal area, described by Stendhal as 'an uncertain land, a sort of blue and grey reflection', once harboured wreckers, whose living came from the sea – the trick of the trade was to tie lights to the horns of cattle and let them wander on the sands; unsuspecting mariners, seeing these lanterns bobbing up and down in the dark, thought they were the lights of fishing boats, and would steer straight onto the sand banks and into the hands of the waiting wreckers, who would appropriate the cargo; barrels of rum were a favourite prize.

Little *esquirres* – white shrimps – and *crabes verts*, used for making crab soup, are reared here by the same farmer, M. Bertrand, an enterprising ecologist who works with nature in an area of seashores, marshes, estuary shores and rivers. If you have a long fork, wild cockles and clams known as *coques* and *palourdes* can be found South of Médoc, in the Arcachon basin and many hopeful fishers go out in the spring to dig them out of the sand at low tide.

Razor clams

Razor clams, *couteaux,* which are a bit stupid, can be lured out of hiding with a pinch of salt.

Once you have spotted their holes in the sand – they look a bit like a key hole – pour in salt and then watch them emerging.

Grab the clam, give it a shake and pull it out. They are strange to look at, but very good to eat. Discard any that are broken or that do not tighten up when tapped. Leave them in a bucket of cold salted water for an hour. Give the sandy creatures a very good wash, in three changes of water. Open them quickly in a pan with a few tablespoons of boiling water. Remove and shell them. Heat some olive oil and sauté them very briefly with a chopped shallot or two, some chopped garlic and a handful of parsley – no salt. Eat them with your fingers.

Arcachon Oysters
Gravettes, Gigas and Crépinettes

Gravettes, the sweet, nutty, flat native oysters of the Bassin d'Arcachon (*Ostrea edulis*) – enjoyed by Romans, and gathered in quantities (75 million oysters per year in the early nineteenth century), ran out in 1850 and since then oysters have had to be cultivated, emerging from the Bassin, green and dripping, at low tide. The Bassin d'Arcachon oysters, from some 350 family farms, are in full season from September to April, but available all the year round, now that better hygiene, refrigeration and fast trains and lorries mean they can be eaten fresh.

A few remaining *gravettes,* often called *les plats,* because their shells are flat, are occasionally for sale, but generally eaten by the locals, who like them best.

Today Pacific oysters (*crassostrea gigas*) called '*les creuses*' because of their deep shells, are farmed here in vast numbers and a characteristic sight is the row of huts where the *ostreiculteur*s clean and pack their oysters, ready to be shipped off all over France.

Women – *les parqueuses* – have always worked in the oyster beds; they were among the first French females to be seen wearing trousers, definitely more practical than long flouncy skirts when wading in a foot of water. They looked charming in their matador pants, topped off with a blue pleated shirt and a frivolous, ruffled sun bonnet.

Everyone in Arcachon and around the Bassin eats oysters – they are everyday events. They insist on perfect attention to detail when serving them. There must be very cold oysters, a burning hot sausage and a bowl of *mignonette* (red wine vinegar mixed with a little salt, pepper and some finely chopped, raw shallots). There must also be lemon halves of course, plus cold butter with rye bread alongside and baguette on the table. Perhaps you like Tabasco? A bottle of chilled Entre-Deux-Mers dry white wine? And *voilà*, lunch is ready.

Oysters with Hot Sausage Patties
Huitres Comme à Bordeaux

I first had oysters with these little sausage patties, called *crépinettes* at the Hôtel Restaurant de France et d'Angleterre on the river quays in Pauillac.

Their recipe was simple – coarse well-seasoned fatty minced pork, rolled into a little ball, slightly flattened and covered with a piece of caul. This is how they can be made at home, but you could serve grilled pork chipolatas or fried cocktail sausages with your oysters, which are hopefully being opened by someone else while you cook the sausages.

2 dozen fresh oysters, chilled and kept on ice
400g (14 oz) fatty minced pork or pure pork sausage meat
100g (3½ oz) pig's caul (which can be ordered from the butcher)
1 medium slice *pain de campagne* or coarse white bread, crusts removed
3 tablespoons dry white wine
2 shallots, finely chopped
1 tablespoon chopped parsley
1 egg, beaten
salt and plenty of freshly ground pepper
45g (2 oz) butter
2 tablespoons olive oil

Soak the caul fat in warm water to soften it. Put the minced pork or sausage meat in a bowl.

Sprinkle the bread with half the white wine and crumble it.

Mix the meat with shallots, crumbled bread, parsley, egg and seasoning; mix in the remaining white wine.

Shape into 24 little flattish, round patties. Untangle and spread out the caul on a board.

Cut the caul into 24 squares and envelope each patty in its square of caul, which keeps it from crumbling and adds to the flavour and juiciness of the *crépinette*.

Fry in hot buttter and olive oil for 10 minutes.

Serve *crépinettes* burning hot with the iced oysters.

If you want to serve this country style, add two finely chopped onions to the sausage meat and make it into 4 large rectangles. Cover with caul fat, brown on the outside and fry for 15 minutes. (Serves 4 – 6)

Scallops with Green Herb and Walnut Oil Sauce
Coquilles St Jacques au Coulis d'Herbes à l'Huile de Noix

A refreshing, very slightly bitter emerald green sauce from Pau, useful for enhancing fish and shellfish, particularly scallops.

12 scallops or 36 queen scallops, cleaned, washed and dried
100g (3½ oz) of mixed young rocket, flat parsley and baby spinach
1 tablespoon of small capers, drained
2 – 3 tablespoons herb cooking liquid
2 tablespoons olive oil
2 tablespoons walnut oil
2 tablespoons flour
30g (1 oz) butter
squeeze of lemon
salt

Wash the herbs.

Bring a pan of water to the boil and plunge in the herbs. Push them under the water with a spoon, and let them cook for 1 minute.

Reserve some of the cooking liquid, strain the herbs with a sieve, and immediately hold the sieve under the cold tap for a minute, to fix the bright green colour. Drain well, put the herbs in a blender with 1 tablespoon of the cooking liquid and the capers, purée them to a fine texture, adding more liquid if necessary, then slowly blend in the oils. Add a little salt.

To cook the scallops:

Prick the orange corals gently with the tip of a knife.

Season the scallops and sprinkle generously with flour, tapping off the excess.

Heat the butter and when it starts to brown, put in the scallops and let them cook for 1 minute on each side. They should be a light golden brown when they are cooked. Remove the scallops. Add a good squeeze of lemon to the browned butter and let it froth up, then pour it over the scallops.

Serve the scallops on top of the green herb sauce. Have bread at hand, to mop up the juices. (Serves 4)

Crab Rillettes as a starter
Rillettes de Crabe au Piri-Piri

Even the dictionary does not really know the definition of *rillettes*; it is described in the massive Harrap's French and English dictionary as 'potted mince', and elsewhere as 'potted meat', or 'minced spread of pork'. The meat, often pork but sometimes duck, goose or rabbit, is seasoned and spiced and cooked for a long time in fat and then shredded, not minced. They may also be made with fish or shellfish. Rillettes of seafood, such as tuna, sea bass, bream, salmon or crab, are fairly widespread in the South West, and are made with fish or shellfish. They are light and fresh, an ideal starter in hot weather.

These rillettes come in all shapes and sizes, and can contain spring onions, mayonnaise, cream cheese or cream, sea water jelly, caviar, chives, avocado. I like this good straightforward one containing chilli and fromage frais or cream cheese.

Serve it on toast or on slices of bread brushed with olive oil on both sides and grilled. These rillettes should be eaten the same day that they are made.

200g (7 oz) white crab meat, or ⅔ white to ⅓ coral or brown meat
125g (4 oz) cream cheese
green part of 2 spring onions, finely chopped
1 tablespoon parsley, finely chopped
2 strips lemon zest, finely chopped
½ teaspoon *piment d'Espelette* or cayenne pepper
1 teaspoon Dijon mustard
Salt, freshly ground pepper

Fork the red and white crab meat together in a bowl, then add the remaining ingredients and blend, still using a fork, as lightly as possible. Taste for seasoning, pack into a terrine or several small pots and serve chilled. (Serves 4 – 6)

Spider Crab

The Atlantic Spider Crab *(Maja brachydactyla)*, can grow to a monstrous size. The meat is luscious and white and it is a favourite of the Basques. Armed with a thick spiny carapace, quite hard to get into, the crab also has meaty legs that are worth picking out with a skewer.

Crab with Home-made Salad Cream
Araignée Labourdine

This is originally made with spider crab but is equally good with fresh brown crab *(Cancer pagurus),* which is more likely to be available, although spider crab is very delicious, and there is no reason why our fishmongers do not supply it, other than the fact that in Northern Europe we are not used to seeing it.

200g (7 oz) white crab meat

Salad cream as follows:
2 eggs
I teaspoon Dijon mustard
I tablespoon red coral from the crab
5 tablespoons olive oil
I tablespoon white wine vinegar or lemon juice
2 teaspoons freshly chopped mint
salt, *piment d'Espelette* or hot paprika

Boil the eggs for 4 minutes and then let them cool. Peel the eggs carefully and transfer the half-cooked yolks to a bowl.

Stir in the mustard and the red coral from the crab. Add a pinch of salt.

Gradually add the olive oil a few drops at a time to start with, then in a thin trickle. Use a small whisk to blend it in with the egg yolk mixture. Add a little vinegar or lemon juice to taste and finally season and stir in the mint. Serve with the crab meat. (Serves 4)

Gambas with Black Aïoli and Smoked Paprika

Aniseed is a flavour used in the cooking of the little white shrimps of the Gironde, but it is equally good with larger *gambas* (prawns).

24 large raw prawns, either in their shells or shelled
1 star anise
1 clove fresh, juicy garlic
2 egg yolks
coarse salt
1 packet cuttlefish ink (*Nero de sepia*)
¼ teaspoon smoked paprika
100ml (3½ fl oz) sunflower oil
100ml (3½ fl oz) olive oil
salt, plenty of freshly ground pepper
1 lemon cut into 6 pieces

Bring a pan of salted water to the boil with 1 star anise.

Simmer the prawns for 1 minute if shelled or 2 minutes if in their shells; drain them.

Purée the garlic on a wooden board, together with some coarse salt, mashing them together with a fork or the flat side of a knife blade.

Add the purée to 2 egg yolks in a bowl and stir in the squid ink and paprika until thoroughly blended.

Gradually whisk in the sunflower oil, starting drop by drop, as if you were making mayonnaise. You are looking into an inky black, shiny pool. Keep adding the oil gradually, then slowly add the olive oil. Taste for seasoning. Put it in a small dish and serve with the pink, aniseed flavoured prawns and the slices of lemon. (Serves 4)

Mussels with Chorizo

This is a really clever way to cook mussels, the tradition of eating fish and shellfish with sausage is well-established on the Atlantic coast. You can use chorizo or sausage or pieces of ham to flavour the sauce.
You could traditionally include some fresh breadcrumbs, but you may find the sauce is muddied by this addition.

2kg (4½ lbs) mussels, cleaned
100g (3½ oz) fresh chorizo, or pure pork sausage, skinned and broken into small pieces
3 tablespoons olive oil
4 large tomatoes, skinned and chopped
3 cloves garlic, thinly sliced
1 teaspoon *piment d'Espelette* or hot paprika
250ml (8½ fl oz) white wine
1 tablespoon chopped chives and parsley
salt if needed

Heat the butter or olive oil in a large deep pan, fry the chorizo and when it has started to brown, add the tomatoes and the garlic and season with chilli powder or hot paprika. Simmer, uncovered, for 5 minutes, then add the white wine. Simmer a further 5 minutes, allow to cool a bit, blitz in a blender and return the sauce to the pan, then add the mussels. Or you can leave the chunks of chorizo whole.

Cover the pan and steam over a high heat for 1 or 2 minutes until the mussels open. Taste for seasoning and sprinkle in the parsley and chives. Serve with plenty of sliced fresh baguette to mop up the juices. (Serves 4)

Pan-Fried Mussels
Poelés de Moules

Le Bouchon is a large noisy brasserie by the Bassin d'Arcachon in the Quartier Ostréicale of Cap Ferret, full of the macho sound of clashing pans and loud fishing tales.

They often serve tiny, juicy super-fresh moules, just opened in a very little white wine, with very finely chopped shallot and then dressed with fresh olive oil, chopped parsley and red pepper flakes. The parsley can be blanched before chopping to keep it green.

2kg (4½ lbs) small mussels, cleaned and bearded
3 tablespoons olive oil
3 shallots, finely chopped
3 tablespoons white wine
2 teaspoons chilli flakes
2 tablespoons chopped parsley

Heat the olive oil gently in a wide shallow pan, such as a paëlla pan. Soften the shallots without letting them brown.

Pour in the wine and let it evaporate, then add the mussels, stir in the chilli flakes and cover the pan. Shake it over a fairly high heat until the shells have all opened. Cook very lightly, just a minute will do, as small mussels can easily overcook. Scatter in the parsley and stir it through. Ladle into bowls and eat with good *pain de campagne* and unsalted butter. (Serves 4)

Squid Ink

The first time I drove over the French border into Spain in 1960 – flashing along in an open top car – I was thrilled to find much of the food, apart from red tomato salad and rose-red ham, appeared to be black, a colour I had not, until then, envisaged on a plate. These dark dishes were usually made with either black pudding, with mushrooms or with squid or cuttlefish ink; if these were followed by black figs my happiness was complete.

Squid (*Loligo vulgaris*), *encornet or calamar* (*Txibia* in Basque), contains a silvery sac of blue-black edible ink, tasting of salt and iodine, which can be bought in packets or jars, or extracted from the body of the fresh squid, and is used both in sauces for fish and shellfish and in cooking rice.

In season from the end of September until January – squid aren't easy to fish. They are caught *à la ligne* – with rods loaded with hooks –

when they are landed on the boats they often jettison their ink and the boats return to port dyed black.

Ink is produced by the ink glands in most cephalopods, and is squirted out when there is danger, to darken the water, so the disturbed and angry creature can disappear to safety.

Natural sepia, a powerful, edible, dark brown dye, is made from the ink of the cuttlefish (*Sepia officinalis*), known as '*seiche*' in French, '*txoko*' in Basque and '*sepia*' in Spanish. It was once used extensively in drawing and painting. This can be bought in little packets, ready to squirt into your sauce or rice dish; there are several good suppliers on the internet.

Octopus (*Octopus vulgaris*) known as '*poulpe*' or '*pulpo*' (in Basque '*ologarro*') has black ink.

Petits Calamars à l'Encre

Petits calamars, known as '*Chipirons*' or, in Arcachon, '*Casserons*', are small squid in this area, while in the Mediterranean the name *chipiron* is used for the tiny curled cuttlefish (*Sepiola rondoletti*) caught off the Languedoc coast.

1kg (2¼ lbs) small squid
3 tablespoons olive oil
1 large onion
1 long red pepper (called *corne de boeuf*) grilled, skinned and cut into small strips
3 cloves garlic
2 teaspoons hot paprika
1 tablespoon tomato purée
200ml (7 fl oz) white wine
3 packets of squid or cuttlefish ink
200ml (7 fl oz) of fish stock or water
salt

Wash, clean and drain the squid thoroughly.

Heat 1 tablespoon of olive oil in a wide, shallow pan, over a brisk heat. Fry the squid a few at a time until just beginning to brown.

Transfer them to a dish. Add more oil if necessary.

In the same pan, over a low heat, soften the onions, red pepper and garlic in the remaining olive oil. When they are tender stir in the paprika and tomato purée and then add the white wine.

Return the squid, add the ink and stock or water and season with salt. Cover and simmer for 30 – 35 minutes for smaller squid, 40 – 45 minutes for larger ones.

Serve with rice. (Serves 4)

Squid and Potato Stew

Although the Basques, traditionally, are not potato eaters, they make an exception when cooking with fish and particularly squid and octopus. The sumptuous sauce has marine and earthy flavours summoned from the depths.

1kg (2¼ lbs) squid, prepared but whole
125ml (4 fl oz) cloves of garlic, sliced
1 tablespoon chopped parsley
1 dessertspoon tomato purée
1 teaspoon *piment d'Espelette* or chilli flakes
200ml (7 fl oz) red wine
200ml (7 fl oz) fresh tomato sauce, sieved or *passata*
150ml (5 fl oz) fish stock or water
200ml (7 fl oz) water
1kg (2¼ lbs) King Edwards or other starchy potatoes, peeled and broken into walnut sized chunks (use an oyster shucker for this)
a small glass of Armagnac (optional)
salt

Check the squid for sand and wash thoroughly. Drain well.

Cut the squid bodies in half lengthwise. Cut each half into 2 or 3 long strips. Cut large legs in half and chop any long tentacles into short pieces.

Heat a couple of tablespoons of olive oil in a large pan and sauté the pieces of squid a few at a time over a brisk heat for 2 – 3 minutes.

Set them aside on a plate and add a bit more oil each time. Lastly sauté the legs.

Turn down the heat and sauté the garlic and parsley together with the tomato purée. When the garlic starts to smell cooked, but is still very pale, add the chilli and the wine, scraping the bottom of the pan. Then add the tomato sauce and the stock and water.

Return the squid and any juice it has made. Add the potatoes, pushing them down, season with salt, cover and simmer for 35 minutes (larger squid will take 40 minutes), stirring occasionally, add extra water if needed. At the end, if you want to be very authentic, add a small glass of Armagnac. (Serves 4 – 6)

Percebes, Gooseneck Barnacles or Devil's Fingers

These curious edible barnacles (*Lepas anatifera*) have long necks and short, shell-like beaks; they grow on driftwood and the sides of ships as well as on rocks.

At one time, because geese migrate North to breed, Southerners had never seen a barnacle goose nesting, and it was thought that these strange barnacles hatched out into geese.

In Galicia, young men in wet suits risk everything at low tide to clamber down the dangerous cliffs to the rocks below, in order to gather valuable *percebes*, a great and costly delicacy. Galicians always boil them briefly in plain salted water, and think Basques get it all wrong when they add olive oil.

They are served with bread and a bottle of wine.

1kg (2¼ lbs) goose neck barnacles
2 – 3 tablespoons olive oil
salt

Bring a large pan of salted water to the boil. Add the olive oil and plunge in the *percebes*. Bring the water back to the boil and then drain and serve hot.

In order to eat them, break the head part or beak away from the neck where it joins, by picking it open with you finger nail. Then slip the shell off the cylindrical section, which is the part you eat. Take a bite of bread and a sip of wine after each one. (Serves 4)

Clams with Beans
Pochas aux Palourdes

Wild cockles and clams, *coques and palourdes,* are fished in the sublimely beautiful Arcachon basin in Spring and many hopeful amateurs in wellington boots go out onto the sands at low tide, with forks and buckets, to try and dig them up.

Long razor clams, also known as jack-knife clams, are also to be had. To fish for razor clams, take a pot of fine salt with you and look for small holes shaped something like keyholes. Pour in some salt and the clam will obligingly pop up out of the sand. Work it to and fro a bit and then pull and it is yours.

This inspired combination comes from Navarre. The recommended beans are the flat white Tarbes beans; butter beans work just the same.

300g (10 oz) butter beans or large white haricot beans, soaked for 24 hours
500g (1lb 2 oz) clams
1 onion, chopped
4 cloves garlic, chopped
1 – 2 green chillies, seeds removed, sliced
1 bay leaf
1 packet of saffron
60ml (2 fl oz) white wine
1 tomato, skinned and diced
4 tablespoons olive oil
1 tablespoon chopped parsley
salt

Soak the saffron in the white wine.

Put the soaked beans in a pan with the onion, half the chopped garlic, chillies and bay leaf and enough water to come two fingers above the beans. Stir in the saffron flavoured white wine. Bring to the boil, then add some cold water to bring the temperature of the water down below boiling point. This is known as 'scaring the beans' and should be done twice again while they are being cooked. They will take about 2 hours to cook, depending how long ago they were harvested. After one hour, add 2 tablespoons of olive oil.

Simmer, covered, for a further hour or until the beans are just tender. Add more hot water if necessary. Remove the bay leaf.

Fry the remaining garlic gently in a large pan with 2 tablespoons of olive oil, without browning. Add the diced tomato. Sauté briefly and add the clams. Cover the pan and keep on the heat, shaking the pan, until they open. Sprinkle with chopped parsley and then pour the mix over the beans. Serve in large soup plates, with spoons and forks. (Serves 4)

Pan-Fried Eels
Anguilles Poelés

There are eels everywhere in the Gironde Estuary and the salt marshes of the Médoc, and they are everyday food either cooked in red wine, like lampreys, or eaten fried.

As we know, eels are slippery things and while alive, they wriggle – to hold onto an eel in order to bash it on the head (eels are usually sold live), you will need a dish cloth or a piece of muslin so it does not slip away from you. An old Médoc trick is to cover it with wood ash, which makes it easy to grip. After killing it, you cut it in pieces and then wash the ash off; all the slime on the skin will come off with the ash. Dry the pieces well afterwards.

If you have had the eel killed and skinned for you, cut it in short lengths and dip the pieces in flour before frying.

1 fresh eel
flour for frying
3 tablespoons olive oil
2 tablespoons chopped shallots
2 cloves garlic, chopped
4 tablespoons parsley, chopped
1 lemon, cut into quarters

Cut the eel into 2 cm (1 inch) pieces, with the skin on. Heat the olive oil, flour the eel pieces and fry for 12 – 14 minutes altogether, turning them, until they are very well-browned; transfer to absorbent kitchen paper and season well. Put the pieces of eel in a hot dish, and throw the shallots, garlic and parsley into the pan.

Let them cook, stirring for 2 minutes and sprinkle over the eel. Squeeze on a bit of lemon juice and eat them as a snack, preferably with your fingers, or serve with *Pommes Écrasées*, crushed potatoes, (page 264) with olive oil.

Chapter Seven

Poultry and Feathered Game

When it isn't forest, it is prairies of maize to the horizon, soaking up water from irrigating booms wide enough to sprinkle half a football pitch in one sweep.

Travelling through the pinewoods of les Landes, the shady silence goes on interminably.

Quite a relief, from time to time, to reach a clearing with a small farm surrounded by flowering meadows, in which pecking fowls enjoy the sun.

There is a long tradition of poultry rearing in les Landes, locals say it goes back to the eighth century. Always the women's job, the poultry yard was where birds were reared, geese, *mulard* ducks, the fat males ideal for foie gras, *magrets* and *confit*, and a few guinea fowl as well as hens. This was a good source of income for the small farms – although up to half the geese, chickens and eggs had to be given to the landlords and the priests always got some too.

Maize from South America, destined to replace the basic grains, millet and buckwheat, had arrived by ship towards the end of the sixteenth century. This alien corn thrived in the hot summers of les Landes, and made the rearing of fine poultry a speciality of the area, and it still is.

This is the land of duck, duck and more duck – the breasts sold as *magret* and the legs and wings as *confit de canard*. There are cured duck saucissons and fresh duck sausages, there are duck breasts galore, fresh or cured, some stuffed with duck sausage or, a delicacy, smoked and sliced, ready for salads; perhaps on a gorgeous Salade Royale, together with asparagus and foie gras, and in the autumn, some fresh ceps and apple. *Aiguillettes* of duck, sometimes rolled round a juicy *pruneau d'Agen* and cooked on a brochette, are the small strips of tender meat close to the breastbone, beneath the *magret*.

A dish not much in fashion, but which suggests a motto, 'waste not want not', is *desmoiselles grillés*, these are the duck carcasses, with the *aiguillettes* still on them, cut into pieces, seasoned with *gros sel* and grilled on the barbecue. The meat is picked out with fingers, from between the ribs and under the carcase, and it is very good.

Then there are the giblets, *gésiers* and hearts, *coeurs de canard,* which can be bought in quantity, and made into a little stew, or skewered and grilled on a brochette, or served fried, or made into confit and then fried, to be thrown onto a salad.

Occasionally one sees piles of strange-looking curling confit duck tongues on a market stall, also destined for salads. Duck skin is washed, drained, rendered and then minced up with duck fat, and turned into a sort of pâté when it is called *chichons*, or into *grattons de canard* which are a sort of rillettes.

Then, just to be confusing, there are another sort of *grattons* also called *fritons,* which are duck scratchings made with crisp pieces of duck skin and tissue, eaten like pork scratchings, with drinks. They can be a filling for an omelette or sprinkled on a salad.

However *Gratton de Bordeaux*, similar in texture to rillettes, is more like a sausage for slicing.

The plentiful duck fat is invaluable, use it to fry or roast vegetables, it tastes good, particularly with potatoes and with mushrooms, and it gives a lovely golden colour. It can be bought in jars or collected from roast duck or fried duck breasts. Goose or duck fat is necessary in large quantities to make *confit de canard*. It is also the best thing for bean dishes such as *cassoulet*.

When it comes to chickens, look for the label of Les Poulets Fermières des Landes also known as Poulets Rouges. Free to run skittishly after every butterfly or cricket, or take a dust bath in the sunshine, these are the best and most delicious of chickens; they scratch in the meadows and wild forest, living on a diet of heather, small insects and maize, and have a happy life for at least 81 days (the unhappy factory farmed chicken, unable to exercise at all, gets to roasting weight in just 42 to 49 days). During their carefree weeks outdoors, the farm birds have time to develope a deep, old-fashioned flavour and firm, juicy flesh. Turkey, ducks, capons, pigeons and quails are raised in the same way.

The large Poularde Saint-Sever is also reared outside and is fed 80% maize and then fattened up at the end of its life with skimmed milk, amongst other things, which makes the meat tender, melting and well flavoured.

A *poulet* weighs 1.3kg – 1.4kg (2lbs 8oz – 2lbs 10oz) and is slaughtered at about 84 – 96 days

A p*oularde* weighs 1.6kg – 1.8kg (3lb 9oz– 4lb) and is slaughtered at about 112 –120 days.

A *capon*, which is a castrated cockerel (capon) can weigh 2½ kg – 3½ kg (4½ lbs – 6½ lbs) and is slaughtered at 150 days.

Alicot with Chestnuts and Mushrooms

Throughout Southern Europe the tradition still lingers on – every single bit of the domestic bird, chicken, duck or goose, is good to eat, and even the guts are welcome, once they have been scrupulously cleaned and put in with the mix of necks, carcases, unlayed eggs, wing-tips, gizzards, livers, feet and heads that make *alicot*. These ingredients, so often discarded, do in fact make an excellent little stew (which will happily feed a whole family when supplemented with *milhas* – polenta). You can buy these in Lisboa, a Portuguese grocer in Golborne Road, north Kensington, London.

For centuries, most agricultural workers did not own their own land, and after the *seigneur* had his fair share of their produce (I don't know how fair it was that he had half of everything), they were able to make a few francs from the poultry yard. Some of the fowls and ducks or geese would be sold at the market, some ducks or geese would be made into foie gras for the Christmas *marché au gras*, and *confit* for the winter soups.

Other than that the family who reared the poultry would have been glad to eat this *alicot* with its foraged chestnuts and wild mushrooms. If you can find salsify, a hardy root, this can also be included.

600g (1lb 5 oz) chicken or duck giblets, including wings, necks, feet, gizzards, hearts, backs and possibly heads and feet (keep the livers separate)
2 tablespoons goose fat
6 ceps or 250g (9 oz) Portobello mushrooms, cleaned and cut into thick slices
12 chestnuts, *Clément Faugier Marrons Entiers* in tins are good or use fresh, shelled
500g (1lb 2 oz) carrots
4 sprigs thyme
1 bay leaf
bunch of flat parsley, chopped
nutmeg
1 litre (34 fl oz) chicken stock
1 - 2 tablespoons tomato sauce
salt, freshly ground pepper

Fry the chestnuts and mushrooms in a tablespoon of goose fat until golden.

Chop up the chicken or duck necks and the backs if using them. Heat a tablespoon of goose fat in a casserole and brown all the chicken giblets except the livers. Add the carrots, mushrooms and chestnuts. Put in thyme, bay leaf and parsley. Season with nutmeg, salt and pepper. Lastly cover with stock and add the tomato sauce. Cook gently, with a tilted lid for 4 hours. Add more stock or water as needed. (Serves 4)

Fried Chicken Livers

Be careful not to overcook the livers – it takes a few minutes only and you have to stay on the case; use tongs or a spatula to turn them over, the smaller ones first, and watch carefully.

They will quickly turn a lovely brown; when no raw bits are visible, they are done. They sometimes explode so do not cook them wearing a bikini!

500g (1lb 2 oz) fresh chicken livers, trimmed of fat, green patches and strings
1 dessertspoon flour
1½ tablespoons goose fat
3 tablespoons sherry
3 teaspoons sherry vinegar
1 shallot, chopped
1 large clove garlic, chopped
1 tablespoon parsley, chopped
2 – 3 tablespoons chicken stock
salt, plenty of coarsely ground black pepper

Dredge the chicken livers with flour and sprinkle them with black pepper (no salt at this point).

Heat the half the goose fat in a wide frying pan. When it is sizzling hot, put in half the chicken livers and sieze them, so that they do not start losing their juices. Fry them carefully, turning them every minute, and when there are no raw sides visible, after three or four minutes, sprinkle with half the sherry, and a teaspoon of sherry vinegar and scatter on half the finely chopped garlic and parsley. Stir well, then remove from the heat and season with salt. Repeat with the second batch. Put them all back in the pan and moisten with the stock. Heat through and serve. (Serves 4)

Quails with Peaches

You could serve this very fragrant dish from the Dordogne on a plate decorated with peach leaves or vine leaves. Peaches are also traditional with duck or goose.

8 quails
4 peaches
60g (2 oz) butter, melted
2 chicken livers, trimmed
75ml (2½ fl oz) dry white wine
1 tablespoon pomegranate molasses, grenadine or honey
4 rashers streaky bacon
salt, freshly ground pepper

Preheat the oven to 200°C (400 °F).

Carefully cut two of the peaches in half, skin them and remove the stones. Chop the two remaining peaches into small pieces, discarding the stones.

Fry the chicken livers in butter for 2 minutes on each side. Chop them finely and mix them with the chopped peaches, season with salt and pepper.

Stuff the quails with this mixture, coat the breasts with melted butter and put the birds in a roasting tin.

Cover each with half a slice of bacon, flattened and stretched on a board with the flat side of a knife blade. Place the peach halves around them in the tin. Brush them with melted butter.

Roast the quails for 25 minutes.

Let them rest on a heated dish, keeping them warm.

Spoon some of the fat from the roasting tin, deglaze it with the white wine, and stir in the pomegranate molasses, grenadine or honey to make a sauce. Reduce if it is too thin. Taste for seasoning and serve with the quails and their stuffing and the roasted peaches. (Serves 4)

Grilled Quails with Lentils
Cailles aux Lentilles

This recipe is based on one in José Pizarro's Spanish Flavours, published in 2012. Good quality green lentils are needed, they are grown in the Laurageais, near Castelnaudary.

4 large or 8 small quails

Marinade:
4 cloves garlic
2 tablespoons olive oil
juice of ½ lemon
I teaspoon hot smoked paprika
2 teaspoons cumin seeds
salt and coarse ground black pepper

Lentils:
200g (7 oz) green lentils
3 – 4 tablespoons olive oil
100g (3½ oz) soft (cooking) chorizo, diced
I onion, chopped
2 cloves garlic, chopped
I – 2 carrots, diced
I leek, chopped
I – 2 sticks celery, chopped
I bay leaf
½ teaspoon dried thyme
I tablespoon tomato purée
300ml (10 fl oz) chicken stock or stock made from quails' backbones
I tablespoon sherry vinegar
salt, freshly ground pepper

Remove the backbones from the quails, by cutting either side of the spine with kitchen scissors. You can use these bones to improve your chicken stock.

Press down on each quail and flatten them out.

Mix the marinade ingredients in a bowl and put in the quails one by one, spooning some of the marinade over the breasts and legs, and undersides of each one as you do so. Leave for an hour to absorb the flavours.

   To cook the lentils, put them into a large pan, cover them with water and boil them without salt for 15 – 20 minutes, until soft but with a bite, add salt just before the end. Drain, reserving the liquid.

Meanwhile, heat the olive oil in a frying pan and soften the chorizo, onions, garlic and other vegetables except the tomato, over a low heat until tender. Add the sherry vinegar, then add the herbs, tomato, and chicken stock and simmer for 5 minutes and then add the lentils and stir them in. Keep them warm.

To cook the quails, preheat the oven to 180°C (350 °F).

Heat a ridged grill pan or barbecue and sear them until brown on each side, squashing them down flat. Remove to a roasting tin, breast side up. Dribble remaining marinade from the bowl over the breasts and roast for 15 – 20 minutes. Allow to rest for 5 minutes before serving the quails with the lentils. (Serves 4)

Chicken Stuffed with Herbs and Garlic Bread
Poulet Farçi au Pain à l'Ail

I particularly like the way this simple dish makes much out of little, a skill not much in evidence recently. The stuffing mingles its flavours with the bird, while keeping it very succulent and providing a purpose for yesterday's bread with fine results. A more rustic Landaise way of stuffing a full size chicken is to cut a 10cm (4 inches) length of baguette in half lengthwise, rub the two halves all over with plenty of crushed garlic and a bit of goose fat, season them and push them into the chicken.

1 large free-range chicken
day old *pain de campagne* or *baguette*
2 cloves garlic
3 tablespoons olive oil
1 teaspoon chopped fresh marjoram, or dried marjoram
1 tablespoon goose fat or butter
1 onion, finely chopped
2 carrots, finely chopped
2 sticks celery, finely chopped
salt, black pepper,

Preheat the oven to 180°C (350 °F). Season the chicken and rub it with olive oil. Cut 2 or 3 x 1 ½ cm (½ inch) slices of bread, or 4 slices of *baguette* and remove the crusts. Mash the garlic and mix it with two tablespoons of goose fat or olive oil, the chopped or dried marjoram, salt and black pepper, brush this mixture over both sides of the bread slices and stuff them into the bird. Let the bird absorb these flavours for an hour or longer. Season the outside of the chicken.

Heat a tablespoon of goose fat and one of olive oil in a deep casserole large enough to hold the chicken, (but not too large or the vegetables will burn) and soften the onion for 10 minutes, over a low heat. Add the carrots and celery and soften for a further 10 minutes. Place the chicken on top of the vegetables, breast downwards, in the pot and roast in the oven, uncovered, for 20 minutes. Turn the chicken on its side, cover the pot and roast for 20 minutes. Turn it over and roast on the other side, covered, for 20 minutes.

Now turn the bird breast side up and cook uncovered for a further 20 – 30 minutes. It may not be very brown, but it should be extremely succulent and well flavoured. Test to make sure the chicken is done; if the juices run clear when you stick a skewer into the thigh, remove the bird to a dish and allow to rest while you spoon the fat from the juices and vegetables in the pan.

Carve and serve with the vegetables and pan juices and spoons of the bread stuffing. Serve the following really quick Red Sauce with Capers to freshen the flavours. (Serves 4 – 6)

Red Sauce with Capers
Sauce Rouge aux Câpres

1 tablespoon white wine vinegar
2 teaspoons Dijon mustard
1 tablespoon tomato purée or tomato sauce
3 tablespoons olive oil
½ shallot finely chopped
2 – 3 teaspoons capers, roughly chopped
salt, freshly ground pepper, *Piment d'Espelette* or cayenne pepper.

Combine the wine vinegar, mustard and tomato purée or sauce in a bowl. Gradually whisk in the olive oil, season well and stir in the chopped shallot and capers. It will separate, but it still looks beautiful and the flavours are rich and zesty. (Serves 4)

Poulet Chilindron

Originally this would have been cooked in an earthenware *cazuela*; the chicken, dark red and glistening, looks its best in this homely terracotta dish; *cazuelas* are oven proof, and can still be bought on line, or at Garcia, the superb Spanish shop in Portobello Road, London. If you choose a flat-bottomed *cazuela*, you can even put it to cook over a gas burner; use a diffuser if you are on the cautious side.

In Spain (and in Garcia) it is possible to buy slices of shank of Serrano ham sawn up like logs, after the rest of the ham has been carved away. These come as little discs which are vacuum packed, and which when added to a casserole or stew, give an extra dimension to the flavour of the dish.

1 medium sized chicken cut into 8 pieces
3 dried red choricero or ancho peppers (or 2 dried red chillies, soaked, chopped and put in skin and all)
4 tablespoons olive oil
1 red onion, chopped
2 large cloves garlic, chopped
1 ham bone or gammon knuckle (or a thick slice of *pancetta*)
2 teaspoons sweet paprika
¼ teaspoon *piment d'Espelette* or cayenne pepper
4 tinned tomatoes, drained and chopped
2 fresh red peppers or 3 long green peppers
125ml (4¼ fl oz) chicken stock
splash of brandy
1 tablespoon chopped parsley
salt

Pour boiling water over the choricera or ancho peppers, and let them soften. Season the pieces of chicken with salt and pepper.

Scrape the thin inner pulp from the soaked peppers and chop it, discarding the skins.

Heat the olive oil in a wide pan and sauté the chicken on all sides until lightly browned.

Remove the chicken pieces to a dish as each one is properly browned and then put in the onions, garlic, and ham bone and cook over a moderate heat until well-softened. Add more oil if needed.

Add the pulp from the dried peppers or the chopped red chillies, stir them in with the paprika and cayenne and then add the tomatoes and chicken stock. Return the pieces of chicken, season with salt, cover with a lid and simmer for 20 minutes.

Meanwhile char the fresh peppers over a gas flame, or in a very hot, dry frying pan until soft and charred – this adds a smoky flavour to the dish. Peel off the charred skin (you can do this under the tap), remove the seeds and add the peppers to the chicken, stir in the brandy and parsley and cook for a further 10 minutes. Rest the chicken for 20 minutes. Serve with potatoes, *milhas* (polenta) or rice and some good, strong, tannic red wine. (Serves 4)

Spanish Chicken with Olives

1 medium chicken (1½ kg or 3⅓ lb), cut into 10 pieces
1 – 2 teaspoons sweet paprika
2 tablespoons olive oil
6 cloves of garlic, mashed (you can use a garlic press)
1 generous tablespoon tomato paste (use the one in a tube)
30ml (1 fl oz) sherry vinegar
500ml (17 fl oz) chicken stock
2 red bell peppers, grilled and deseeded
100g (3½ oz) stoned green olives, cut into pieces
2 tablespoons chopped, fresh parsley
salt

Preheat oven to 200°C (400°F). Season the chicken pieces on both sides with salt and paprika. Heat a large ovenproof frying pan over a medium heat and add the oil. Add half the pieces of chicken to the pan and cook until browned. Transfer the chicken to a plate as it is browned. Brown the remaining chicken adding more oil if needed.

Reduce the heat and add the garlic and tomato paste, scraping up browned bits with a wooden spoon. Return the chicken to the pan, increase the heat a bit and pour in the vinegar. Boil, stirring, until the liquid is reduced to a glaze. Turn chicken pieces to coat all over.

Stir in the stock and bring to a boil. Add the peppers, cut into strips and the olives. Season with pepper. Transfer to the oven and braise for 25 - 30 minutes. Rest for 10 minutes. Sprinkle with parsley.

Poulet Basquaise

Based on a recipe from Marie Haran, who presides over the Bastanondo Chambre d'Hôte, Gastanchoanea, Bidarray.

This is a rather more mellow dish than the usual version, in which the peppers are not roasted beforehand.

I medium chicken, cut into 8 pieces
4 red peppers
4 – 5 tablespoons olive oil
2 large onions, sliced
2 long green chillies, cut in half and deseeded
2 cloves of garlic, coarsely chopped
6 medium tomatoes, skinned and roughly chopped
2 rosemary sprigs and 2 bay leaves
½ teaspoon *piment d'Espelette* or hot paprika
flour for dusting
salt, pepper

Roast the red peppers as in the recipe on page 66. Skin them, remove the cores and seeds and slice into pieces.

Heat 2 tablespoons of oil in a frying pan and add the sliced onion. Fry without browning for 10 minutes, then add the red peppers, green chillies and garlic. Soften the vegetables for a further 5 minutes, then add tomatoes, herbs, and seasoning of hot *piment* or paprika, salt and pepper.

Cook gently, covered for 20 minutes. Remove the lid and allow the liquid to evaporate if it looks watery – it must not be!

Next fry the chicken, doing this well is crucial for this dish, they must be evenly brown and they must not burn. Heat three tablespoons of olive oil in a casserole. Dust the pieces of chicken with flour and fry them for 10 minutes, turning the pieces frequently so that they become generously golden all over, add more oil if necessary. Add the pepper and tomato mixture and lower the heat. Simmer for 15 to 20 minutes or until the chicken pieces are cooked to your liking, turning them over once or twice. (Serves 4)

Poule au Pot Henri IV

I ate this famous dish in Pau, in the Restaurant Henry IV, in the Rue Henri IV, right next to the Château where Henri IV was born; it is the dish he wished all his subjects to be able to eat once a week – poached, stuffed chicken – a generous, plentiful, soothing dish to eat with lots of people.

The best way to make it is to make some really good chicken bouillon first, and then to cook the chicken and vegetables in this. Some of the uncooked stuffing, wrapped in cabbage leaves and then simmered in the broth, makes excellent dumplings. The bird is served in a bit of bouillon, with its vegetables, cabbage parcels and a brilliant Red Sauce.

1 large chicken
125ml (4 fl oz) white wine
2 litres (34 fl oz) bouillon or stock made with 1 stock cube
6 leeks, cut in half
8 whole carrots,
8 small potatoes,

For the stuffing:
2 slices bread, crusts removed
5 tablespoons milk

2 – 3 chicken livers
400g (14 oz) pure pork sausages
1 clove garlic, chopped finely
1 egg, beaten
1 tablespoon chopped parsley
½ teaspoon grated nutmeg
salt and freshly ground pepper
1 tablespoon Armagnac
1 Savoy cabbage
Béarnaise Red Sauce from Pau (see page 41)

Make the stuffing:
Soak the bread in milk, squeeze it and crumble it into a bowl.

Chop the chicken livers finely. Remove the sausage skins and crumble the meat into the bowl. Add the chicken livers, garlic, egg, parsley and seasoning and a splash of Armagnac. Mix everything together. Put half the stuffing inside the chicken.

In a large pot put the chicken, the wine, the carrots and leeks, add the bouquet garni and 2 litres of stock.

Bring to simmering point and cook at a slow simmer for 1 hour. Add the potatoes and cook for a further 20 minutes.

Meanwhile, make the stuffed cabbage dumplings.

Remove 8 good sized leaves from the outside of the cabbage and blanch them for 2 minutes in a large pan of boiling water. Plunge them into cold water and then pat them dry. Put a tablespoon of the remaining stuffing in the centre of a leaf and fold the leaf round it into a parcel. Tie with string. Make eight parcels.

Remove the chicken and let it rest in a warm place. Carefully scoop out the vegetables and keep them warm too. Put the cabbage dumplings into the broth and simmer the broth for twenty minutes to reduce it. Lift out the dumplings and remove the string. Taste the broth for seasoning.

Carve the chicken, which should be very succulent, and serve in wide shallow bowls with the stuffing, vegetables, cabbage dumplings and Red Sauce on the side. (Serves 4)

Duck Cottage Pie
Pâté de Gueux

Although this simple, rustic dish is called a pâté, it's almost a cottage pie, and can be made with left overs of ox cheek or braised oxtail for example, or roast lamb or beef – or game (add some gravy to keep it from being dry), but is probably at its best when made with duck confit.

The secret is to flavour the potatoes with herbs and to make them into a very light '*pommes purées*' by softening the mash with a ladle of the potato cooking water.

500g (1lb 2 oz) potatoes
1 bouquet of bay leaves, parsley, marjoram etc.
2 confit duck legs, tinned, in a jar or vacuum packed (500g or 1lb 2 oz)
or use left over ox cheek, oxtail stew or roast lamb
2 large or 4 small shallots, finely chopped
1 – 2 cloves garlic, finely chopped
2 tablespoons chopped parsley
butter
salt, plenty of freshly ground black pepper

Preheat the oven to 200 °C (400°F).

Peel the potatoes and boil them with a bouquet of herbs – bay leaf being the main flavour. Cook until very soft, remove the herbs, drain and purée the potatoes, adding half a ladle of their cooking water. Season well, adding plenty of pepper.

Remove the fat from the confit and keep it for roasting potatoes.

Skin the duck legs and take the meat off the bones, pulling it into pieces. (Pull ox cheek or oxtail into pieces, off the bone. If using left over roast beef or lamb, cut it into small dice). Mix the meat with the finely chopped shallots, garlic and parsley. Spread the mashed potato in a gratin dish, cover with a layer of the meat you are using, pushing it lightly into the potatoes. Scatter the top with little pats of butter.

Bake for 15 - 20 minutes and serve with red onion confit and green salad. (Serves 4)

Duck Confit Pie
Parmentier de Confit de Canard

This comforting, simple dish has been a standby in Bordeaux for at least 200 years, according to local food writer François Martin, who has a new take on the dish, replacing the usual mashed potato top with puréed pumpkin, a favourite winter vegetable in the South West. I make this version with butternut squash.

3 whole legs of duck confit
I large butternut squash or pumpkin, peeled with a potato peeler, seeds removed
I tablespoon olive oil
2 cloves garlic, chopped
2 shallots, finely chopped
I bunch parsley, chopped
4 tablespoons thick cream
salt, freshly ground pepper, pinch nutmeg

Heat the oven to 220°C (425°F).

Cut the butternut squash or pumpkin into cubes and put them in a roasting tin with the olive oil, cover with foil and roast until soft, 15 to 20 minutes. Crush to a rough, golden mash with a potato masher and season well.

Place the pieces of duck in the oven in a small roasting tin for 5 minutes until the fat runs out.

Cook the shallots and garlic slowly in a tablespoon of the duck fat until soft.

Remove the skin and bones from the duck and pull the meat into rough pieces. Mix it with the garlic, shallots and parsley.

Put the shredded duck in layer in a gratin dish, spoon over the cream and carefully spread the mashed squash over the top. Bake until hot, about 15 - 20 minutes. (Serves 4)

Duck au Vin

Daube de Canard au Pruneaux d'Agen

This rich, bronze coloured daube was originally made with an elderly duck in need of a good long stewing; it can be made just as well with duck legs, turning them into a rich, dark brew, sweetened in this case with Agen prunes.

The recipe is my version of one by Francine Claustres in her book *Discovering the Cookery of South-West France*. Like all daubes it takes a bit of time to marinate the meat – you can leave this stage out, but it gives a certain richness to the flavour of the duck. Madiran usually seems to be the wine chosen for the marinade.

4 fresh duck legs

For the marinade:
2 onions, sliced
2 sticks celery, sliced
2 cloves garlic, sliced
1 bunch thyme
500ml (17 fl oz) red wine such as Madiran

12 prunes
50ml (1¾ fl oz) Armagnac
8 shallots, peeled
1 tablespoon goose fat
2 – 3 tablespoons good tomato sauce (page 46)
500ml (17 fl oz) chicken stock
salt, freshly ground black pepper

Put the duck legs in a bowl with the sliced vegetables and pour on the wine. Push in the herbs and leave to marinate for 6 to 8 hours or overnight.

Soak the prunes in the armagnac for 2 hours or overnight. Drain the meat, keeping the marinade, which can be strained.

Pat the meat dry, heat the goose fat in a casserole and sauté the pieces, especially on the fat side until they are a dark bronze colour. Keep spooning away excess fat as it collects. Remove the duck and brown the shallots (and sliced vegetables from the marinade if you are using them) in the same fat. Pour in the wine from the marinade and boil for 5 minutes. Add the duck, add stock and seasoning and simmer gently for 40 minutes, covered.

Add the prunes and Armagnac and simmer very gently, uncovered for a further hour, turning the pieces of duck from time to time. Add more chicken stock if it becomes too thick. Test to make sure that the meat has become very tender.

Allow to cool a bit and spoon off most of the fat from the surface, Better still leave in the refrigerator overnight, which mellows the flavours and makes it easier to remove the fat. Reheat gently. (Serves 4)

Spiced Duck Breasts with Honey and Mustard
Magrets de Canette, Sauce au Miel Chez Paulette

Duck breast is an everyday dish, as familiar as beefsteak, in Bordeaux' Chez Paulette and is handled confidently – rapidly slashed, glazed with honey, cinnamon and star anise and fast-grilled.

To do it in Paulette's style, instead of crosshatching the fat (cutting careful diagonal slashes in both directions), make three deep decisive slashes lengthwise almost from end to end, on the fat side, cutting through close to the flesh.

This is my version of her *magrets*.

4 small duck breasts (Gressingham duck is good – very large duck breasts can be tough)

For the glaze:
3 tablespoons runny honey
2 teaspoons mustard
1 tablespoon tomato ketchup
generous pinch ground cinnamon
1 star anise, pounded
salt

Make two or three deep, lengthwise slashes in the fat on the duck breasts.

Mix all the ingredients for the glaze together and reserve. Place the slashed duck breasts fat side down in a hot iron pan. Let them sizzle and if copious amounts of fat come out, pour it into a bowl to use later.

Let them cook for 4 minutes, turn them over and sear the underneath for 4 more minutes. Turn down the heat. Spoon the glaze onto the fat side and turn the breasts fat side down and cook for 3 minutes. Now glaze the flesh side and turn the breasts again; cook for a further 3 minutes. Repeat once more if you like the meat just pink.

You can tell when the meat is done by poking it with your finger – it should be slightly resilient not soft or wobbly to the touch, but definitely not hard. Remove the *magrets* to a dish, pour any juices in the pan over the top and allow to rest for 5 minutes before serving them whole or sliced. They should be pink inside. (Serves 4)

Duck Breasts with Honey and Orange

This one came from Jean-Marie Laplace, owner of a chambres d'hôte near Bayonne.

4 small duck breasts
4 tablespoons runny honey
juice of an orange or clementine
4 tablespoons cider vinegar
I star anise, crushed (optional)
salt

Put all the ingredients, except the duck, in a small saucepan and reduce by half to make a glaze Cook as in the previous recipe.

Duckburger
Burger du Sud Ouest

We had this in a transport café near Ascain. We had been looking for a *cidrerie*, but instead we found Restaurant Eguzki, which means, in Basque, the Sun. It was a transport café-restaurant. Plumbers and electricians were eating duckburgers topped with foie gras instead of bacon. As well as this brilliant take on a burger, the wonderful crunchy sliced potatoes that accompanied it were cooked on the *plancha*. It was a great combination.

The large, flat bun contained duck breast cut into little pieces, quickly browned and served in a sticky glaze with its juices and a thin slice of fried raw foie gras, (or you could use duck liver pâté). Sliced shallot rings cooked in duck fat accompanied the succulent duck.

1 large duck breast

2 thin slices of foie gras or fine duck liver pâté

2 banana shallots, sliced into rings

2 tablespoons milk

1 dessertspoon cornflour, preferably yellow cornflour

olive oil

a handful of rocket

2 bread rolls

For the marinade:

2 dessertspoons runny honey

2 teaspoons red wine vinegar

2 teaspoons soy sauce

1 clove garlic

½ teaspoon *Espelette* pepper

Remove the fat from the duck breast and cut the meat and half the fat into very small pieces, as if for a steak haché. Mix the marinade ingredients in a bowl and put in the pieces of duck.

Put the remaining fat, cut in pieces, into a frying pan with a little olive oil and let it melt down. Remove the pieces of crisp skin remaining after the fat has melted. Dip the shallot slices into milk, then drain them well and dredge with cornflour. Fry them in the duck fat until crisp and light brown.

Drain the pieces of duck, and keep the marinade. Brush a heavy frying pan with oil and heat until it is very hot.

Put in the duck pieces and sear them hard on all sides. They need to brown quickly on the outside and remain pink inside.

Remove them to a bowl.

Pour the marinade into the pan and swish it round, let it bubble until reduced by half, it only takes a second, then pour it over the duck. Drain the shallot rings on kitchen paper. Cut the rolls in half, pile the duck on the lower halves, place a slice of foie gras or duck liver pâté on top if you like and put the shallot rings on top. Add the rocket. Cover with the top of the rolls and serve straight away. (Serves 2)

Home Made Duck Confit

4 fresh duck legs
15g (½ oz) coarse sea salt
5 green peppercorns
5 black peppercorns
5 juniper berries
25g (just under 1 oz) parsley stalks
1 tablespoon fresh thyme leaves
1 fresh bay leaf
500g (1 lb 2 oz) duck or goose fat

Rinse the duck legs and pat them dry with kitchen paper.

Using a spice grinder or other grinder blitz the salt with all the herbs and spices until it is very fine.

Rub each duck leg all over with the green salt and allow to cure in the refrigerator for 12 hours. If they are particularly small, reduce the time by 3 hours.

Rinse off the salt and dry the legs with absorbent paper again.

Preheat the oven 170°C (325°F).

Heat the duck fat until it is completely melted.

Put the duck legs in a casserole and cover with the duck or goose fat. After 30 minutes reduce the heat to 100°C (200°F) and leave to cook for a further 3 hours. Allow to cool in their fat.

Use within 10 days. (Serves 4)

FOIE GRAS

Terrine de Foie Gras

There may be a ban on Foie Gras in California, but in Bordeaux and the whole of the Médoc there isn't a restaurant serving French food that does not have it on the menu at least once and quite probably three different ways.

Grand Hotel de Bordeaux, opposite Bordeaux' classical eighteenth century Grand-Théâtre, has a delightful restaurant which manages to provide that priceless combination of luxury and kindness. Stuffy formality, which Bordeaux was once famous for, has completely disappeared – nothing to be seen but jeans and sweaters, short skirts, black tights and long hair.

The Grand Hôtel specialises in top quality Foie Gras des Landes, which is served with a quince compôte; (Membrillo works almost as well, providing exactly the right balance of roughness, sweetness and sharpness to set off the smooth silky foie gras).

Around the corner from the Grand in the Rue St Rémi, dozens of ways of serving foie gras were on offer on one single November evening, in one single street, right in the heart of town. This street is lined with bistros and zinc bars, some clinging to their old traditions, dark, candlelit, full of music-hall or bull-fighting posters, wine-barrels and carafes, others with cool, industrial décor, stainless steel counters and high bar-stools, but all serving more or less the same food!

These are just some of the ways in which they serve fresh foie gras – an everyday food for shoppers – you can see that chutney is a popular accompaniment, as it cuts the richness.

Foie gras maison et son chutney. Home made foie gras with chutney.
Terrine de foie gras, pain d'épices et confiture de pomme, poire et noix. Terrine of foie gras with spice bread and apple, pear and walnut jam.
Duo de foie gras (pannacotta et foie gras) Pannacotta of foie gras and terrine of foie gras.
Terrine de foie gras et ses toasts. Terrine of foie gras with grilled sourdough bread.

Poelée de foie gras frais aux cépes (this is fresh, fried with fried ceps).

Foie gras maison, confiture Corse (with jam made with Clementines or Cédrat – a huge, thick-skinned citrus fruit)

Foie gras maison au Tariquet. (Tariquet is an Armagnac from Gascony, a good alternative to Sauternes).

Bocal de foie gras. (Foie gras preserved in a jar).

Oeuf Cocotte au foie gras. (Baked eggs with foie gras).

Foie gras maison au Sauternes. (Foie gras served with sweet Sauternes jelly. see recipe below).

Mystére de foie gras aux noisettes, chutney de Chasselas de Moissac. (Foie gras with hazel nuts and chutney made with the golden-coloured Chasselas table grape with a honeyed flavour).

Terrine de foie gras mi-cuit au Lillet, chutney d'oignons rouge. (Foie gras cooked with Lillet Blanc, a vermouth, locally made, golden in colour with candied orange, honey, pine resin, lime and fresh mint flavours, and served with red onion chutney).

My own feeling about foie gras, after watching many films both for and against the practice, is that it can be produced without harm or suffering to the birds, but we do need to insist on ethically reared foie gras, as we now do on free-range poultry.

Gavage

Ducks and geese have a natural ability to store fat in the liver, to prepare for their migratory journeys; this stored fat is used as fuel for the flight.

Ducks and geese will therefore gorge on large quantities of food to prepare themselves for migration.

For more than 4,000 years humans have known about the tendency of these birds to gorge themselves and have perfected the art of feeding geese and ducks to reproduce and enhance the natural fattening of the liver.

Detailed stone friezes from Saqqara in the Nile Valley, dating 2,500 B.C. show geese and ducks being fed through funnels to increase their fattiness. Jews, Greeks and Romans all followed the practice – the Romans used figs for fattening and no doubt enjoyed the resulting foie gras.

For their first months the ducks or geese destined to be used for foie gras production are reared in normal ways, and it is only for the last two or three weeks of their lives that they undergo the *gavage*; this involves being fed directly into their crops through a tube, with a mixture of maize kernels, water and oil or fat to help it slide down.

Because the oesophagus of ducks, geese and other water birds such as cormorants, is designed to make it possible to swallow large things such as frogs and snails, there is no gag reflex and the lining of the neck is extremely strong and flexible. So there is none of the pain, choking or retching associated with swallowing tubes or large objects in humans.

In addition, the birds are prepared beforehand by being fed a fairly large amount only once a day, so they are used to eating large quantities at once. As the feeding continues, the liver is enlarged, but if *gavage* stops, then the liver goes back to normal size unharmed, as the fattening is a natural process.

Duck foie gras can be cooked in a number of ways. Always remove it from the refrigerator at least 2 hours before starting work. This makes opening it out and removing the veins a lot easier.

Any of these methods can also be used for the larger goose foie gras, but the cooking times should be doubled.

Recipe for Terrine de Foie Gras with Armagnac

The texture of the foie gras will be smooth and silky and making it, as Michel Guérard puts it, child's play - '*jeu d'enfant*'.

To provide a very generous slice of foie gras each for 8 – 12 people:

1 fresh raw duck foie gras weighing 500g (1 lb 2 oz)
1 tablespoon Armagnac, port, or sherry or 1 teaspoon of Armagnac and sherry and 2 teaspoons of port
sprinkling of fine salt
pinch of nutmeg
pinch of sugar
a few grinds of black pepper
2 tablespoons duck fat or goose fat

Soak the foie gras in warm water for an hour or leave at room temperature for two to three hours, to soften it.

Each liver has two lobes. Open out the two lobes, remove all sinews, greenish traces and veins as far as possible, trying to keep the lobes fairly intact, and then sprinkle both lobes with a little Armagnac, port and sherry and a little salt, nutmeg, sugar and pepper. Put the two lobes back together, place in a tight-fitting terrine, leaving as few gaps as possible. Leave in the refrigerator overnight to absorb the flavours, and then bring back to room temperature; this is important.

Spread a little duck fat mixed with a few drops of Armagnac over the liver.

Preheat the oven to 150°C (300°F) and heat a roasting tin of water, deep enough to come at least half way up the terrine. When the water reaches 70°C (160 °F), put the covered terrine into the water bath and poach for 35 – 40 minutes.

Test the liver by inserting a meat thermometer; the correct temperature for the centre of the terrine is from 70°C (160°F) for very pink to 110°C (230°F) for longer keeping. Any fat that comes out will go solid when chilled and can be eaten as a sort of aromatic butter. However the aim is not to shrink the foie gras too much, hence the importance of the water bath and temperature control.

When it is cooked, let it cool, then put the terrine in the refrigerator overnight.

Always let it mature for at least a day (but preferably two or three days) after cooking, before serving it country style, with slices of grilled pain de campagne and your chosen accompaniment. Try thinly sliced apples fried in duck fat, or a dandelion salad with lardons. (Serves 8)

Poached Foie Gras

This is the professional way to serve foie gras for a big occasion, such as a New Year feast, and if you make a Sauternes jelly to go with it, it will be something really special.

After trimming the veins and seasoning the foie gras with a little sugar, salt and some black pepper as described above, and sprinkling it with Armagnac, port or sherry, push the two lobes back together and shape them into a cylindrical roll 30cm (12 inches) long.

Wrap it very tightly in muslin or a thin, clean linen teatowel. Tie with string at each end. Allow it to absorb the flavours for several hours or overnight in the refrigerator.

Let it to come back to room temperature.

Prepare a large basin of very cold water.

Heat a litre of Sauternes to 90°C (190°F), (never let it boil), lower the foie gras into the liquid and let it cook gently for 10 minutes. Keep the Sauternes cooking liquid to make the jelly. Remove the foie gras in its cloth, plunge it into the cold water and then hang it up in a cool place (this bit is messy) and allow to cool and dry out for 24 hours. Remove the cloth, which will be covered in fat. (Scrape it off with a knife.)

Place the roll of cooked foie gras on several flat, overlapping sheets of cling film – you will need the cling film to be at least 40cm (16 inches) long, so that the cylinder of foie gras can be rolled up and sealed at each end with little cling film handles sticking out at the extremities.

Repeat the cling film twice more, so you have three layers. Twist the handles until the foie gras is pressed tight in its casing. Now roll it gently to and fro with the flat of your palms, like a rolling pin, to make the cylinder smooth, to even it out and to remove any holes.

Let it set, in the cling film, in the refrigerator for at least a day or two. Carefully remove the cling film.

Slice the roll into thickish rounds with a knife dipped in a jug of very hot water. Serve with the Sauternes jelly.

Sauternes Jelly

the sweet wine in which you cooked the foie gras.
6 gelatine leaves, soaked in water in the refrigerator overnight (this will give a firm set.)

Chill the Sauternes and remove the fat from the top. Drain the gelatine thoroughly.

Heat the defatted wine to 65°C (150 °F), hot enough to melt the gelatine, do not overheat it. When all the gelatine has completely dissolved, stir once and pour the liquid into an oblong gratin dish and chill in the fridge. When it is set, cut the Sauternes jelly into cubes to serve with the foie gras.

Fried Foie Gras

Open the two lobes of the liver and carefully remove any green traces and veins with a small knife. Cut the raw foie gras into small escalopes, 1½ cm (½ in) thick, with a very sharp knife, dipped in very hot water after each cut. At the last minute, season the slices and coat them with flour.

Fry in hot oil for 2 – 3 minutes on each side. Serve on a salad with asparagus, or with confit figs or with slices of fried quince or apples.

Keeping Foie Gras:

	Presentation	Storage*
Raw Foie Gras	- vacuum packed - unpackaged	- See label - 7 days (0 to 4 °C), wrapped in a tea towel
Semi-preserved or semi-cooked Foie Gras (mi-cuit)	- in sealed cans, jars and containers - shrink-wrapped, vacuum packed (semi-cooked) - in pastry, brioche, or terrine shrink-wrapped or vacuum packed	- 6 months (2 à 4°C) - 21 days (2 à 4°C) - 15 days (2 à 4°C)
Preserved Foie Gras	- in jars or cans	- several years (10 to 15°C)

GAME

There are plenty of pheasants in the forests of Lot et Garonne, and I know of one long-standing pheasant farm by the Dordogne river, which replaced tobacco farming, their fragrant crop until the eighties, when airy tobacco drying barns became second homes for foreigners from Brive, 20 miles away.

Most of their birds are turned into pâté, because pheasants can so often be disappointing, with dry breast meat and tough legs and because in the South West, game pâté of any kind is a favourite.

But pheasant should be so good – not only do they look gorgeous in their exotic plumes, but they have plenty of flavour after a life spent outdoors eating all sorts of little aromatic plants and crickets.

One possibility is to brine the birds briefly before cooking and to cook the legs for a long time and the breasts very briefly.

The two recipes below could resolve the problem.

Confit Legs of Pheasant, Partridge or Quails
Cuisses et Jambes de Faisan Confit

4 pheasants or 8 partridge or quail
2 litres (68 fl oz) cold water
200g (7 oz) coarse salt
8 bay leaves
8 tablespoons duck fat

Dissolve the salt in 500ml (17 fl oz) of the water in a pan, add the bay leaves, bring to the boil and then add the remaining water and allow to cool completely. Immerse the whole birds, making sure that the brine enters the cavities and let them brine in a cool place for 1 hour. Partridge or quail will only need 40 minutes. Drain, remove the birds from the brine, and dry.

Slide a small sharp knife between a bird and its leg, feeling your way to the ball and socket leg joint tucked under the body. Remove the leg from the body with a small sharp knife, keeping drumstick and thigh in one piece. Repeat until you have removed all the legs. Reserve the breasts to use for another dish (see next recipe).

Heat the oven to 160°C (325°F).

Put the legs, packed in as tight as possible, in a casserole and pour in enough melted duck fat to cover them completely. Cook for 1 hour then turn down the heat to 100°C (200°F) and cook a further 3 hours.

Allow to sit in the fat for at least 3 days before eating. They will keep, in the fat, which can be used again, for two weeks or more.

Serve fried in a little duck fat with a salad of lentils, with fried apple or quince or on a green salad with lardons. Watch out for the long, sharp tendons in the drumsticks, they are not good to eat!

Pheasant Escalopes

The pheasant should be brined for an hour as described above (page 211), before being cut into legs and breasts.

4 pheasant breasts
plain flour
1 large egg
50g (2 oz) fresh white breadcrumbs
30g (1 oz) hard sheep's milk cheese, grated
30g (1 oz) butter
1 tablespoon olive oil
1 lemon

Preheat the oven to 200°C (400°F).

Put the beaten egg on one plate and the crumbs mixed with the cheese on a second plate. Skin the pheasant breasts and flatten them firmly with the palm of your hand, pat them quite hard to make fairly even escalopes.

Flour them lightly and dip them into the beaten egg. Lastly dip them into the crumbs to coat them.

Heat the butter and oil in a frying pan and fry the breasts, like veal escalopes, for 1 – 2 minutes on each side, depending on the size, until nicely browned and crisp. Place in the oven for 4 – 5 minutes. Take them out and let them rest for a minute or two. Serve with Béarnaise

Red Sauce (page 41) or Wild Garlic Oil (see page 52) and sliced lemons. (Serves 4)

Quail Wrapped in Vine leaves
Cailles à la Feuille de Vigne

You can eat the grape vine leaves as well as the quails and the bacon; cooked, the leaves have a fresh, lemony taste.

4 large quails
30g (1 oz) butter
4 thickish slices of streaky bacon, *poitrine fumée*
8 large young, fresh grape vine leaves (some may be too small in which case you will need two)
2 tablespoons goose or duck fat
salt and pepper

Preheat the oven to 200°C (400°F).

Brown the quails and the bacon in a frying pan in the butter.

Wrap a slice of bacon over each quail breast. Season with plenty of freshly ground pepper. Cover with a vine leaf, wrap it round and tie it in place with string like a small parcel.

Place the birds in a small roasting tin and put a teaspoonful of goose fat on top of each quail. Put the rest of the fat in the bottom of the tin.

Roast for 25 minutes, basting twice.

To serve the quails, untie the string, remove the vine leaves and bacon and place both on hot plates beside the quails. Moisten with some of the cooking juices. (Serves 4)

Pheasant with Apples and Prunes
Faisanne au Pruneaux d'Agen

This dish comes from the Arcachon Bassin area, which is surrounded by endless pine and oak woods, where hunting game for the table is more important than life itself. Here pheasants, formerly wild, wily birds, hard to hunt, are now reared in pens and then released semi-tame.

Often fed corn in the woods, to keep them in a particular area, they will soon be shot.

It's not very sporting, but it means that pheasants are plentiful, fat and fairly tender in les Landes. Choose hen birds if possible and allow one bird for two people.

2 young pheasants (you could brine them, see page 211)
200g (7 oz) cream cheese
I teaspoon thyme leaves
salt, plenty of freshly ground black pepper
2 cloves garlic
4 eating apples, peeled, cored and quartered
20 soft, stoned Agen prunes
100g (3½ oz) small lardons
4 tablespoons duck fat
4 slices of toasted *pain de campagne*
salt, freshly ground pepper

Heat the oven to 200°C (400°F).

Mix the cream cheese with thyme, salt and plenty of coarsely ground black pepper. Stuff the birds with the mixture and push a clove or two of garlic inside.

Place them in a large earthenware oven dish or gratin dish. Arrange the apples, prunes and lardons round the outside. Coat the birds and fruit with duck fat.

Roast for 20 minutes, then remove the dish from the oven and turn the birds over, breast downwards. Return to the oven for 15 – 20 minutes. Meanwhile make the toast.

To serve the birds, remove the pheasants to a carving board and spoon the creamy stuffing onto 2 pieces of toast and keep hot.

Remove about a third of the prunes and apples to a bowl and mash roughly with a fork. Spread this mixture on the remaining toast and keep hot.

Carve the birds and return the slices of breast and the legs to the hot oven dish. Let them absorb any juices and serve each person with slices of breast and leg of pheasant, some apple and prunes and the juices in the dish. Cut the toasts in half and place a cream cheese toast and a prune and apple toast on each plate, alongside the pheasant. (Serves 4)

Pheasant Patties
Crépinettes de Faisan

Make these well-flavoured rissoles towards the end of the season in spring, when pheasants are not very young and on the tougher side. Brine the pheasants if time allows (see page 211).

2 pheasant breasts, chopped finely
2 – 3 chicken livers, or a slice of duck liver pâté, chopped
400g (14 oz) Toulouse or other fatty pork sausages
1 egg, beaten
50g (2 oz) of fresh breadcrumbs
1 shallot, finely chopped
1 clove garlic, finely chopped
1 tablespoon chopped parsley
1 tablespoon Armagnac
½ teaspoon grated nutmeg
salt and freshly ground pepper
100g (3½ oz) caul fat, (see page 171)
olive oil for frying

If using chicken livers, fry them briefly in butter. Chop them finely.

Mix all the meats together, including the pheasant, with the egg, breadcrumbs, shallot, garlic, parsley, Armagnac and seasonings. Allow to mature for 3 hours or overnight.

Make 8 patties with the mixture.

Place the caul fat in a bowl of hot water to soften. Take it out a piece at a time, tease it open to make flat squarish sheets. Cut 8 squares and trim the edges with a knife. Wrap each pattie in a sheet of caul, folding it round carefully.

Fry very gently in olive oil until just cooked through (test by pressing with a finger – it should be springy, not soft and not too firm).

Serve with braised cabbage, which can have little slices of streaky bacon and garlic sausage embedded in it. Or serve with fried eggs sprinkled lightly with paprika, a slice of orange and a red endive salad. Makes 8 x 70g (2½ oz) patties.

Soupy Pigeons with Apple
Palombes en Sauce

Migrating doves are the darlings of the Basque skies. In spring and in autumn they come to the Pyrenees in swirling flocks, flying fast with the wind; some 500,000 birds spend the summer in the North in Scandinavia and Northern Europe, migrating in Autumn to the South West of France, the Pays Basque and the Iberian peninsula.

Hunters relish the sound of their wings as they clatter through trees; at times they skim the hilltops and rooftops as they fly. La Chasse à la Palombe is a special sport and has a huge place in Basque and Gascon culture.

I have been on a Gascon pigeon hunt; it was a lot to do with sitting in wait, fortifying the spirits with a flask of Armagnac.

You reach the hide by ducking through long netting tunnels camouflaged with oak leaves.

Lookouts are perched high up on wooden platforms, ready to inform the chaps in hides below. Some hunt with lures of tethered tame birds that are made to flap their wings as if alighting safely. Lulled into a false sense of security, the wild birds fly down to drink or rest, and are then ambushed with nets, trapping a dozen or more at a time.

In the mountains, men armed with guns and dogs wait in hides for the flocks to fly overhead. White flags are waved to drive the birds towards the guns, everyone uses mobile phones to plot their course, and on a good day, the quantity of birds culled is considerable.

Afterwards or a day or two, later, the pigeons are plucked, cooked and eaten.

These migratory doves, with their blue-grey plumage, blush-pink breast feathers, white stripes on the wings and, in adults, a patch of white neck feathers, are in fact the same as wood pigeons. They are eaten either roasted whole or breasts only, but very pink indeed, or, for older birds, in a sort of *salmis* (a game stew).

I like this Basque soupy-stew with chocolate and apples in the sauce.

4 pigeons plus their giblets if possible
2 tablespoons sunflower oil or olive oil
1 carrot, chopped
1 onion, chopped
2 cloves garlic, chopped
1 leek, chopped
2 green apples, peeled and chopped
250ml (8 oz) white wine
700ml (25 fl oz) chicken stock
1 tablespoon of goose fat
4 slices of country bread
2 squares dark chocolate
salt, freshly ground pepper

Heat the oil or goose fat in a casserole and brown the pigeons. Remove them to a dish. Brown all the vegetables and the apple and continue cooking until light brown.

In a small frying pan, heat a tablespooon of goose fat and brown the pieces of bread on both sides. Chop up the fried bread.

Return the pigeons to the casserole of vegetables and apple, pour on the white wine, let it bubble for 10 minutes, then add enough boiling water or chicken stock to cover the pigeons. Add the fried bread. Season and simmer until the legs are very tender, 45 minutes should do.

Remove the birds and strip the meat from the carcasses, removing the tendons from the legs; keep the meat hot.

Reheat the vegetables and stock, stir in the chocolate until it is melted and well mixed in. Pile the pigeon meat in the centre of four bowls and spoon the apple and vegetables and their juices round and over the meat. Serve with toast. (Serves 4)

Roast Pigeon with Garlic

The trick with roasted pigeon is to eat it very rare, otherwise it gets tough. Perhaps you may find it too rare? Cook it a little longer, but down in Gascony they love them *saignant* and, possibly, they will pour the heated Armagnac over the roasted bird and set light to it at the end of the cooking.

4 farmed pigeons
24 cloves garlic, peeled
40g (1½ oz) butter
1 shallot, finely chopped
2 tablespoons Armagnac
2 tablespoons port
250ml (8 fl oz) red wine

Preheat the oven to 240°C (465°F).

Blanch the cloves of garlic in boiling water for 2 minutes. Drain them.

Season the pigeons with salt and pepper, inside and out.

Melt the butter in a casserole or a frying pan that will go in the oven, and brown the birds lightly all over for 10 minutes.

Transfer the dish to the oven and after 5 minutes throw in the cloves of garlic and baste them and the birds. Cook for a further 10 minutes for very rare, 15 for rare. Take care not to touch the frying pan handle – I have burned myself many times by forgetting that the handle is hot.

Remove the birds and let them rest, cover them with foil; also remove the nicely browned cloves of garlic and add the shallots to the pan, letting them soften over a lowish heat for a few minutes. Add the Armagnac, flame it if you like, then add the port and the red wine. Reduce the liquid to half its volume. Taste for seasoning and serve the pigeons, which should be very rare, and their garlic and sauce.

Chapter Eight

Meat and Furred Game

The high peaks of the Pyrenees can usually be seen from a great distance when the sky is blue and transparent, the peaks snow-covered from winter to late in the year. This is the remote home of chamois, boars, bears, and three kinds of vultures. Hunters, climbers, cyclists and skiers think this place is daunting.

But when the South wind, a warm, dry *foehn* wind, starts to blow, the snow thaws, revealing meadows in flower and whole hillsides of oaks with the sun dazzling through their golden spring leaves; it comes to life and the mountains become the summer home of hundreds of thousands of sheep, cattle and pigs and their herders.

In September, when they come back down, some ewes are already getting ready to lamb.

In order to get the highest yield of sheeps' milk, which is made into cheeses such as Ossau Iraty, these lambs are sent to the butchers when very young, three to five weeks old – hence the local taste for milk-fed lamb in early spring.

Pyrenean lambs are tiny. A strong Basque and Béarn farmers cooperative known as Amatik, with thirty participating local farmers, take their lambs to the market before they taste grass. Their super fine lambs, called Fermier Label Rouge Agneau de Lait, are purely milk fed and have had no antibiotics or other medication, one whole lamb will weigh 6 – 8kg (13 – 17lb).

Delicate, white and succulent when roasted, some lambs are available as early as December and are offered on market stalls by the producers, complete with miniature sweetbreads, liver and kidneys, a great delicacy; they continue until March or April and are in great demand for Easter.

In Northern Europe they are sold as Pyrenean milk-fed lamb. The tiny legs or shoulders are delicious.

Today many sheep farmers take their animals up to the mountains in trucks, some grazing is 3,000 metres up; in the past these flocks, decked with bells and coloured collars, all followed after their shepherds and dogs, some from as far as the pine forests of les Landes.

The herders, the Gitanes of les Landes, would return with their packs loaded with olive oil pastries and spicy red sausage, and with new ways to cure maladies, to cook a *méchoui* over a firepit, or to make an omelette. They were the explorers who returned with new ideas, the story tellers, who talked of wolves and bears and strange customs.

One such custom was the making of *jambon de mouton,* mutton ham – which was usually made from the gigots of the Manech sheep, the old race loved by the Basques for their rich, flowery milk, the milk of Roquefort and Ardi Gasna (sheep's cheese).

Writer Michel Doussy has a recipe for mutton ham in his book *La Cuisine du Bassin d'Arcachon* (2005). He compares it to *viande de Grisons* (air-dried beef), and recommends that it is served without the fat, which does not have the same texture as ham fat from pigs.

The sheep needs to be bled before ham can be made with it; a leg from a halal lamb, properly bled, will serve the purpose.

Jambon de Mouton

Originally this would have been a large leg of mutton, as large as possible, not easy to find today. However it is just as easy to make a mutton ham with a leg of lamb.

I whole leg of halal-butchered lamb, knuckle uncut
I tablespoon coarsely ground black pepper
I teaspoon Prague powder
I tablespoon cane sugar
5 tablespoons coarse sea salt
I tablespoon hot paprika

Hygiene is very important. Wash your hands and use only spotlessly clean dishes.

Mix the ingredients together. Trim any excess fat from the gigot and put it into a shallow porcelain dish that will fit in the refrigerator.

Rub it thoroughly with the salt mixture, including the Prague powder, a mixture which includes sodium nitrate, used to cure meat. It is dyed pink to avoid confusion with table salt, and gives meat its pink colour. Make sure you rub the end of the bone and all the nooks and crannies of the meat, massaging the salt and other seasonings into it as hard as you can. Put it in the refrigerator for 10 days, turning and rubbing it thoroughly and massaging the salt mixture into it with your hands every day, especially the cut surfaces and the shank.

Rinse off all the salt, dry the ham well and wrap it in a loose cloth.

Place in a very cold, airy place or in the refrigerator for 3 – 4 days to dry the surface. Coat the cut surfaces and the shank end of the bone with lard and paprika to exclude bacteria. Hang again in a clean dry place such as a larder at 15 – 30°C (60 – 85°F) for 5 weeks.

Roast Baby Lamb
Lechazo

It was no good ever hoping to find our chosen lunch spot, booked at the elusive famous starred restaurant of Alain Delteil in the Basses

Pyrénées; we asked everywhere, but nobody had heard of it. Having driven up and down hills, between banks of primroses, for over an hour, we were saved by a telephone engineer who directed us firmly to the Hotel Etchebarne in the village of Mendionde, where we were offered a table in a small, modest Basque family restaurant.

Nothing any clever chef could have come up with would have been better than the red bean soup, the tiny fried fresh trout, the size of goldfish, followed by the local milk-fed lamb, roasted golden brown – this lamb is served *à point*, not rare – with a pool of creamy haricot beans.

The Pyrenean baby lamb is easy to serve as it is quite often roasted already chopped through the bone into manageable pieces (but still on the bone), so that each plate gets a chunk of the miniature leg, some melting shoulder, a piece of juicy loin and some tasty neck cutlets.

The lambs are very small, and a leg or shoulder will feed just three people. Cook a small joint of about 1 kilo (2¼ lb) for 60 – 70 minutes and a larger joint, 1½ kilos (3⅓ lb), for up to 90 minutes. Typically, an onion flavours the gravy, but you can equally well add a whole head of garlic, sliced across in half.

Roast Milk-fed Lamb with Summer Savory

Alain Ducasse uses the herb *sarriette*, summer savory, when he cooks the baby lamb his way, a peppery, sweet herb. Summer savory is easy to grow, pretty and rather neglected in our repertoire of herbs. Romans called it the herb of love and found it effective for sexual deficiencies; it is now known to be a stimulant and an excellent anti-oxidant. It lies, in flavour, somewhere between rosemary, sage and thyme.

Ducasse also recommends cooking the lamb briefly after browning it well, and making a special lamb gravy – it makes a lot of sense as the lamb has fairly scant juices.

1 leg of milk-fed lamb
1 head of new season's garlic
20ml (1 fl oz) milk
1 bay leaf

½ bunch summer savory (or use a mix of thyme, sage and rosemary)
2 tablespoons olive oil
coarse sea salt, freshly ground pepper

For the jus:
500g (1lb 2 oz) neck of ordinary lamb, cut up
1 tablespoon olive oil
2 cloves of garlic
5 sprigs savory or thyme
1 bayleaf
1 litre (34 fl oz) stock or water
salt, freshly ground black pepper

To make the gravy:
Roll the pieces of the lamb neck in flour and fry in a tablespoon of olive oil until very well browned. Cover with stock or water, scrape up the juices on the bottom of the pan and add the garlic, savory or thyme, bayleaf and seasoning. Simmer for 40 minutes or until you have reduced the stock to one third.

To cook the lamb:
First make sure that the meat is at room temperature.

Preheat the oven to 180°C (350°F). Simmer the cloves of garlic in milk with a bay leaf for 10 minutes, until soft.

Heat 2 tablespoons of olive oil in a heavy pan that will go into the oven and brown the leg of lamb all over. Season the meat and put the pan in the oven to roast for 20 minutes (or more if you do not like it pink). Allow the lamb to rest in a heated dish, while you spoon the fat from the roasting tin and pour in the *jus*. Stir and simmer for two minutes to make the gravy. Mash the garlic well with a fork and put it onto a small plate for those that want it; new season's garlic, when cooked this way, is mild and will not overwhelm the delicate taste of the lamb. (Serves 2)

Agneau de Lait au Four

This long cooking is more traditional than the previous recipe and is
how it is often served.

half a milk-fed lamb
I clove of garlic
olive oil
salt and pepper

Ask the butcher to cut the gigot, the loin and the shoulder through the
bone into 4cm (1½ inch) slices.

Preheat oven to 180°C (350°F). Rub the lamb pieces with salt,
pepper and olive oil, and put them in a roasting tin. Slice the clove of
garlic lengthwise and tuck pieces into the meat here and there.

Roast for 40 – 45 minutes basting frequently with olive oil.

Cover the meat with aluminium foil and roast a further 10 – 15
minutes. Serve with haricot beans, see page 281. (Serves 2)

Sherry Kidneys

Fresh kidneys from young lambs are so different from frozen. It is
worth having a talk with the butcher about keeping some aside, as
quite often they will otherwise put them straight in the freezer. A
fresh kidney is firm and springy, not floppy, and has a blueish, thin,
transparent membrane on the outside, which is quite resilient and has
to be removed.

10 lamb's kidneys
I onion, finely chopped
4 tablespoons olive oil
100g (3 oz) *poitrine fumée* or *pancetta*, cut into lardons
I clove of garlic, finely chopped
I tablespoon flour
125ml (4¼ fl oz) fino dry sherry
I tablespoon tomato concentrate
2 sprigs fresh thyme, finely chopped

salt and freshly ground black pepper
½ to 1 teaspoon cayenne pepper

Remove the membranes from the kidneys, cut them in half and cut out the tough, fatty core from the centre.

Heat 2 tablespoons of oil in a large frying pan over gentle heat. Sauté the onion until soft and transparent, add the lardons and garlic and cook for 10 minutes.

Remove the onion and bacon from the pan, keep them warm. Add 1 – 2 tablespoons more olive oil to the pan and, when it is hot, put in the kidneys, a few at a time, over the highest heat and stir occasionally. When they are seared, pull them to the sides of the pan and add more kidneys. When they are all seared and coloured, return the onions and bacon, sprinkle with flour and stir it in.

Add the sherry, tomato concentrate and thyme, taste for seasoning, add the cayenne, and bring to a simmer, cook gently for 5 minutes. Season to taste.

Navarin of Lamb with Baby Vegetables

I have no faith in the idea that this lovely spring dish was named after the Battle of Navarino in the early nineteenth century, but that is the story. One other suggestion is that it is called this because it contains turnips, (*navets*) but it could also originally have been a dish from Navarre,[1] which is a Basque sheep-rearing area in the Basse-Pyrenees

Whatever the origin, it is an old favourite in the South West; young spring vegetables such as peas, asparagus and broad beans, added towards the end, make it Navarin Printanier (spring Navarin). I have also come across a Navarin d'Automne, which has chanterelles or oyster mushrooms and the herb summer savory added towards the end of the cooking.

1½ kg (3⅓ lb) shoulder and best end of lamb, on or off the bone, cut into big pieces (or 4 small lamb shanks) ask the butcher to do this.
6 slices *poitrine fumé* or *pancetta*, cut in pieces, or 200g (7 oz) lardons
3 tablespoons olive oil

[1.] An ancient breed of horses from Navarre are called *navarins* or *navarraises*.

25g (just under 1 oz) butter, cut into dice
8 shallots, halved lengthwise
12 – 16 young carrots, Chantenay if possible, tops removed
400g (14 oz) new potatoes
8 baby turnips, halved, a small length of stalk left on if possible
chicken stock or lamb stock
4 sprigs fresh thyme
salt, freshly ground pepper

Preheat the oven to 150°C (300°F).

Season the meat with a little salt and plenty of pepper. Heat 3 tablespoons of olive oil in a large frying pan or skillet and fry the pieces of lamb to brown them lightly on all sides.

Dot the bottom of a casserole with butter and spread it round, arrange the lardons on top. Place the shallots on top of this in a layer. Cover with a layer of half the carrots, potatoes and turnips and season with pepper only. Next put in the meat, sprinkle with thyme, and lastly put in a layer of the remaining vegetables. Heat the stock, pour it over the top and cover the casserole. Braise in the low oven for 2 hours. Allow to cool, and when it has set solid, pick out the fat with a spoon. Reheat slowly and serve very hot. (Serves 4 – 6)

Chuletas de Cordera alla Navarra

The sheep of Navarra are mountain sheep, with a good strong flavour, so their meat can take this very intense way of cooking.

8 – 12 nice lamb cutlets, trimmed
4 sprigs of thyme or a teaspoon of dried thyme
3 tablespoons olive oil
1 large onion, finely chopped
1 thick slice Bayonne or Serrano ham cut into small batons or lardons
4 tomatoes, skinned and chopped
100g (3 oz) fresh, soft chorizo, cut into batons
salt, freshly ground pepper

Rub the chops with olive oil and sprinkle with thyme leaves. Allow them to sit for a while to absorb the flavours.

Heat the olive oil in a frying pan that will take all the cutlets in one layer (or heat 2 pans).

When the oil is just starting to smoke, add the cutlets and cook for 1 minute on each side.

Remove the meat to a plate, reduce the heat and put in the onions, ham and chorizo. Soften the onion and cook the ham and chorizo for 5 minutes, add the tomatoes and then put the chops back.

Let them cook a further 1 – 2 minutes on each side. Press with a finger to see if they ready – they should feel vibrant, juicy and springy, not soft and definitely not firm. Sprinkle with salt crystals and freshly milled pepper and serve hot with crushed potatoes, see page 264. (Serves 4)

Txilindron

If you prefer you can cook this splendid stew with boned lamb shoulder, but keeping the bone gives depth of flavour to the dish. Paula Wolfert, author of *The Cooking of South West France* (1983), suggests that cooking meat with plenty of fat on it adds to the taste. If you prefer to take the fat off, do so after the meat is cooked. Make the dish a day ahead if possible, let it get cold and the fat on top can then easily be removed with a spoon.

half a large lamb shoulder, cut in fairly large pieces, on the bone
1 – 2 whole dried choricera or ancho peppers
4 long green pimentoes or 2 green peppers
1 large red pepper
4 – 5 tablespoons olive oil
2 onions, chopped
2 cloves of garlic, chopped
100ml (3½ fl oz) white wine
1 teaspoon *Piment d'Espelette* or ½ teaspoon sweet paprika and
½ teaspoon cayenne pepper
3 medium ripe tomatoes, skinned and chopped

1 teaspoon fresh thyme leaves
350ml (12 fl oz) stock or water
salt

Preheat the oven to 180°C (350°F).

Pour boiling water over the dried peppers and let them soften. Remove the seeds. Roast the green and red peppers under a grill in a roasting tin until the skin blackens and puffs up or grill them over a flame or on a hotplate, turning them over, until the skin chars and can be removed and the flesh is just tender (the green take less than 5 minutes to grill, the red twice as long), put them in a covered saucepan or a plastic bag until cool. Remove the skins and seeds. Cut the flesh into strips.

Heat the olive oil in a casserole and brown the pieces of lamb on all sides. Remove the browned meat to a plate, turn down the heat and soften the onions until tender and turning brown. Add the garlic and the peppers including the choricera peppers. When the garlic begins to smell cooked, add the wine and let it bubble for a few minutes. Add *piment d'Espelette* or cayenne pepper and paprika and stir it in, then add the tomatoes and thyme. Season with salt and allow to reduce a little for 10 – 15 minutes.

Add the lamb and any juice that has run from it and the stock or water and cover the pan. Cook in the oven, covered, for an hour and a half. (Serves 4)

Sunday Roast Lamb with Potatoes and Shallots
Gigot d'Agneau de Dimanche

The celebrated pré-salé lambs of Pauillac feed on the salt marshes of the Médoc during summer. It was the custom, from the thirteenth century, to pasture these sheep on the vineyards in winter, where all sorts of flavourful wild herbs and alliums grow. With the advent of weedkiller this looked perilous, but many wine producers are now going bio, and hopefully the custom can continue.

This is a very easy way to make a rustic and very enjoyable Sunday lunch.

1 leg of lamb weighing 2 – 2½ kg (4½ – 5½ lb)
olive oil
several sprigs of rosemary
2 cloves of garlic cut in slivers
25g (1 oz) butter
6 potatoes, peeled and diced into large cubes
4 banana shallots, halved lengthwise
2 cloves of garlic, sliced
125ml (4 fl oz) water
200ml (7 fl oz) stock
salt, freshly ground black pepper

Preheat the oven to 200°C (400°F). Brush a roasting tin with olive oil.

Pierce the leg of lamb here and there with the point of a knife blade and push a small sprig of rosemary and a sliver of garlic into each cut. Put any rosemary left over with the potatoes.

Lay the potatoes in the middle of the roasting dish leaving a margin round the edge, mix in the shallots and garlic, season and dot with butter. Lay the lamb on top. Sprinkle with 125ml (4 fl oz) of water.

Put the lamb into the middle of the oven and roast for 20 minutes, turn down the heat to 180°C (350°F) and continue to roast – allow 1½ hours altogether. Keep an eye on it to ensure that the potatoes do not burn too much – a bit of dark brown crispiness round the edges is fine.

Move the lamb to another dish and leave it to rest while you transfer the potatoes and shallots to another dish also, and keep them hot. Add the stock to the roasting pan and place on a low heat. Scrape all the juices and stuck pieces of potato into the gravy and when it has bubbled for a few minutes, taste for seasoning and pour through a sieve into a gravy jug.

Serve with green beans, see page 281. (Serves 4)

Marmite Navarraise

The Marmite is a cooking pot, originally an iron cauldron, which hung from a hook in the chimney or was placed on a trivet over the glowing embers of a wood fire.

This rich and fragrant stew can be made more rustic by adding one or two small birds such as pigeons (or blackbirds, thrushes etc.) with the meat. Use lamb off the bone if you prefer and you can make it with any stewing cut, such as best end of neck.

half a shoulder of young lamb, cut in large pieces on the bone
2 tablespoons pork, goose or ham fat
1 onion, chopped
500g (1lb 2 oz) potatoes, washed and roughly diced
100g (3½ oz) soft chorizo, cut in thick slices or diced into chunks
6 cloves of garlic
1 x 400g (14 oz) tin tomatoes, chopped
1 small glass (50ml or 2 fl oz) Armagnac
250g (9 oz) white stalks of chard, sliced
250g (9 oz) shelled broad beans (frozen are fine)
250g (9 oz) jar or tin of artichoke hearts, drained (or use fresh artichoke hearts)
salt, freshly ground pepper

Melt the pork, goose or ham fat in a casserole. Brown the pieces of meat all over, a few at a time, and set them on one side. Soften the onion in the same fat, adding more if necessary, then add the potatoes and sauté them for 5 minutes.

Stir in the chorizo and chopped garlic and cook for a few more minutes. Add the meat and its juices, the Armagnac and chopped tomatoes, season, cover and simmer over a low heat for one hour and 40 minutes.

Add the remaining vegetables to the pan. Simmer a further 20 minutes and serve. (Serves 4)

PORK

In the mid 1980s, a group of Basque charcutiers, fed up with the poor quality of ham produced on an industrial scale and of pork imported from Normandy, decided to restore the traditional Basque way of rearing pigs and began producing pork and charcuterie in the old way.

The young and enthusiastic Louis-Ospital, whose father was a charcutier before him, was one of these, but first he decided on doing a *stage* in Paris, before settling into the family business. There he made friends with the up and coming young chefs of the day. These chefs, who now have their own successful restaurants, have watched his enterprise with interest and today buy his ham and charcuterie.

To make sure of the quality, he has a dedicated young pig mid-wife, kept busy in Spring delivering all the babies for this production. Any that are too small or thin are sold on, only the strongest and best are kept and from the age of three months they are reared outside; there are very few pigs per acre and they are fattened for a year. So they live long and much healthier lives – from the spring onwards, they enjoy clear air and sunshine and in Autumn, gorge on the nuts that are dropping off the trees. Allowed to grow much longer than industrially reared pigs, free of chemicals and GM foods, they become gigantic; these mature, lardy beauties make the most delicious, delicate, juicy and well-marbled ham, pork saucisson and chorizo.

Another group of Basque pig farmers formed the collective who produce Kintoa pork and ham. The Kintoa was the tax of one in five pigs which had to be given to the king from every herd.

The black and white '*pie noir*' pigs are reared in the Kintoa region of Les Aldudes in the hills of the Pyrenees, a lush farming commune, half French and half tied to Spain, where 20 pig breeders have revived an ancient, almost extinct race of Basque pigs.

In the Autumn, towards the end of their fattening they graze in the high meadows and forage for acorns, beechnuts and chestnuts under forest trees. They provide the most exquisite pork.

In my first travels in The South West, nearly two decades ago, I found most *jambon crû*, which is served at every opportunity in every restaurant throughout Aquitaine, hard, dry and salty, very inferior to Parma ham for example.

But the picture has changed, thanks to these farmers and their decision to get together and return to the traditional Pyrenean way of rearing old breeds of pigs for pork and old ways of making ham.

Basque Roast Leg of Marinated Pork

Start the marinading three days before you want to serve the meat. The spiced wine bath gives a deep rich flavour, which can be enhanced with mustard and cream at the end. The resulting roast, if any is left, is also extra good eaten cold with salad.

1½ kg (3⅓ lb) leg of fresh pork, skin removed (use the skin to make cracklings) but make sure the fat is left on
4 cloves of garlic, crushed
1 tablespoon salt
12 peppercorns, crushed
8 allspice berries, crushed
8 juniper berries, crushed
1 tablespoon fresh thyme leaves
2 bay leaves, crushed
1 onion, quartered
2 x 8cm (3 inches) strips orange zest
250ml (8½ fl oz) red wine
100ml (3½ fl oz) chicken stock
2 – 3 tablespoons *crème fraîche*, optional
2 teaspoons Dijon mustard, optional
salt and freshly ground black pepper

Combine garlic, salt, peppercorns, allspice, juniper, thyme, and bay and crush them roughly with a pestle and mortar or in a spice grinder.

Rub the pork with this mixture and place it in deep porcelain bowl. Add the onion and orange zest. Pour in the red wine. Let the meat marinate in this mixture for 3 – 4 days in the refrigerator, turning it once or twice a day.

Remove the pork from the marinade, dry it well and allow it an hour or two to come to room temperature. When you are getting ready to cook the pork, heat the oven to 200°C (400°F). Rub the meat all over generously with olive oil and put it in a clean roasting pan. Roast at 200°C (400°F), allowing 15 minutes per 250g (9 oz). Baste every 30 minutes with the marinade.

When it is cooked, transfer the pork to a hot platter to rest, while you deglaze the pan with chicken stock, scraping up the caramelized juices. Skim some of the fat off the top. Strain any remaining marinade and add it to the roasting juices. Cook the juices down to half their volume and then add the *crème fraîche* and mustard if you want to. Whisk it in well, season with salt if needed and plenty of black pepper. (Serves 6)

Roast Pork with Honey and Rosemary
Roti de Porc au Romarin et Miel

2 pork fillets
4 tablespoons clear honey
1 tablespoon grain mustard
4 sprigs rosemary
1 star anise, smashed in a pestle and mortar
4 tablespoons dry white wine
salt, pepper

Preheat the oven to 200°C (400°F).

Strip the leaves off the twigs of rosemary and chop the leaves finely. Mix together the honey, mustard, chopped rosemary and star anise. Brush the pork with the mixture. Season. Put the pork in a roasting tin, add the wine and roast for 25 minutes. Turn the pork occasionally.

After the pork is cooked, put the roasting pan on the top of the stove with the pork in it, and reduce the liquid, turning the meat all the time until the juices have caramelized and the meat is golden in colour. Serve sliced with a green salad. (Serves 4)

Fluffy Eggs and Bacon

This is a recipe from Jean Suhas, author of *Les Trois Cèpes de Michel, Histoires Gourmandes du Sud-Ouest et d'Ailleurs* (2007), inspired by a Gascon childhood memory that he cherished.

Xingar eta arrolze, black pudding and white sausage cooked together, was a favourite with Suhas' Aunt Justine, amongst other things, when she was organising supper. Another dish she loved consisted of fluffy eggs. To make it:

> "Beat the whites with two forks until they make a soft snow. This mattress of egg white is cooked gently in a frying pan. Then little nests are made in it with the back of a spoon, and a yolk is slipped in and cooks there; around this were placed some slices of fried *ventrèche*, streaky bacon. *Merveille, ô merveille.* Wonder of wonders, not just bacon and eggs!"

This is a charming little dish and would appeal to any child; keep the yolks in two separate cups when you break the eggs and fry the whisked up foam from two egg whites in a non-stick pan in a tablespoon of butter, making a sort of fluffy platform. Press two holes with the back of a soup spoon and slide a yolk into each one, like two eyes. When the egg whites get warm they cook the egg yolks just enough; serve it with two rashers of streaky bacon, one on each side. (Serves 1)

Marinated Pork Fillet

This fragrant and delicious mixture of aromas is very popular in the Pays Basque. The rub is massaged onto pork chops or fillet and allowed to flavour it for as long as you have got – 24 hours if possible, or 1 or 2 hours if not.

2 pork fillets, at room temperature
2 red peppers and 2 yellow peppers grilled, deseeded and skinned
1 tablespoon olive oil
1 tablespoon sherry vinegar
salt

For the marinade mixture:
2 teaspoons smoked hot paprika
1 teaspoon *piment d'Espelette* or ½ teaspoon cayenne pepper
2 teaspoons dried oregano
2 teaspoons ground cumin
1 teaspoon dried thyme or 4 sprigs fresh thyme
4 cloves of garlic, crushed

4 tablespoons olive oil
salt, black pepper

Mix the marinade mixture ingredients in a bowl and put in the fillets. Rub the mixture all over the meat with your hands, massaging it in as much as possible and allow to marinate for up to 24 hours.

Preheat the oven to 200°C (400°F). Let the pork come to room temperature.

Cut the skinned peppers into broad strips. Sprinkle them with olive oil and a little salt.

Lay out the peppers in an oiled roasting tin, and roast for 10 minutes, then put in the pork and baste with any marinade remaining in the bowl. Roast at the top of the oven for 12 - 15 minutes. Allow to rest for 10 minutes. Slice the pork, sprinkle with olive oil, sherry vinegar, salt and the roasting juices and serve with the roasted red and yellow peppers. (Serves 4)

Cured Pork Fillet

1 fillet of pork weighing 400 – 500g (14 oz – 1lb 2 oz)
gros sel
pinch of Prague powder no 2 (see page 221)
piment d'Espelette or hot smoked paprika
sweet paprika
black pepper
muslin or large gauze dressings and string

Hygiene is important when curing pork, so scrub up well.
Mix the salt with the Prague powder.
Put a good layer of *gros sel* in a porcelain dish. Put the fillet on top and then put another layer of salt over the top of the meat. Cover the dish and refrigerate overnight for 12 hours, not longer

Take out the fillet and wash it briefly. Dry it carefully with kitchen paper.

Put a good thick layer of *piment d'Espelette* and paprika on a board, grind some black pepper over it and roll the fillet in the spices until it is completely covered all over.

Wrap the meat in muslin, long enough and wide enough to contain the fillet, or wrap it in dressings to cover. Tie it with string at 5cm (2in) intervals.

Put the fillet in the vegetable drawer of the refrigerator for 4 days and then hang in a larder or other dry room (at between 20°C and 30°F) for 3 weeks – it is now ready to eat. Slice it thinly and eat it raw like ham.

Black Pudding with Beans
Morcilla con Fabadas

The best *morcilla* for this splendid dish is the one from Burgos with rice and a flavouring of cumin. You can also add a bit of chorizo, cut in slices and fried, and some lardons, but not too much, they can swamp the very unique taste of the black pudding.

200g (7 oz) morcilla, preferably morcilla de Burgos
350g (12 oz) very large dried white beans (alubias grandes) or butter beans
1½ l (51 fl oz) water or stock
150g (5 oz) potatoes, cut in chunks
2 carrots
3 large cloves of garlic
2 teaspoons marjoram
1 teaspoon cumin
2 large fresh red chillies, seeded and cut in strips
2 dried choricero peppers
200g (7 oz) spinach
3 tablespoons olive oil
sweet paprika
salt

Soak the beans overnight in cold water.

Drain and put them into a large casserole with 1½ litres water or stock. Bring to the boil, skim off the foam that rises and simmer for 1 hour or until the beans are tender. Add a splash of cold water (scare the beans) every now and then.

Add potatoes, carrots, garlic, marjoram, cumin, fresh chillies and salt. Bring back to the boil and cook until the potatoes are tender.

Pour boiling water over the dried chillies and when they are soft, open them and discard the seeds. Either throw them in whole or scrape the flesh off the skins with a knife and transfer this paste to the beans, stirring it in. Simmer for 20 minutes. Add the spinach and let it just wilt.

Skin the morcilla and crumble it into pieces the size of a walnut. Heat the olive oil in a frying pan and put in the morcilla. Fry until very crisp, then scatter it over the top of the beans. Sprinkle with paprika and serve in bowls. It should be quite soupy, add more liquid if it is needed. (Serves 4 – 6)

Braised Pork Loin with Quince
Rouleau de Porc Noir

Any good free-range pork will do for this recipe, but best of all are the rustic black Gascon pigs, *les porc noirs de Bigorre*, survivors of a very ancient line; they have much more fat than a modern pig and this fat is tender and luscious to eat and makes superlative charcuterie.

The black pigs live at liberty in the Pyrenees and are partly fed in the traditional way on acorns and beech nuts to improve the quality of their meat. These wonderful animals are not suited to industrial farming and are not particularly easy to raise, and consequently would have disappeared without the hard work of devotees, who brought the breed back from the edge of extinction.

1½ kg (3⅓ lb) boned, rolled loin of pork (with plenty of fat but no skin)
6 shallots, halved
4 cloves of garlic
100ml (3½ fl oz) cider vinegar
100ml (3½ fl oz) stock
1 quince, peeled and cut across into 1cm (⅓ in) rounds
50g (1¾ oz) butter
salt, freshly ground pepper

Preheat the oven to 180°C (350°F).

Heat a tablespoon of olive oil in a casserole. Sear the meat, turning it to brown on all sides, then add the shallots and garlic and the cider vinegar.

Add enough stock to make about 1cm (⅓ inch) of liquid in the bottom of the casserole. Season the meat, cover and roast for 40 minutes; turn the meat once or twice and top up the liquid with more stock if necessary.

Fry the sliced quinces in butter, then add 2 teaspoons cider vinegar and cook for 2 - 3 minutes. Add them to the casserole and cook the meat for a further 15 minutes, just under an hour altogether. Transfer the pork to a serving dish with the quinces, and allow to rest for 15 minutes while you reduce the gravy if necessary. (Serves 6)

Long-cooked Spare Rib Chops
Échine de Porc Confite

The nearest cut we have to *échine de porc,* is what my butcher calls 'pork spare rib chops'. It can be cut into individual chops or kept in one piece, it is a superb cut for braising, well marbled with fat.

2kg (4½ lb) spare rib chops, preferably in one piece
1 teaspoon hot paprika or *piment d'Espelette*
1 – 2 teaspoons thyme leaves
1 – 2 tablespoons goose fat or pork dripping
4 red onions, coarsely sliced into crescents
4 cloves of garlic, sliced
300ml (10 fl oz) red wine
200ml (7 fl oz) chicken stock
3 – 4 tablespoons tomato coulis
salt, freshly ground pepper

Preheat the oven to 150°C (300°F).

Season the meat on all sides with salt, pepper and paprika or piment d'Espelette and rub this in together with the thyme leaves.

Heat 1 tablespoon of the fat in a casserole just big enough to hold everything and brown the meat until golden on all sides. Remove it and lower the heat. Put the onions and garlic into the pot, sprinkle them with a little salt and add more fat if needed. Let them wilt down, stirring often. Return the meat and pour in the wine and let it bubble for a few minutes. Add the stock and tomato and cover the pot.

Bring to simmering point and transfer to the oven, Cook for 2 hours, turning the pork once.

Turn off the heat and rest the meat, covered, for 20 minutes before serving. (Serves 6)

Migas de la Vallée de Roncevaux

Migas comes in many forms, the unifying factor being bread. This can be cut in cubes, crumbled coarsely or broken into larger pieces and added to a frying pan full of fried onions and either breast of lamb or lardons of cured pork belly or streaky bacon, salt cod, vegetables or bits of confit duck.

This recipe comes, via Anne Marie Gale's book *Recettes du Pays Basque* (2011), from the region of Roncevaux, a remote high mountain pass between France and Spain, site of a famous eighth century battle. Roland, leading the French against Charlemagne, was defeated here and the story, somewhat twisted to make it a battle between Moors and Christians, became the Song of Roland.

A really great comfort dish comparable to hash or bubble and squeak, this is a very useful dish when you do not have quite enough of anything to go round. This *migas* can be served with poached eggs, with cooked peas stirred in and with the chopped green tops of spring onions on top.

400g (14 oz) bread, not too fresh, crusts removed
2 potatoes, peeled
4 tablespoons pork fat or goose fat
1 onion, chopped
4 cloves of garlic, chopped
100g (3½ oz) sliced ventréche – streaky bacon, or pancetta – cut into lardons or small, thick slices

salt, I teaspoon *piment d'Espelette* or hot paprika
4 eggs
2 – 3 spring onion tops, sliced across

Break the bread into pieces about 1 – 2 cm (½ in) in size, or smaller. Dice the potatoes, fairly small, about 2 cm (¾ in).

Heat the pork fat or goose fat in a frying pan and add the onions, garlic, bacon and potatoes, season with hot red pepper, sprinkle with a little water, cover the pan and fry until the onions are soft and the potatoes just browned and cooked. Turn the heat down if they are getting too brown, they must not burn.

Add the bread and continue to fry, gently, sprinkle with a little water and cook until the bread is brown, a little bit crisp and tender, not hard. Fry the eggs and put them on top, sprinkle with chopped green onion tops.

BEEF

Bazas Beef - *Boeuf Bazardais*

A little Roman town South of Bordeaux and the Sauternes vineyards, Bazas is a well known for its cattle markets.

In February, a special Festival is held here in honour of the champion fat beef cattle of Aquitaine. On a cold, sometimes snowy, day the marching pipe band strikes up and a parade of massively muscular, rippling beasts, dressed up in tall flowered crowns, with bunches of roses sprouting from their tails, files past the local crowd.

They come to a stop in front of the splendid Gothic Cathedral and receive a blessing there. Next the judging; after much serious prodding of deeply padded rumps, a King is crowned. After the parade a meal – mainly beef – is served, starting off with Beef *Pot-au-feu* with Green and Red Sauce.

Historically, apart from dairy cows, the domestic cattle reared in Aquitaine were bred to carry wood and fodder and to pull carts and wagons, ploughs and harrows – they were not butchered much below 8 years of age and being tough, did not make good beef, which was once considered a lower grade meat – cheaper than pork or veal.

But since the mid nineteenth century there have been huge efforts to improve the beef cattle and now the brindled Bazas steer is a very serious contender, its only rivals the Blonde d'Aquitaine, the Boeuf de Chalosse and the Boeuf Limousin; all provide superb beef, from pastured mature animals – tender and finely marbled, but the Bazas beef is prized for its 'inexpressibly fine' flavour, and the quality of its lesser cuts.

Cattle raised traditionally on grass and hay, can live to a great old age.

Top dollar in the Basque country, is grilling steak from animals up to 12 or even 14 years old and beyond; I have eaten it and it is sublime, and very expensive.

This aged meat is from traditionally raised animals, often cows, who live mostly outside on grass. According to environmental author and scientist Michael Pollan, if all steers were raised outside and mainly grass fed, they would live much longer and be a lot healthier themselves and a lot healthier for us. Look for grass fed beef and you cannot go wrong.

Pot au Feu with Red and Green Sauce

This recipe is based on the *Pot au Feu* served at the Bazas beef festival, it uses leeks instead of onions and is served with marrow bones and a fresh sauce. It is important to get the right cuts of beef for this, you will be rewarded by splendid results. You may have to order the marrow bones from the butcher; get him to saw them into 4 – 5cm (around 1½ in) lengths. Serve with Red and Green Sauce

400g (14 oz) chuck steak, cut into 5 – 6cm (around 2 in) pieces
400g (14 oz) blade stake, cut into 5 – 6cm (around 2 in) pieces
middle part of 2 marrow bones, cut into pieces 4 - 5 cm (1½ inch)
3 leeks, washed and trimmed and cut across into two
6 carrots, peeled
3 turnips, peeled
2 cloves
1½ litres (51 fl oz) good stock (or use a stock cube)
gros sel

Red and Green Sauce:
2 tablespoons white wine vinegar
5 tablespoons olive oil
I clove of garlic
3 tablespoons tomato paste
2 tablespoons chopped parsley
2 tablespoons chopped chives
2 shallots, finely chopped
4 chopped cornichons
2 tablespoons capers, roughly chopped
salt and pepper

Cut the carrots into lengths of 4 – 6cm (around 2 inches).

Quarter the turnips. Sprinkle the cut ends of the marrow bones with salt. Put the vegetables into a large casserole with the marrow bones and the cloves. Place the meat in amongst the vegetables. Pour in enough stock to cover the meat. Season with *gros sel*. Bring to the boil and skim off the froth and scum. Cover the pan, lower the heat and simmer for 3 hours.

To make the sauce, put the vinegar, olive oil, garlic and tomato paste into a small food processor and whizz them together. Season and stir in the herbs and the shallots, cornichons and capers.

Serve the meat and vegetables in small individual terracotta or earthenware bowls (*cazuelitas*) with some of the broth, sieved if necessary. Serve the sauce in a bowl to pass round. Spread the marrow from the bones on pieces of hot toast, and sprinkle with *gros sel*, to serve with the *Pot au Feu*. (Serves 6)

Pot au Feu de la Queue de Boeuf de Bazas

Cooking marrow bones with the oxtail adds tremendously to the texture and flavour of the sauce. Ask the butcher for the middle part of the marrow bone cut into 6cm (2 inch) pieces, the top part by the joint is not the best bit as it has no marrow, and is too big to go in most pans! The cooked bone marrow can be spread on toast to serve with the oxtail. If you do not like bone marrow, serve toast with grated hard mountain cheese such as Ossau Iraty – ewe's milk cheese is traditional. Place the toast under the grill for a moment to melt the cheese.

1 oxtail, jointed
4 marrow bones, centre cut, in lengths of 4 – 6cm (around 2 inches)
1 stick celery
1 clove of garlic
a bunch of bay leaves, parsley and thyme
120g (4 oz) or streaky bacon, cut into 4 pieces
1 teaspoon *piment d'Espelette* or ½ teaspoon cayenne
1 x 400g (14 oz) tin of plum tomatoes, chopped
3 litres (100 fl oz) of stock, or water and stock cubes
3 whole leeks, washed, trimmed and tied in a bundle
4 carrots, peeled
2 turnips, peeled and halved
2 onions, skinned and quartered
4 potatoes, washed
salt, freshly ground pepper

To serve with the oxtail:
4 slices *pain de campagne,* toasted
75g (3 oz) sheeps' cheese, grated, if not using the marrow from the bones
Red and Green Sauce (see previous recipe)

Put the oxtail and marrow bones in a large casserole with the celery, garlic, herbs and the bacon, season with *piment d'Espelette* or cayenne, add tomatoes and a little salt and cover with stock or water and stock cube. Bring to the boil, skim and simmer 3 hours.

Remove from the heat, allow to cool in a cold place, letting the fat solidify on the top. Remove the fat.

Break the potatoes into walnut sized chunks with an oyster knife. This will release their starch and help to give substance to the broth.

Add all the vegetables to the pot, add a little more stock if necessary, bring it to the boil, season well and lower the heat so the liquid just bubbles. Cook for 30 minutes. Remove the marrow bones and scoop the marrow into a small bowl. Keep it hot, the bones can be discarded.

Remove the meat and vegetables to a hot dish and cover to keep warm. Strain the broth through a fine sieve and leave the bottom, cloudiest part behind, as you want the broth to be free of bits. Taste for seasoning and reheat without boiling.

Prepare some toast and spread the slices with warm marrow from the bones; season with salt crystals and freshly ground pepper. Put briefly under the grill. If using cheese instead of marrow, do the same.

Serve the hot toasts alongside the oxtail and vegetables moistened with the broth, together with the Red and Green Sauce.

Beef Cheeks with Sherry

The traditional Basque attitude, not always apparent when eating in most restaurants, is to enjoy all the bits; nose to tail is the style. They will throw bits of tripe into soup, grill kidneys and chitterlings *à la plancha* , make *pot au feu* with tougher bits, and turn tongue or tail into a hot, fiery, delicious stew. Underpinning the flavour of this version of braised ox cheek, tough as you like unless it is cooked for 4 hours, is sherry. Any sherry will do, but recommended for this really simple dish is deep, dark, sweet sherry made from the Pedro Ximinez grape, tasting of chocolate, coffee and spices. The carrots add further to the sweetness.

1½ kg (3⅓ lb) large beef cheeks cut in 4 (or one small one per person)
6 tablespoon olive oil
2 onions, chopped
1 whole head of garlic
12 baby carrots
500ml (17 fl oz) Pedro Ximinez sherry
500ml (17 fl oz) red wine
500ml (17 fl oz) stock
3 bayleaves
1 teaspoon dried thyme or 4 sprigs fresh thyme
salt, *piment d'Espelette* or cayenne, ground black pepper

Trim all the fat and the sheet of sinew off the cheeks.

Heat half the olive oil, brown the cheeks all over and remove to a plate. Turn down the heat a bit, add the remaining olive oil and brown the onions and garlic lightly, add the carrots. Put back the beef cheeks, stir in the sherry, wine, stock and herbs. Season well and simmer very gently for 3 – 4 hours, turning the cheeks occasionally, until the meat is very soft when stuck with a knife. Remove the cheeks to a dish and reduce the gravy by a third. Serve with mashed potato to soak up the juices. (Serves 4)

Daube de Joues de Boeuf aux Cèpes

Beef cheeks are hallowed, and should be so, as they are quite the most rich and melting stew meat you can find – just keep the tough and odd-looking things simmering away and they will transform themselves into something deeep, dark and melting. Start this dish a day ahead, the marinade should help to tenderise the meat a bit.

2 ox cheeks (about 1½ kg or 3⅓ lb)
100g (3½ oz) *poitrine fumée* or streaky bacon cut into lardons
1 – 2 carrots, sliced
2 cloves of garlic
small bunch thyme
2 bay leaves
½ bottle robust red wine
3 – 4 tablespoons olive oil
1 onion, finely chopped
1 stock cube
1 teaspoon sugar
300g (10½ oz) open cap Portobello mushrooms, *cèpes* or other wild mushrooms
salt, freshly ground pepper

Trim the cheeks and remove the sheet of membrane on one side, if the butcher has not done so. Cut each of the ox cheeks into 6 pieces if they are large, or 4 if smaller.

Place in a bowl with the bacon, carrots, garlic, herbs and the bottle of red wine. Marinate in a cold place or the refrigerator for 12 to 24 hours, turning once or twice.

Drain the meat well over a bowl, keeping the marinade, and pat dry. Coat the pieces with flour.

Heat half the olive oil in a large casserole and fry the pieces of meat several at a time, until browned on all sides, adding more oil as needed, then remove them to a plate. Fry the chopped onion in the same pan until soft and starting to brown, then add the marinade and carrots, scraping the pan to pick up any caramelized juices.

Put in the meat, add enough stock almost to cover, about 300ml (10 fl oz), and add sugar, salt and pepper.

Cover the pan, bring slowly to simmering point and simmer for 3 hours. Test the meat, if it is meltingly tender add the cleaned, quartered mushrooms to the casserole and simmer for 10 – 15 minutes before serving. (Serves 4)

Basquaise Tripe
Gras-Double à la Basquaise

Authentic flavours are sometimes hard to capture but this tripe dish made with tarragon, garlic and chilli has a real smack of the South West. It is cooked with pork or goose fat – a winter dish – and a couple of beaten eggs are stirred in, eventually, to thicken the sauce. A glass of cognac livens it up at the end.

If you want to be very authentic, serve the tripe in little individual earthenware dishes, *cazuelitas,* which can be heated up in the oven, but not too hot or the eggs will curdle.

1kg (2¼ lb) honeycomb ox tripe, prepared by the butcher and ready to cook
1 calf's foot cut in 6 pieces or 2 pig's trotters, each cut in 4
3 red peppers
3 tablespoons pork or goose fat
200g (7 oz) lardons
4 carrots, sliced into rounds
2 onions, finely chopped

1 bottle white wine

4 sprigs tarragon

4 tablespoons chopped parsley

3 cloves of garlic

2 cloves

1 teaspoon *piment d'Espelette* or ½ teaspoon cayenne pepper

salt, coarsely ground black pepper

2 eggs, beaten

3 tablespoons chopped cornichons

100ml (3½ fl oz) Armagnac or brandy

Put the tripe and calf's or pig's trotters in a large pan, cover with water, bring to the boil, skim off any rising froth, and drain the meat in a colander.

Heat the oven to 200°C (400°F), roast the peppers and put them in a covered saucepan or a plastic bag to cool. Skin them, remove the seeds and cut them into short strips.

Heat the pork or goose fat in a casserole and brown the lardons, carrots and onions. Cut the tripe into irregular pieces.

Add the tripe and peppers to the casserole with the feet and pour on a bottle of white wine.

Chop tarragon, 1 tablespoon of parsley and the garlic all together and add to the tripe. Add two cloves, the piment or cayenne, salt and black pepper.

Cook at a gentle boil for 30 minutes, then turn the heat right down and simmer for 4 hours. Allow to cool, chill and skim off the fat.

Reheat and taste for seasoning, thicken by stirring in the beaten eggs, off the heat; add the remaining parsley and the cornichons and lastly add a glass of brandy. (Serves 4 – 6)

Wood Grilling

Cooked over a wood fire, as in the Pays Basque, beefsteak gains a unique sweet, smoky, slightly charred flavour. In fact any barbecue can give a great flavour, provided you use hardwood; oak is good, or olive or applewood. For a fast, last minute burst of heat, you can use dried vine or apple prunings from the garden, or you can buy hickory chips.

Unfortunately, although convenient to light and very reliable, charcoal briquettes will not give the same result.

It is possible to have this authentic smoky wood flavour if you have a fireplace. If so, you can arrange some bricks in the hearth, on either side, so that they will contain the fire. Balance a large sturdy grill on them to cook the meat over the embers. It is as easy as that.

Spread the embers out evenly with a poker, and then start grilling at once, as they soon die down.

Trim and major bits of fat off the steaks. Rub or brush the steaks lightly with olive oil and some crushed garlic. Season with plenty of pepper.

Have your oven gloves, tongs, a big hot dish and a jug of water nearby. Heat the metal grill well over the fire before you put on the steaks. Put thicker bits where the fire is hotter. If the fat drips off and starts a flame, dip you hand in the jug and flick some of the water off your fingertips onto the flames, to douse them.

After one or two minutes lift the steaks with tongs to see if they are nicely browned – they are better tasting if not black. Turn them over carefully.

Do not overcook the steaks, they will cook very fast if the fire is just right – press with a finger to see if they are done, they must be springy and a bit soft, but not too soft – if they feel hard, they are already overdone – very underdone is better.

Transfer the meat to a hot dish with tongs, season with salt and let the steaks rest, after they are cooked, for a few minutes. The salt must only be added once the meat has been seared.

I like rib-eye steaks because they have the right amount of fat, but in South West France entrecôte steaks with plenty of fat are the first choice and they are cut thicker than ours, so they do not dry out.

l'Entrecôte Bordelaise with Shallot and Red Wine Butter

Christian Coulon, author of *Le Cuisinier Médoquin* (2000), quaintly states that while stews and daubes are watched by women, it is men who take care of the grill. More credibly, he recommends that steak be cooked in the fireplace (see above), over dried vine prunings (there are plenty of these to be had around the Médoc of course), or outdoors on the barbecue. The fire should be lit with pine needles or a dry copy of Le Sud Ouest, as newspapers from Paris, for various reasons, do not work![2]

2 beautiful thick entrecôte steaks (two fingers thick, they say) at room temperature
150ml (5 fl oz) red wine
1 medium banana shallot finely chopped
125g (4½ oz) softened butter
salt, plenty of freshly ground black pepper
a little olive oil

To make the Shallot and Red Wine Butter:
Put the red wine in a saucepan with the chopped shallot, a little seasoning and a bay leaf, and simmer until almost dry. Allow to cool, remove the bayleaves and when cold add the shallot mixture to the butter and combine. Chill in the refrigerator until needed.

To cook the steaks:
Let the meat come to room temperature. Rub a little oil into the steaks. Heat the grill. Grill the steaks for
2 – 3 minutes on each side. Transfer them to a very hot dish and spread with Red Wine Butter. Cover the dish and let the steak rest for 5–10 minutes. (Serves 2)

Beef Chop
Txuleton Txogitzu

Txogitzu beef from Galicia is described as some of the best in the world, as good as Wagyu, tender and succulent, oozing creamy fat with a great flavour. It is the meat of 'very old, very fat cows'. The fat on this beef is yellow and the favourite piece for grilling, rib, has almost as much fat as meat on it. You can do something similar if you buy the fattiest piece of fore rib you can find.

[2.] And, according to Parisians, north of the Loire everything works, south of the Loire, nothing works.

A beef chop is a whole rib of beef on the bone, about 8cm (3in) thick, grilled over wood or charcoal, or cooked on the *plancha*, or on a griddle, and served very rare. The meat is carved into thickish slices, at right angles to the bone. It is definitely for meat lovers.

Remove the joint from the fridge 2 hours before you want to cook it, to make sure the beef is at room temperature.

Grilled Rib of Beef

1 rib of beef on the bone weighing about 800 – 900g (1¾ – 2lb)
2 – 3 handfuls of coarse salt

It is vital to have the beef at room temperature when you start to cook it.

Light the fire or preheat the *plancha*, griddle or hot plate, the temperature should be very hot, 250°C (480°F). Preheat the oven to 100°C (200°F). Put in a dish large enough to hold the beef rib.

First sear both sides of the beef, fat and all, on the hot *plancha* or griddle, until dark brown.

Quickly shower both sides of the meat with 2 handfuls of coarse salt crystals and put the meat back on the hot plate. Cook, turning once, for about 3 minutes on each side (until, the inside of the meat is 56°C (130°F) then knock the salt off. Turn the oven down to 90°C (195°F). Place the meat on the very hot dish inside the oven and leave for 15 minutes to rest and relax. If you have a digital probe or meat thermometer you can test the doneness, roughly speaking:

55 – 56°C is rare (120 – 130°F)
58 – 60°C is medium rare (130 – 140°F)
63°C is medium (145°F)

When it has rested, place the rib flat on a board, cut away the bone, and with a sharp carving knife, slice the meat, like a loaf of bread, into thick slices at right angles to where the bone was. (This cut is not carved across the grain in thin slices, like a roast).

Serve with Béarnaise Sauce (see page 46) and plenty of rocket dressed simply with oil and *fleur de sel* – salt flakes. (Serves 4)

VEAL

In the seventeenth century, while Louis XIV was building Versailles, the Médoc was still untamed; the wild, deserted region was notorious for its *'lédounes'*, vast herds of wild cattle. Thousands of these untamed animals – scrawny, undernourished and vicious – wandered the sand dunes, marshes and woods of the Médoc and in the forest of les Landes, grazing on the undergrowth, on acorns, arbutus, broom and heather, and to some extent clearing the brush that would otherwise be the very thing to set off dreaded fires.

These animals were wild – both bulls and cows with young would charge any human being foolhardy enough to wander alone and unarmed on the dunes.

A number of these cattle were still roaming free until the mid twentieth century; they belonged to whoever owned the land and once a year were rounded up, in scenes reminiscent of the hilarious film *Blazing Saddles* (1974), for one purpose only – veal.

The cattle themselves were scrawny and tough and gave no milk – not one had ever seen the inside of a cattleshed. But the young bull calves were tender enough, and were slaughtered to be eaten at weddings and family fêtes.

The region still has a great taste for veal, even though there are now splendid beef cattle reared in the area around Bazas.

Veal Chops with Onions and Cheese
Côtelettes de Veau comme à Bordeaux

This is a great recipe, unsophisticated but so good. The veal should be just slightly pink – cook it longer and it will dry out.

2 veal chops or one large T-bone chop
1 tablespoon olive oil
30g (1 oz) butter
1 onion, sliced
a squeeze of lemon juice
50g good Gruyère cheese
salt, freshly ground pepper

Rub the chops with a little olive oil.

Melt half the olive oil and half the butter in a frying pan and cook the onion until it is transparent and beginning to turn golden.

Heat the remaining butter and a bit of olive oil in a large frying pan and put in the chops; fry over a medium heat for 5 minutes on each side for a small chop or 7 minutes on each side for a large chop.

Put them in a well-heated gratin dish, season and squeeze lemon over them. Cover them with the onions and then grate the Gruyère cheese loosely on top, on the coarse side of the grater. The heat will slightly melt the cheese.

A large T-bone chop will feed two people. (Serves 2)

Basque Meatballs
Boulettes de Veau Basquaise

These very fragrant and light meatballs can be served with roasted peaches.

500g (1lb 2 oz) minced veal
25g (1 oz) short grain rice, cooked and rinsed in cold water
1 tablespoon basil leaves
1 tablespoon thyme, stalks removed
1 tablespoon parsley, stalks removed
1 tablespoon mint leaves
1 – 2 cloves of garlic, mashed
1 large egg
2 teaspoons *piment d'Espelette* or hot paprika
1 teaspoon salt
3 tablespoons olive oil

For the Basquaise Sauce:
4 small green peppers or 1 red bell pepper
4 tablespoons olive oil
1 onion, finely chopped
2 cloves of garlic, sliced
125ml (4 fl oz) white wine

1 x 400g (14 oz) tin of tomatoes
1 bay leaf
½ teaspoon *piment d'Espelette* or hot paprika
salt

First cook and drain the rice, and rinse it in cold water.

Let it drain. Chop the herbs and mix thoroughly with the meat in a bowl, together with the rice, garlic, egg and seasoning. Fry a teaspoon or two of the mixture to check it for seasoning. Form into balls the size of a golf ball and chill.

To make the sauce:
Burn the peppers under the grill or on a gas flame, until wilted and scorched, this gives an authentic smokey flavour. Put them in a covered pan or plastic bag to cool. Skin them, remove the seeds and slice into small strips.

In a casserole, soften the onion and garlic in olive oil for 10 – 15 minutes without browning. Add the white wine and let it bubble for 3 minutes. Add the peppers and cook gently 5 minutes more, then add the tomatoes, bayleaf and seasoning. Cook the sauce over a low heat for 30 minutes adding 125ml (4 fl oz) of water if it gets too thick.

Roll the meatballs in flour and fry in a large frying pan with 3 tablespoons olive oil, until brown all over. Cover with the sauce and cook gently, on a low heat, covered, for 15 – 20 minutes. (Serves 4)

Chopped Veal with Peppers
Axoa – Hachua de Veau

Axoa is the favourite lunch in the Pays Basque and, more particularly in the canton of Espelette, the village devoted to growing the very superior chillies that make the hot red pepper *piment d'Espelette*, used in so many of their dishes.

In the village of Espelette, at the splendid traditional Restaurant Daraidou, the veal is cooked for a short time and that is how they like it.

600g (1lb 5 oz) veal escalope, veal shin or beef *bavette d'Aloyau* (flank steak)
2 slices of raw ham such as Bayonne or Serrano, with fat
3 tablespoons olive oil
2 shallots, finely chopped
2 cloves of garlic, chopped and crushed
2 green peppers, grilled, skinned, deseeded and diced
1 red pepper, grilled, skinned, deseeded and diced
1 teaspoon *piment d'Espelette* or 1 teaspoon chilli flakes
1 teaspoon finely chopped rosemary
2 teaspoons flour
3 tablespoons stock or water
salt

Cut the veal or beef into very small dice. Dice the ham finely, keeping the fat on one side.

Heat the olive oil and ham fat in a sauté pan until sizzling hot (hot enough to seize the meat at once, so no liquid comes out) then add the veal, shallots, garlic and peppers, season with *piment d'Espelette* or cayenne and rosemary and toss the mixture on the high heat for 1 minute. Stir in the flour and let it cook for a minute then add the stock, simmer for 2–3 minutes and leave to rest in the pan for 1 minute. Serve immediately. (Serves 4 – 6)

Curnonsky's *Axoa*

A more bourgeois version, invented by Curnonsky, Prince of Gastronomy, who coined the phrase 'Good cooking is when things taste of what they are', instructs us to cook the veal for much longer.

Follow the directions above, sprinkle the meat with flour after browning, then add 250ml (9 fl oz) of stock, but hold back the peppers. Let the meat simmer for 2 hours, adding more stock as necessary, then add the peppers and the hot red pepper or chilli flakes and cook a further 20 minutes.

GAME

Today, as Christian Coulon[3] tells us, *la chasse, la pêche* and *la ceuillette* which roughly translates as hunting, shooting, fishing and foraging, are practices that still mean 'much more than mere material pleasures or sport; they are the symbols of a certain form of autonomy and of freedom'.[3] Over the centuries, the collective right of the rural population to hunt and forage has been a hugely important part of traditional life to the country communities. This feeling still holds true in many parts of France, and particularly so in the parts that shared and lost a common language, Oc. This is certainly true of his beloved Médoc.

One way in which the Médoquins like to cook the game they take home is in a *civet*. For a *civet* you need the animal's blood. Should you ever feel like making a *civet* and you do have the animal's blood, just mix it with a little vinegar to stop it curdling. Make a red wine stew of the hare, rabbit or whatever animal you have according to the *Civet de Sanglier* recipe (page 259), and add the blood to thicken the sauce at the end.

Rabbit in Sauce
Lapin en Sauce

'La Sauce' can mean two things in the South West, a sauce that you serve separately with steak or fish, or it can mean meat or game braised in its own sauce – a sort of stew.

This rabbit *en sauce* is made with plenty of garlic and small green peppers – you can use Gernika peppers, Padron peppers or *Piments du Pays*, and you can also use ordinary green bell peppers for the dish.

1kg (2¼ lbs) fresh farmed or wild rabbit, cut in pieces with the liver if possible
10 cloves of garlic
400g (14 oz) Padron or Gernika peppers, or *piments du pays*, seeds removed, or green bell peppers
125ml (4¼ fl oz) olive oil

Notes: If you prefer, cut down the garlic by half.
3. Christian Coulon, author of Le *Cuisinier Médoquin*.

100ml (3½ fl oz) white wine
150ml (5 fl oz) chicken stock
1 teaspoon hot paprika
2 teaspoons marjoram
1 bayleaf
1 teaspoon thyme leaves or a small bunch of fresh thyme, stalks removed
sea salt

Separate the cloves of garlic, peel them and crush them either with a knife blade or a garlic crusher.

If using large green peppers, peel them with a potato peeler and remove the seeds; cut them into strips.

Heat the olive oil and fry the pieces of rabbit and the liver until they are lightly browned on all sides.

Put the rabbit on a plate and drain some of the olive oil from the frying pan. Turn down the heat and put in the peppers and, after 5 minutes, add the garlic.

When the peppers have wilted and started to brown, add the wine, let it bubble for a few minutes, then add stock, paprika and all the herbs and seasonings. Put back the pieces of rabbit and simmer for 35 – 40 minutes, less for farmed rabbit. Leave to rest for 5 minutes before serving with olive oil mash.
(Serves 4)

Rabbit with Saffron Potatoes
Lapin aux Pommes de Terres

Like many rabbit dishes, this is a cross borders dish; originally from Rioja; like the previous recipe it uses Basque Gernika or Galician Padron peppers for flavour, but any green peppers will do.

1 rabbit of about 1kg (2¼ lbs), farmed or wild, cut into 8 pieces
3 tablespoons olive oil
20 small green peppers or 3 green bell peppers
750g (1lb 10 oz) potatoes
2 bayleaves
4 cloves of garlic, sliced

Aligot - mashed potato with
cheese (above)

Fish from the Gironde on ice
in the market

Whitebait

Cans of confit - pigeon
and sausage

Beautiful Basque cakes with black cherries

Ossau Iraty cheese, quince membrillo and walnuts

Walnut cake

Pantxineta - a cream puff

Meringues and local treats in the South West

Café in les Halles, St Jean de Luz

Galettes Maison ready to take home

1 red chilli pepper
500 – 600ml (17 – 20 fl oz) chicken stock
2 large pinches saffron or 2 packets of saffron substitute / paëlla
seasoning (Spigol or la Dalia are both reliable)
salt

Snip the stalks off the small green peppers.

If using larger peppers, peel them with a potato peeler, deseed them and cut them into strips. Peel and slice the potatoes.

Heat the olive oil in a casserole large enough to take all the rabbit and vegetables. Fry the pieces of rabbit with the bayleaves and when they are nicely browned, remove them and put the garlic and peppers and chilli into the same oil, adding more oil if needed. When they are limp and soft add the sliced potatoes. Return the pieces of rabbit, almost cover them with stock, season and add the saffron or paëlla flavouring. Simmer until the rabbit is done; it takes 35 – 40 minutes (less for farmed rabbit). (Serves 4)

Venison Steaks with Honey and Walnuts

I first found this sauce 25 years ago, in a little book called *Recettes de Quercy* by Claudine Duluat and Jeanine Pouget. I also encountered for the first time the word *terroir* used in the context of food. It conjures an earthy picture of food that is steeped in the influence of the land it comes from and that includes, as well as the actual soil, the particular amount of sun, the winds, the length of the various seasons, the geography (mountains, sea, river valley etc) and how this influences the local livestock, flowers, plants and fish, cooking fats and oils and even the honey, giving them their special local flavour. This recipe comes from the Dordogne, walnut paradise, and it works well with young wild boar (*marcassin*) as well as venison.

4 x 125g (4½ oz) venison steaks (the fillet steak is best of all but leg
steaks will do)
1 tablespoon marc or Armagnac
2 tablespoons walnut oil
salt, freshly ground pepper

1 – 2 tablespoons olive oil

For the sauce:
1 tablespoon good quality red wine vinegar such as le vinaigre vieux de Cahors
100ml (3½ fl oz) good chicken or beef stock
3 tablespoons flower honey
24 walnut halves, toasted and roughly cut into large pieces
¼ teaspoon cardamom seeds, ground
salt, freshly ground pepper

Season the steaks with pepper and sprinkle them with marc and walnut oil. Let them steep in this mixture for 3 hours.

In a small pan heat the vinegar and stock, add the honey, the nuts and the cardamom. Season, bring to the boil and simmer for 5 minutes.

Strain the liquid from the venison steaks and pat them dry. Heat the oil in a frying pan and cook the steak for 2-3 minutes on each side, salting each side after one minute, when it is seared.

Transfer them to the heated dish and allow to rest for 5 minutes, then serve them with the walnut sauce. (Serves 4)

Wild Boar Basque Style
Sanglier à la Basquaise

For stunning life-sized images of boar hunting and all other forms of *la chasse,* from the sixteenth century onwards, visit the Château of Henri IV in Pau. Here the tapestries are a marvel and give complete insight into hunting - the methods, hats, breeches, weapons, triumphs, disasters and dogs, and how the game was carried home. The heaviest prize was the wild boar.

Wild boar, *sanglier*, still runs wild in the forests of South West France and is a nuisance everywhere, ruining crops. The meat can be tough and may need to be cooked for a long time. This recipe uses boar shoulder meat, but this glorious, ruddy stew could easily be made with diced pork shoulder.

1 kg (2¼ lbs) wild boar shoulder meat, cut into pieces or diced pork
shoulder
6 red peppers
1 glass white wine
2 onions, chopped
2 cloves of garlic, chopped
400g (14 oz) tomatoes, skinned and cut into quarters, or use tinned
tomatoes
500ml (17 fl oz) stock or water with a stock cube
4 tablespoons olive oil
salt, black pepper, *piment d'Espelette* or hot paprika

Peel the peppers with a potato peeler, removing seeds and stalks. Cut
them into strips.

Heat half the olive oil in a heavy casserole and sear the pieces of
boar, and when they are nicely browned remove them to a plate.

Turn down the heat and soften the onions and garlic in the same
pan, in the remaining olive oil. Next add the peppers and cook gently
for a further 10 minutes. Turn up the heat and add the white wine, let
it bubble a few minutes, then add the tomatoes.

Season the mixture with salt, plenty of pepper and hot paprika. Put
back the boar, with its juices, add stock or water and the crumbled
stock cube and cover the pan. Simmer over a very low heat for 2½
hours or for pork shoulder 1 hour 15 minutes. Serve with triangles of
bouille de mäis (polenta), see page 141. (Serves 4 – 6)

Wild Boar Civet
Civet de Sanglier

Wild boar, known as *basurde*, is a great source of well-flavoured meat,
but it can carry trichinosis – the way hunters avoid this problem is to
freeze the meat for a month before they cook it.

Basques are very fond of cider and there are many *cidreries* scattered
around. A natural extension of making cider is making calvados, and
there is Basque calvados available there, but any calva will do for this
recipe. Add a splash at the end as well.

1kg (2¼ lb) wild boar shoulder, cut in large pieces, or use pork shoulder
500ml (17 fl oz) red wine
1 small glass Calvados
1 carrot, sliced
1 onion, sliced
2 cloves of garlic
1 small cinnamon stick
1 tablespoon flour
500ml (17 fl oz) stock or water and 1 stock cube
30g (1 oz) butter
dash of sherry vinegar
3 tablespoons pork fat or olive oil
100g (3½ oz) lardons
150g (5 oz) *cèpes* or Portobello mushrooms, cleaned carefully and
quartered
salt, freshly ground pepper

Put the meat in a bowl and cover with the red wine and calvados. Add
the carrot, onion, garlic and cinnamon. Leave the meat to marinate in
the refrigerator overnight.

Drain the meat well and pat it dry with kitchen paper and dust with
flour. Heat the olive oil and fry the meat, turning it to brown it all over.

Add the marinade, with its vegetables, and 500ml (17 fl oz) of stock
or water and stock cube. Season well, cover and simmer for 2 – 3 hours
until very tender (pork will take 1½ hours). Stir in the vinegar, butter
and salt.

Sauté the lardons with the ceps or other mushrooms, until a deep
golden brown. Season them with plenty of pepper, add them to the
civet and cook for a further 15 minutes.

Chapter Nine

Vegetables, chillies, and pulses

It is said that one hardly ever gets a vegetable in France, apart from *pommes frites* and a bit of salad with a steak. It is not true, of course, and it is particularly untrue in the South West where they almost worship their vegetables (as well as Saint's Day Festivals they have Vegetable Festivals) and put one vegetable – garlic – in just about every dish.

At Saint-Clar de Lomagne, in Gascony, garlic-worship has continued since the thirteenth century. Their Lomagne white garlic is highly prized and Saint-Clar, a pretty fine example of an arcaded mediaeval village built of golden stone, boasting a venerable, ancient covered market, holds an annual garlic festival in August, with fancy garlic windmills and towers on display, and a rustic garlic museum, open during the summer months.

On May 1st at Pontonx, on the Adour river South of les Landes, there is the Fête de l'Asperge.

At this merry fête, to the strains of a raucous brass band, eight or ten people are busy cracking hundreds of eggs, while five men in aprons and berets light a log fire, on top of which they balance a huge, two metre (six foot) omelette pan. First of all, the pan is scrubbed out with salt over the flaming logs. Then something like 50kg (110 lb) of small white asparagus, chopped into little pieces, is cooked in oil over the logs, stirred vigorously by five men with wooden paddles. Then the bucketfuls of eggs go in. The omelette is a lot of work to make, so wine is handed round now and then, and it ends up more like scrambled eggs than tortilla, but there are plenty of takers.

For home cooks, spring in les Landes is an inviting time; along with the freshness of lilacs breeding out of the dead land is the freshness of this pearly white asparagus breeding out of sand and of bouquets of baby violet artichokes, which, being thistles, like the poor sandy soil too.

Spring comes early in Spanish Basque markets; in San Sebastian and Bilbao, delicious small green peppers from Galicia follow after the peas and broad beans from Tudela.

This city, rich with arcades and towers, was once a Moorish seat, strategically placed on the banks of the Ebro in Navarra, a vegetable growing area bordering the Pyrenees on the Spanish side. Here, in Tudela, they have not just one but several Fiestas de la Verdura – Vegetable Festivals – starting in March, with several weeks of conferences and fêtes to celebrate the importance of their local vegetables. I couldn't agreee more. Broad beans fried in olive oil is one of their excellent specialities (perhaps the descendant of a Turkish dish brought over by the Moors in 802 AD), dried white beans another.

In the rich soil of the Garonne river valley, once called the land of Cockaigne, is an area described by Kate Hill, owner of a most brilliant cookery and charcuterie- making school, who has lived here at Caumont for the last 20 years, as the bread basket of France. I know she means the bread, vegetable and fruit basket.

Here grow the splendid, giant, almost seedless tomatoes of Marmande, the mediaeval town of Marmande is proud of its heirloom varieties (Marmande tomatoes date back to the nineteenth century) and the town holds a jolly Tomato Festival every July.

Further down the river, the Bordelaises have the pick of everything, laid out beautifully on the huge open air markets on the quays of

Bordeaux. They have their own market gardens too, at Éysines, North of the Gironde, where baby new potatoes are a great speciality. And of course they have their own fête too, the Fête de Patates at midsummer, to celebrate these 'little pearls'.

In the Autumn, wild mushrooms from the forests of the Médoc and les Landes and from Périgueux, flood into these markets - great piles of ceps and little baskets of golden girolles. As the days get shorter, in the French Basque countryside the hot red chilli peppers of Espelette are harvested and hung up to dry on the whitewashed walls of the village houses.

Winter brings pumpkins and dozens of different kinds of squash, roots, leeks, bitter chicories, wild herb salads, giant chard leaves, and massive cabbages and as winter recedes, there are also bunches of inviting secondary onion shoots called *ognasses* or *cébars*, looking like fat spring onions, but red in colour, which are eaten in omelettes.

The South West is an undisputable cornucopia of vegetables; it may be that few vegetables are served in restaurants in some parts of France, but they really love them here and are oblivious of the myth that there are no vegetables to be had in France.

Potato Gratin with Goat's Cheese

Potatoes combined with cheese, wonderful and a very typical taste in the South West, one that I really enjoy. In this version two kinds of cheese melt together inside a succulent potato gratin.

1kg (2¼ lb) potatoes (charlotte or similar buttery salad potatoes are good for this)
30g (1 oz) butter
500g (1lb 2 oz) small onions, sliced
450g (1 lb) firm goat's cheese *bûche* (log)
100g (3½ oz) Ossau Iraty (ewe's milk cheese) or gruyère cheese, grated
4 bay leaves
700ml (23½ fl oz) chicken stock
salt, pepper, *piment d'Espelette* or cayenne pepper

Preheat the oven to 200°C (400°F).

Sweat the onions in the butter for 15 minutes, until soft and golden. Remove the onions and deglaze the pan with the stock.

Slice the goat's cheese.

Peel and wash the potatoes, cut them lengthwise in quarters and slice them thinly. You can use the food processor for this.

Put half the potatoes in a gratin dish and spread them out. Spread the onions on top in a layer. Place the sliced goats' cheese on top, then the grated cheese and then put in the rest of the potatoes; push the bay leaves in here and there. Season with salt, pepper and hot red pepper.

Pour on the hot stock. Dot with butter and cook in the oven for 1 hour. (Serves 6)

Pommes de Terre au Jus de Poule

In Pau's enormous, plain-looking, covered market one stall sells nothing but huge quantities of spit-roasted chickens and other poultry. Beneath the spit, underneath the shining, golden chickens as they turn, is a tray of juicy potatoes, which are spooned into the bag with the roasted chicken.

To make these potatoes at home, quarter the potatoes lengthwise and brown them in goose or duck fat. Place them in a roasting tin and put the chicken on top. Roast as usual.

Crushed potatoes
Pommes Écrasées

Use a good mashing potato such as King Edward for this dish.

The skins add an earthy flavour and a rustic look to the potatoes, peel them for a more *soignée* effect.

These potatoes can be flavoured with chopped garlic heated in the oil, with stoned black olives, chopped fairly finely or, very extravagantly, with chopped truffles.

500g (1lb 2 oz) thin skinned potatoes, scrubbed clean and cut in pieces
125g (4½ fl oz) olive oil
salt

Heat a pan of salted water and boil the potatoes, with their skins, for 20 minutes or until just cooked through.

Meanwhile heat the olive oil, just until warm. Drain the potatoes and add them to the oil, break them up roughly with a fork. Taste for seasoning, adding more olive oil if necessary. This should not be smooth, it is the potato equivalent of Rocky Road. (Serves 4)

Pommes Sarladaise

In the Dordogne, these crunchy, golden, garlicky potatoes are served all the time and everywhere. Cooked in goose or duck fat, they are one of the very best ways to eat potatoes. Some parboil them before frying, but I like the texture that results by frying them without pre-cooking them.

600g (1lb 5 oz) waxy potatoes
2 – 3 tablespoons duck or goose fat
2 cloves garlic, finely chopped
1 tablespoon chopped parsley
salt, freshly ground pepper

Peel the potatoes and slice them thinly. Rinse them in cold water and rub them in a tea towel. They must be very dry.

Melt the duck or goose fat in a frying pan and when it is hot put in the potatoes and let them brown, turning them gently and carefully once or twice. They will stick together, which is the way they should be. Season with a little salt and pepper and cover the pan.

Cook a further 15 minutes, then sprinkle with garlic and parsley and turn them over one more time.

Cook uncovered until crisp again. They need not stay separate, but can be stuck together into a sort of cake. (Serves 4)

Pommes Sarladaise aux Champignons

The taste of this dish takes me back to the Dordogne after a summer thunderstorm, and to the sight of a sturdy figure wearing a house overall and a straw hat, with a basket full of ceps on her arm, standing under the chestnut trees by the side of the road, selling her prizes.

We bought the ceps and made this dish. It is perfect in late summer and autumn, when ceps are plentiful. Choose firm young specimens, preferably not too large.

400g (14 oz) firm young ceps or Portobello mushrooms
600g (1lb 5 oz) waxy potatoes, peeled
2 – 3 tablespoons goose or duck fat
2 cloves garlic, finely chopped
small bunch flat parsley, finely chopped
salt, freshly ground pepper

Carefully clean the ceps with damp kitchen paper and the tip of a knife, then slice neatly.

Slice the potatoes into ½ cm (⅓ inch) slices.

Heat the goose or duck fat to medium hot in a large pot such as a le Creuset casserole. Put in the potatoes and let them brown a bit, then turn the heat down low. Cover the pan and let them cook slowly for 15 minutes.

Turn them carefully with a spoon, add more duck fat if needed, add the ceps and sprinkle with salt, pepper, chopped garlic and half the parsley. Cook covered for 15 minutes, then remove the lid and turn up the heat a bit to brown the potatoes.

Serve sprinkled with parsley. (Serves 6)

Giant Chips
Pommes Frites Géantes

The Bordelaise author of one version of these typical Gascon potatoes, Stephanie Béraud-Sudreau, suggests prodigious amounts of butter should be added after the potatoes have already been fried in duck or goose fat. The result, even when the butter is cut down a bit, is very moreish.

1kg (2¼ lb) Bintje or other yellow fleshed potatoes
4 tablespoons duck or goose fat
2 cloves garlic

40g (just under 2 oz) butter, softened

½ desertspoon *fleur de Sel*, such as Guérande

Cut the potatoes into large segments, like the quarters of an apple. Dry them with a cloth or kitchen paper.

Heat the fat in a frying pan and when it is rather hot, brown the potatoes all over, turning them over with tongs so that they brown evenly. Add the garlic, turn down the heat and cover the pan, it will spatter and spit quite a bit.

Cook for 10 – 12 minutes, until just tender, don't let them burn. Pour off the duck or goose fat into a bowl and add the butter in little pieces. Fry the potatoes, turning them, until the butter is absorbed. Drain them well, put them in a dish and sprinkle with plenty of salt. (Serves 6)

Pommes d'Éysines

Disaster struck the Médoc at the end of the nineteenth century, when the killer disease phylloxera rampaged through the rows of vines; it happened so fast, nobody escaped and all the precious vineyards had to be torn up.

North of the river Gironde, in Éysines, now the vegetable garden district for Bordeaux, the grape vines were replaced with rows of potatoes, which were immediately a favourite with the chefs cooking on the packet steamers, plying up and down the Gironde river.

These exquisite potatoes, 'little pearls', are very early and famous for their caramel flavour and edible skin. The usual method of cooking is to steam and then fry them and sprinkle them with salt – this is the way they are served in the streets of Éysines at Midsummer for the Fête des Patates at the celebrations for St Jean, which lasts for four days. When mature they can be used to make a sort of Aligot. This version is based on one by Vincent Poussard *patron* of a cookery school in Bordeaux.

Aligot of Potatoes and Sheep's Cheese

Make potatoes and cheese into something really rich and special. Originally the crushed potatoes would have been beaten until extremely smooth and almost pliable, but this version with a rougher texture has a more rustic appeal.

3 cloves garlic
200ml (7 fl oz) single cream
1kg (2¼ lb) new potatoes
100g (3½ oz) butter
300g (10½ oz) sheep's milk cheese from the Pyrenées such as Ossau Iraty, cut into small cubes plus a further 50g (2 oz) grated cheese
a bunch of flat parsley, chopped
4 slices uncooked ham such as Bayonne,
piment d'Espelette, a little salt

Preheat the oven to 180°C (350°F).

Cook the cloves of garlic in the cream for 10 minutes.

Cut one third of the potatoes into thin rounds and cook for 8 minutes in salted water. Scoop them out, set them on one side and boil the remaining potatoes in the same water until soft enough to make a purée, about 20 – 25 minutes. When cool enough, but still hot, remove the skins and crush the potatoes roughly, adding half the butter and all the cheese, cut into small cubes. Add the cream. Lightly fold in the chopped parsley and season lightly with salt (the ham will be salty) and heavily with pepper. Melt the remaining butter in a frying pan and brown the sliced, precooked potatoes.

Transfer the purée to a gratin dish, cover with sliced potatoes and scatter the top with grated sheep's cheese. Brown in the oven until the cheese is starting to melt.

Sauté the ham in a little butter for a minute, not longer. Serve the Aligot with a slice of ham for each plate.

Eat while very hot. It reheats well. (Serves 4 – 6)

Mushrooms

There is one mushroom eaten in the South West which I would think twice about eating, *bidaou*, (*Tricholoma equestre* or *Tricholoma flavovirens* known in Scotland as Yellow Knight or Man on Horseback) found everywhere in les Landes and the Médoc. Eaten occasionally, it will not cause any problems, but eat them several days running and toxins will build up and cause horrible pains or even death. It is, surpisingly, highly popular, but I would probably stick to ceps and girolles.

Cèpes

Cèpes have a long season in Western Aquitaine, growing amongst abundant moss and lichen, in the frequently sopping undergrowth of the pine forests, or in the lovely oak forests.

They can be found from June onwards until the weather gets too cold. Always choose firm, young, tight-capped specimens where possible, although I have noticed that mushroom hunters in les Landes are not put off when slugs, large and small, have eaten great holes, and they will gather larger, older mushrooms for drying or freezing. After you have picked your mushroom, cutting it carefully at the base of the stalk with a sharp knife, it is wise to cover the stump and disturbed ground with leaves, so others do not notice there has been a mushroom there. You do not want them to find your secret *'nids'* – the places where you find your prize specimens.

The two best types to look for are the classic *Cèpe de Bordeaux*, *boletus edulis* bun-shaped, moss-scented, chestnut brown with massive, imposingly bulbous stems and pale sponge; they grow beneath beech, birch and oaks and you can eat the whole thing and even eat them raw, when young. These are the ultimate, with a fine flavour.

Then come the *Cèpes des Pins, boletus pinicola.* The caps are much darker mahogany brown, and stalks fairly squat and large. They can get very big. The spongey part underneath, at first a light primrose colour, darkens to yellow with age and becomes coarse and slimy. This means the sponge can only be enjoyed when young, otherwise just cut it away with a knife. This variety also has an excellent flavour.

To prepare:

Chose young, firm, clean looking specimens, preferably undamaged by slugs, but that does not matter too much. Some may have tiny worms in the stalks, if so cut and throw away those bits.

Carefully pare the earth, leaf mould etc. from the bottom of the stems of the cèpes with a small sharp knife, brush off any dirt under the cap. Wipe the caps with a damp teatowel or kitchen paper to remove any dirt or leaf mould.

Classic Bordeaux Cèpes Cooking Method 1

cep mushrooms
goose or duck fat or butter
parsley, chopped
garlic, chopped
salt, freshly ground pepper

Cut the ceps into thickish slices. Heat goose or duck fat or butter in a sauté pan until very hot and fry the mushrooms until golden, about 6 – 8 minutes. Season with salt and pepper. If, however, it has been raining a lot and the funghi are full of moisture, you may have to let this moisture come out and keep cooking them until the liquid has been reabsorbed or evaporated. Season with salt and pepper.

The classic way to serve them is with a handful of chopped parsley and garlic added at the end of the cooking.

Another way is to start cooking the sliced caps, then toast some pine nuts and combine these with the caps, at the same time adding the chopped stalks, and some chopped garlic and parsley. Season and cook a few minutes more.

Cèpes à la Bordelaise Cooking Method 2

The Gironde was home for chef Bruno Loubet, and he grew up knowing his mushrooms – foraging is a huge family pastime there. His cep recipe makes it seem very easy, but if overcooked they can be slimy or mushy. Use young ceps and take care to clean them carefully without getting them too wet. Use very fresh duck or goose fat, preheated until it is pretty hot. Fry them in batches and the mushrooms will stay firm and turn a beautiful golden colour.

You can, instead of *cèpes*, use *girolles* or cultivated chestnut or Portobello mushrooms, or any wild mushrooms for this dish.

2 tablespoons goose or duck fat
800g (2 lb) fresh ceps, cleaned and cut into chunky pieces
2 tablespoons finely chopped shallots
2 cloves garlic, chopped
2 tablespoons chopped flat leaved parsley
salt and freshly ground black pepper

In a frying pan, heat 1 tablespoon of the goose or duck fat until fairly hot then add half the ceps, stir to colour them golden on all sides, then remove them to a plate with a slotted spoon.

Add the remaining fat and repeat with the remaining ceps, then remove these to the plate.

In the same pan, cook the shallots and garlic over a medium heat. Return the ceps to the pan and add the parsley.

Season with salt and pepper, toss well for a minute and serve immediately. (Serves 4)

Marmande Tomatoes

Grown right in the heart of the South West, on the fertile banks of the Garonne valley, Marmande tomatoes are the fruit of a land that likes its traditions.

Juicy, fleshy and perfumed, the flavour is intense, nothing like industrially produced tomatoes. This tomato has a season – from the end of July to September, or the beginning of October if you are lucky. They enjoy long sunny autumns in this area.

Tomates Farcies de Bidart

If you are eating a plate of roasted beef or lamb, there is often a tomato on the side. It may be just simple, scattered with garlic and parsley or thyme and roasted with a bit of olive oil.

It may be stuffed with rice and herbs or with sausage meat. I like this version, tomato stuffed with red pepper, and flavoured with anchovy, garlic and thyme.

6 large ripe tomatoes
2 – 3 red peppers
6 anchovy fillets
2 cloves garlic, sliced
1 teaspoon fresh thyme leaves
3 tablespoons olive oil
salt, freshly ground pepper

Preheat the oven to 150°C (300°F).

Halve the tomatoes across the middle and scoop out the seeds. Sprinkle the insides with salt and turn the tomatoes upside to drain in a colander for half an hour.

Grill the peppers as described on page 254.

Skin them, remove the seeds and cut them into strips.

Put an anchovy and a few slices of garlic in the bottom of each half tomato and put a few strips of pepper on top. Place the tomatoes in an oiled roasting tin.

Sprinkle with fresh thyme, and then with olive oil. Bake in the oven for 30 minutes. (Serves 4)

Chard Fritters
Beltaraba Ostozko Kruspetak

The original version of these fritters comes from Gerald Hirigoyen, the Basque food writer, who tells us that they can be made with any greens, mild, bitter or astringent, such as beetroot leaves, chard, spinach or nettles, or you could try any variety or mixture of 'salad' greens such as dandelions, rocket, chicory or raddichio.

500g (1lb 2 oz) Swiss chard or other leaves (will be less when the stalks are removed)
4 tablespoons olive oil

6 – 8 anchovy fillets, soaked in milk for 5 minutes and finely chopped
1 – 2 cloves garlic, crushed
salt

For the batter:
150g (5 oz) plain flour
1 level teaspoon baking powder
2 tablespoons melted butter
250ml (9 fl oz) cold water
olive oil for frying

1 hour ahead:
First make the batter. Mix the flour with the baking powder in a bowl. Trickle in the melted butter and the water little by little, whisking to keep the batter smooth. Allow to sit for an hour.

Wash the greens and drop into a large pan of boiling salted water. Cook 1½ – 2 minutes for tough greens, 30 seconds for spinach and other thin-leaved greens. Plunge them into cold water if you want to keep their green colour.

Drain well, squeeze to remove water and spread out on a cloth to dry. Chop the greens.

Heat ½ cm of olive oil in a frying pan. Stir the greens, anchovies and garlic into the batter. When the oil is hot, drop in the mixture, a tablespoon at a time. Fry until the fritters are brown and crisp on both sides and you can see that they are firm and cooked through.

Put on kitchen paper to drain and serve hot on their own as a starter, with salmon, or with roasted meat or fish. (Serves 4 – 6)

Green Pancakes
Farçous or Galettes de Légumes

Originally from the Aveyron, these small, green pancakes are a big item on the quayside market of Bordeaux. There are galettes with toppings of melted goat's cheese or with slices of black pudding on top, but the best selling galette is the healthy *galette verte* made with chard and spinach, flavoured with plenty of garlic and onion.

100g (3½ oz) flour
½ teaspoon baking powder
2 eggs
200ml (7 fl oz) milk
1 small white onion, chopped
1 clove garlic
200g (7 oz) chard, leaves only
100g (3½ oz) baby spinach
2 tablespoons chopped flat parsley
1 tablespoon chopped chives
2 – 3 tablespoons olive oil
salt, freshly ground black pepper

Mix the flour with the baking powder.

Whisk the eggs and gradually incorporate the flour and the milk to make a thick batter.

Put the onion, garlic, chard, spinach and herbs in a blender, pulse once or twice, season with salt and pepper and add the batter. Pulse until you have a very smooth green batter, a bit thicker than a normal pancake batter.

Cook the pancakes in batches. Heat the olive oil in a large pan and cook the galettes like blinis. Drop small ladles of the mixture onto the hot pan. Cook for 2 or 3 minutes each side. Drain them on kitchen paper. They should be light and crisp outside, soft inside.

Asperges des Sables des Landes

You may think that nothing grows in sand, and in the area between Bordeaux and Bayonne there is nothing much but sand.

But surprisingly, not only pine trees, heather and bracken grow here – asparagus likes it too. It is odd to see, in the fields behind Cap Breton, prairies of asparagus stretching into the distance, as if it were a field of wheat. But this asparagus is delicious, both white and green, and tastes to me as good as if it were home grown.

The spears are picked at dawn and ready to sell in four hours, buy them when they look pearly and crisp – they should be eaten as soon as possible, their delicate flavour changes very fast. Incidentally the white are the same as the green, but they are banked up like potato plants and picked before they have poked their noses above the ground, with a long instrument that reaches deep into the sandy earth. After they emerge they develope a pale violet hue and then turn green, which is preferred by some, but try the white ones with their hint of bitterness; some are thicker than thumbs, and so delicate and juicy that you will be converted.

Asparagus with Blood Orange Sauce
Les Asperges Sauce Maltaise

500g (1lb 2 oz) asparagus

For the Maltaise Sauce:
2 tablespoons blood orange juice
2 egg yolks
200g (7 oz) salted butter
salt, freshly ground pepper

First make the sauce. Put the orange juice, salt and pepper into a deep bowl or jug that you can use with a hand held blender, let them infuse together for 10 minutes.

Blend the egg yolks into the orange juice and whizz them until you have a smooth mixture.

Melt the butter until it just starts to foam, it must not brown. Turn off the heat, wait one minute.

Now pour the butter into the egg yolks in a slow, steady trickle, whisking with a hand held whisk or a wire whisk as you do so. Keep the sauce warm until needed, stirring often.

Bring a large pan of water to the boil. Add salt. Put in the trimmed asparagus and cook for 6 – 8 minutes, depending on how thick it is.

Pierce a stem with a knife at the thick part. If it goes in easily, it is done. Carefully pick up the asparagus spears by middle of the stalk with tongs and drain well, putting them round the edge of a colander, tips facing upwards so they do not break. Serve with the Maltaise Sauce.

CHILLIES AND PEPPERS
Le Piment de Gernika

These tasty little Basque peppers are a glossy bright green; fried and sprinkled with salt they are consumed by the bucketful as tapas, particularly in October, when two large Piment de Gernika markets take place. The Basques are very proud of this pepper, think it vastly finer than *piments de Padron*, and in fact it has its own 'Appelation d'Origine et Specialités Traditionelles'.

Le Piment de Padron

Small, sweet, bright green peppers grown in the village of Padron, in neighbouring Galicia, are in season during late May and summer. They are eaten fried in oil until light brown and blistered, and then sprinkled with salt and served as *tapas*. Pick them up by the stalk and nibble round the seeds. Watch out, most of them are mild but every now and then there is a blisteringly hot (ripe) one; noone can tell the difference until it is too late, but a clue may be that the larger ones may be riper and therefore hotter.

Le Piquillo de Lodosa
(also known as *le Pimiento de Piquillo*)

Piquillos peppers are particular to Navarre and specifically to Lodosa, (an interesting site as the town is over looked by a cliff riddled like a cheese with caves that were the ancient homes of troglodytes and which remained inhabited right up to the twentieth century). The town lies on the river Ebro, just South of Pamplona.

Called Piquillos del Lodosa, they boast a D.O. (denomination of origin). In the season, many doorways have signs over them offering home bottled Piquillos for sale. This beautiful small, neat pepper is smooth and silky, 7cm (2¾ in) long, with a small point at one end.

Unlike other other *capsicum annuum*, these peppers are not hot, but sweet, with a smoky, spicy flavour. The smoky taste comes from the fact that they are traditionally always grilled over wood embers.

Navarre is proud of its beautiful hand-bottled vegetables, particularly artichokes, asparagus and – outstanding by miles – the brilliant scarlet piquillos, definitely a favourite food of Basques, and now finding their way, bottled in jars, to delicatessens in northern Europe.

Taken out of the jar, they form a little pouch ready for any kind of stuffing. They can be whizzed in a blender with or without cream, to make a delicious, silky orange-red sauce, or served straight out of the jar with anchovies, garlic, olive oil and vinegar, as a salad.

Sauce of Piquillos

For the sauce:
1 large onion, thinly sliced
2 cloves garlic, sliced
2 – 3 tablespoons olive oil
6 or 7 bottled piquillo peppers (use the broken ones)
1 teaspoon tomato paste
1 teaspoon of dried choricero pepper pulp (see page 72)
200ml (6¾ fl oz) cream (you may need more)
salt and freshly ground black pepper
1 tablespoon parsley or chives for decoration

Heat the olive oil in a frying pan and gently soften the sliced onions together with the sliced garlic. When very soft and beginning to colour, add the finely diced piquillo peppers and cook a little bit until soft. Stir in some tomato paste and *pimiento choricero* pulp paste. Stir in the cream.

Simmer for a few minutes, just enough to thicken the sauce a little, taste for seasoning, transfer to a blender and pulse until smooth. Serve it with the following recipe for Piquillos stuffed with Salt Cod Brandade or with Aubergine. Sprinkle it with chopped herbs if you like.

Easy Stuffed Piquillos with Salt Cod Brandade

300g (10 oz) brandade, home-made (see page 153) or bought
1 x 300g (10½ oz) jar of whole red peppers – *pimiento del Piquillo,
poivrons piquillo*
1 or 2 tablespoons olive oil

Preheat the oven to 150°C (300°F).

Taste the brandade and add salt, more garlic, pepper or double cream if you think it is needed, but do not make it too liquid.

Remove the *piquillos* from the jar carefully, so they do not break or split. Choose the unbroken ones. Take one and open it up, holding it open in the ring made with your left hand thumb and forefinger, so it looks like a small funnel.

With a small teaspoon, carefully fill the little pocket with brandade and fold the top over if possible. Place it in an oiled earthenware *cazuela* or gratin dish. Fill all the *piquillos* in the same way, laying them side by side as neatly as you can. Sprinkle with olive oil and bake in the oven for 15 minutes. Serve with or without rice, and, if you like, the Piquillo Sauce above or with squid ink sauce (see page 148). It looks magnificent if you pour the sauce on to a plate and place the stuffed peppers on top. (Serves 4)

Stuffed Piquillos with Aubergine Purée

Hôtel des Pyrénées, in the beautiful mountain village of St Jean Pied de Pont, serves this with a *Piéce de Boeuf (onglet)* with chopped shallots and Béarnaise Sauce.

The aubergines taste smoky and the peppers are smooth and silky.

2 medium aubergines
3 tablespoons olive oil
1 small onion, finely chopped
1 clove of garlic, chopped
1 x 300g (10 oz) jar of whole *pimientos del piquillos*
salt, 1 teaspoon red pepper flakes or Espelette pepper

Preheat the oven to 220°C (430 °F).

Put the aubergines in a roasting tin and roast for 35 minutes until soft, then turn on the grill and grill until blackened to get a smoky taste.

Remove the aubergines to a board and when cool enough to handle, strip off the blackened skin. Chop the flesh. Heat the olive oil in a frying pan and soften the onion and garlic gently for 10 minutes, then add the aubergine pulp, seasoning it with salt and hot red pepper. When the juices have evaporated and the mixture has thickened and turned translucent, remove from the heat, allow to cool, and pulse until you have a smooth purée, with a hand held whizzer.

Remove the *piquillos* from the jar carefully, so they do not break or split, choose the best ones. Take one and open it up, holding it open in the ring made with your left hand thumb and forefinger, so it looks like a small funnel.

With a small teaspoon, carefully fill the little pocket with aubergine and fold the top over if possible. Place it in an oiled earthenware *cazuela* or gratin dish. Fill all the *piquillos* in the same way, laying them side by side as neatly as you can. Sprinkle with olive oil and bake in the oven for 15 minutes. Serve with or without rice, and *piquillo* sauce (see previous recipe).

Guindilla Chillies
Le Piment d'Ibarra

These are greeny yellow, long Guindilla chillies, grown in Ibarra and are usually sold in jars, pickled in wine vinegar. Piquant rather than hot, these are the perfect peppers for making Gildas, the delicious *pinchos* made of anchovies, olives and pickles on a cocktail stick (see page 67).

Piments du Pays, Piments des Landes:
Le Piment Doux d'Anglet, le Piment Doux

"My grandmother stirred over the kitchen fire, with great savoir faire, a comfortable frying pan in which she was cooking a few tomatoes and some long green pimentoes such as we grow round here. The wooden spoon would be lifted to my careful lips to see if salt pepper or chilli – *piment d'Espelette* obviously – were needed.'"

Once cultivated by Bernadine nuns, these very long green chillies are exceptionally sweet and mild. They are eaten in omelettes, in piperade, fried with tomatoes, or grilled to accompany roast or grilled beef or barbecued fish.

On top of all that they can be eaten raw in a salad with tomatoes and onion.

Goat's Cheese, Chorizo and Green Pepper Cakes
Cake au Chorizo

These little loaf-shaped soda breads, in all different flavours, are sold as *'cake'* on the markets of Gascony and the Pays Basque. *Cake aux Olives* is very popular

This one is made with long green peppers which are central to Basque and Gascon cuisine, and sold under the name of Piment des Landes, Piments Doux or Piments du Pays. They have a stong sweet flavour but are not at all hot.

3 long, mild green peppers
50ml (2 fl oz) olive oil
2 eggs
50ml (2 fl oz) milk
2 tablespoons white wine
150g (5 oz) plain flour
1 level teaspoon of baking powder
50g (2 oz) hard goat's milk cheese, grated (you can use sheep's cheese)
40g (just under 1½ oz) soft chorizo, cut into small dice
salt, freshly ground pepper

Preheat the oven to 180°C (350°F).

Butter 4 small non-stick individual loaf tins or muffin tins. Slice the peppers across into little rings. Fry the rings in a tablespoon of olive oil for 5 minutes. Allow to cool.

Beat the eggs together with the milk, the rest of the olive oil and the white wine and season lightly.

In a separate bowl mix the flour with the baking powder and stir in the cheese, pimentoes and chorizo.

Add the egg mixture and stir together very lightly. Fill the tins two thirds full. Cook for 25 minutes. Allow to cool before removing from their tins. (Serves 4)

Le Choricero

This is a dried hot pepper; in appearance it is similar to a *piment d'Espelette,* long and pointed, and richly red, one of the most rewarding colouring and flavouring ingredients of Northern Spain; you will find it in Marmitako, a fish soup made with tuna (see page 109), and also in the lovely hot stew called Chilindron or Txilindron (see page 227), which is made either with lamb or chicken. It is also used in chorizo-sausage making (see page 72).

To use dried, hot Choricero:
Pour boiling water over the peppers. When they have softened, drain them well, remove the seeds if you like, and scrape the flesh from the inside of the skin and chop or blend it to make a purée. This can be stirred into sauces, rice or fried potatoes to liven them up a bit.

You can also use dried Ancho chillies imported from Mexico in the same way.

GREEN VEGETABLES AND PULSES

Haricots Verts à la Tomate

250g (8½ oz) fine green beans
2 tablespoons olive oil
2 cloves garlic
500g (1lb 2 oz) ripe sweet tomatoes, skinned, deseeded and cut in pieces
salt, sugar, freshly ground pepper or red pepper

Blanch the green beans for 3 minutes in boiling salted water. Drain them and plunge into cold water. Drain them again. Heat the olive oil and fry the garlic until pale golden.

Add the tomatoes, season with a little salt and pepper, taste and add a little sugar if needed, and let them cook for 5 minutes. Add the beans and cook for a further 5 – 6 minutes. (Serves 4)

Petits Pois à la Mode de Bayonne

1kg (2¼ lb) fresh young peas in their pods or 500g (1lb 2 oz) frozen peas
4 thin slices of Bayonne ham
2 green peppers, grilled and skinned (use the long green peppers, *piments du pays*, if possible)
2 – 3 tablespoons olive oil
1 shallot, sliced
2 tomatoes, skinned and quartered
olive oil for sprinkling

Pod the peas and cook for 3 – 4 minutes in boiling salted water. Drain them. Cut or tear the ham into small pieces.

Grill the peppers in a gratin dish, which will collect their juices, until blackened on all sides, cover the dish and allow them to cool. Remove the seed and skins and cut them into thin strips.

Heat the oil and soften the shallot gently until starting to colour. Add the tomatoes and the peppers with their juice and cook for 2 minutes, then add the peas and the ham. Stir everything together and heat through. Sprinkle with fresh olive oil. (Serves 4)

Braised Green Peas

Braised peas are often served with hake in Basqueland, but they are exquisite with any simply cooked fish, particularly with salmon.

You can use fresh or frozen peas for this dish.

500g (1lb 2 oz) shelled green peas
2 – 3 tablespoons olive oil
2 banana shallots, finely chopped
2 cloves garlic, finely chopped

200ml (7 fl oz) chicken stock
20g (1 oz) butter
salt, freshly ground pepper

Heat the olive oil in a saucepan and gently soften the shallots and garlic for 5 minutes. Add the stock and bring to the boil. Reduce the liquid for a few minutes until almost gone, then throw in the peas. Season lightly, cover the pan and cook for 4 minutes. Add the butter bit by bit, in small pieces, shake the pan to emulsify the juices. Drain and serve the peas hot or cold. (Serves 4)

Broad Beans Fried in Olive Oil

This recipe from the formerly Moorish city of Tudela is very similar to a Turkish dish of fried broad beans in oil. In Turkey, the beans are sometimes cooked in their pods, but only if they are very young and tender.

If you like you can add some thinly cut strips of Serrano ham to this dish.

400g (14 oz) young, tender broad beans (1½ kg or 3lb with pods)
2 tablespoons olive oil
1 clove garlic, chopped
40ml (1½ fl oz) water
½ teaspoon sweet paprika
salt, freshly ground pepper

Heat a tablespoon of oil in a frying pan and sauté the garlic until it turns golden. Transfer the oil and garlic to a cup and mix in 25ml (¾ fl oz), about half, of the water and the paprika. Set on one side.

Add more oil to the frying pan and gently fry the broad beans for 5 minutes.

Add the garlic, paprika and oil mixture, with the remaining water, cover the pan and cook for 8 – 20 minutes, depending on the size of the beans. Serve lukewarm or cold with bread to mop up the flavoured oil. (Serves 4)

Ragoût of Peas, Artichokes, Broad Beans and Asparagus
Menestra

This is a wonderfully fresh, spring like dish, which does credit to all the delicate, early baby vegetables. You can make it with older artichokes and broad beans but it will need considerably longer cooking and the dish will be very different. You will not need salt, as the lardons provide enough.

300g (10 oz) asparagus
6 small purple artichokes
1 lemon, cut in half
5 tablespoons olive oil
2 banana shallots, sliced
150g (5 oz) lardons
300g (10 oz) shelled peas
300g (10 oz) shelled broad beans
1 escarole or frizzy endive
1 tablespoon Gascon vinaigrette (see page 48)
salt, freshly ground pepper

Slice the asparagus thinly into fairly long, diagonal pieces.

Remove all the tough outer leaves from the artichokes and trim off their tops, remove the chokes with a teaspoon. Rub with a cut lemon, then cut them across into thin diagonal slices.

Heat 2 tablespoons of olive oil in a frying pan and soften the shallots together with the lardons. Add a tablespoon of water and the asparagus, artichokes, peas and broad beans and more oil if necessary, season and fry until barely cooked, three or four minutes should do it.

Put the leaves of the escarole, very lightly dressed with vinaigrette, on a large plate and put all the vegetables on top. (Serves 4)

Ragoût de Fèves

The idea of broad beans with carrots is an odd one, but it works surprisingly well, the carrots adding sweetness to the beans.

1kg (2¼ lb) young podded broad beans
4 small, or 2 larger carrots
4 shallots
1 tablespoon olive oil
75g (3 oz) lardons
100ml (3½ oz) chicken stock
20g (1 oz) butter
1 tablespoon chopped parsley
salt, freshly ground pepper

Pod the broad beans. Clean the carrots and slice into thin diagonal slices. Peel the shallots and chop them finely.

Heat the olive oil in a sauté pan and gently fry the lardons and shallots. After 5 minutes, add the carrots and continue to cook for 5 more minutes, then add the broad beans and chicken stock and season with a little salt and freshly ground pepper.

Cook until the beans are just tender and still bathed in their juices, about 5 minutes. Remove from the heat, put in the butter and shake the pan to emulsify the butter with the vegetable juices.

Stir in the parsley. (Serves 4)

Cabbage with Ham
Chou à l'Ibaiama

Basque winter cabbages are massive, one of these sturdy curly cabbages would easily feed a family of eight. You can use any sausage meat or the home made spiced Txistorra (page 71). If you want a very substantial dish, double the amount of sausage meat. There are two ways of finishing the dish, as a cabbage omelette, or with lightly baked eggs on top.

1 small green Savoy cabbage
2 tablespoons olive oil
2 onions, chopped
100g (3½ oz) of sausage meat plain or spiced

2 slices of Ibaiama or other ham such as Bayonne or Serrano, torn into small pieces
4 eggs
salt, *Espelette* pepper or cayenne

Shred the cabbage and blanch for 2 – 3 minutes in boiling salted water; if it is a very large tough cabbage, blanch it for longer. Drain it well.

Heat the olive oil in a frying pan and fry the onions, sausage meat, broken into pieces, and ham. When they are cooked, mix in the cabbage and let it cook for a few minutes. Keep it hot.

Make an omelette:
Beat the eggs with red pepper and little salt. Heat 2 tablespoonss of olive oil in a large non stick frying pan. They should be medium hot. Pour in the eggs and as soon as they start to set, scoop them round once, sweeping the egg off half of the pan, with a spatula. Tilt the pan and let the uncooked egg run over the base once more, then remove the pan to prevent the egg cooking too much, it should not be brown. Do not worry if the eggs are not completely cooked. Quickly pile the hot cabbage on top and, after a minute, fold the cabbage and the layer of egg over two or three times so that the thin strips of egg are distributed here and there through the cabbage. Serve warm. (Serves 4)

Or:
Break 4 eggs into little depressions in the cabbage mixture, cover the pan with a lid and let them cook until barely set.

Haricot Blancs à la Pied de Porc

You can use a couple of *couennes* (rolls of confit pork rind seasoned with salt, pepper, garlic and parsley and tied with string, then cooked in fat) instead of the pig's foot, and for a more substantial dish, add some fried or grilled sausages sprinkled with Armagnac, half an hour before the end of the cooking. Start soaking the beans the day before.

1 pig's trotter or 100g (3½ oz) streaky bacon
2 tablespoons goose or duck fat

1 onion, sliced
2 cloves garlic
300g (10 oz) carrots
1 stick celery
300g (10 oz) butter beans or white haricot beans, soaked overnight
3 tablespoons tomato sauce
2 bay leaves
bunch of thyme
salt, freshly ground pepper

For the sausages:
150g (5 oz) pork chipolatas
1 tablespoon Armagnac
2 tablespoons goose or duck fat

To finish:
2 tablespoons chopped parsley
1 tablespoon lemon juice

Put the pig's foot or bacon in a saucepan of water, bring it to the boil and skim it. Turn down the heat and let it cook for 1 hour.

Put the soaked beans in a casserole cover them with water and let them cook for 30 minutes. Drain them.

Heat the goose or duck fat gently, and sweat the onions, garlic, carrots and celery. Add the beans, the pig's trotter, the tomato and herbs. Cover with 1 litre of water and simmer for 2 hours, adding more water as needed. Remove the pig's foot and cut up the meaty bits, removing the bones. Return the meat to the beans.

Adding the sausage:
At this point, if adding the sausages: remove the skins from the sausages, break them into little pieces so that they look like tiny meat balls, and sprinkle them with a little Armagnac.

Fry them in a little goose or duck fat until browned and place them on top of the beans. Continue to cook the beans, covered, in a low oven, 170°C (340°F), for half an hour.

To finish:
With or without the sausages, the beans can now be finished. Stir the parsley lightly through the beans together with 3 tablespoonss boiling hot water, 1 tablespoon goose or duck fat and a tablespoon of lemon juice. Heat through. (Serves 4 - 6)

Basquaise Chick Peas

These garbanzas, according to Gerald Hirigoyen author of *By the Book: Authentically Basque*, are traditionally cooked without meat, I suppose as a Lenten dish.

But chicken stock instead of water gives a decidedly better flavour. You could also add a handful of lardons, which should first be fried with the onions, or a couple of handfuls of spinach, stirred in 5 or 10 minutes before the end of the cooking.

200g (7 oz) chickpeas, soaked overnight
½ teaspoon saffron or use a packet of Spigol or Dalia
paëlla seasoning
600ml (20 fl oz) chicken stock
I red bell pepper, grilled, skinned and deseeded
3 tablespoons olive oil
2 onions, finely sliced
2 – 3 cloves garlic, chopped
I *choricera* pepper or dried red chilli
I tablespoon coriander seeds
2 bay leaves
salt, freshly ground black pepper

Preheat the oven to 180°C (350°F).
Soak the saffron threads or dissolve the saffron powder or paëlla seasoning in a little of the stock.
Toast the coriander seeds lightly in a dry pan to bring out their flavour. Crush them coarsely in a pestle and mortar or spice grinder.
Cut the grilled red bell pepper into dice.
Heat the olive oil in an iron or earthenware casserole.

Soften the onions in the hot oil together with the garlic, chilli, coriander and bay leaves, over a medium heat.

Add the drained chick peas, grilled red pepper, stock or water and the saffron or paëlla seasoning.

Bring to the boil, cover the casserole and cook in the oven for 1 – 1½ hours. When the chick peas are tender, add seasoning. (Serves 4)

COURGETTES AND PUMPKIN

Petits Flans de Courgettes

This is a real classic of the South West, often appearing with roasted meat. It can be very watery, but in this light version the courgettes are first squeezed to remove their liquid and added to the batter fresh and raw.

200g (7 oz) courgettes
2 eggs
70g (2½ oz) cream cheese
50ml (2 fl oz) single cream
1 teaspoon mustard
1 teaspoon baking powder
30g (1 oz) cornflour
50ml (2 fl oz) 1 milk
60g (2 oz) Abbaye de Belloc or other ewe's milk cheese, grated
salt, freshly ground pepper

Preheat the oven to 180°C (350°F).

Grate the courgettes on the coarse side of the grater.

Press out their juices by picking up a fistful of grated courgette at a time and squeezing with your hand.

Mix the eggs with the cream cheese and gradually add the cream and mustard, whisking them in. Mix the baking powder with the cornflour and gradually add the milk, making sure there are no lumps. Combine this with the egg mixture.

Mix in the raw grated courgettes and the grated cheese and season well.

Grease six ramekins with butter and fill with the mixture. Cook for 25 – 30 minutes, until golden.

Serve in the ramekins or turn them out and eat them with grilled or roasted beef, pork or lamb. (Serves 4)

Pumpkin Gratin
Gratin de Courge

Pumpkins and squashes grown in the South West are good keepers and a great autumn and winter vegetable.

You can use any of the squashes such as acorn or butternut for this luscious dish as well as pumpkin.

1kg (2¼ lb) pumpkin or squash, peeled
2 potatoes, peeled
3 tablespoons olive oil
2 shallots, finely chopped
3 cloves garlic, finely chopped
200ml (7 fl oz) double cream
pinch of nutmeg
salt, freshly ground pepper

Preheat the oven to 180°C (350°F).

Slice the pumpkin and potatoes fairly thinly. Heat the olive oil in a large frying pan and fry the vegetables in batches, until just starting to brown and caramelise.

Mix together the pumpkin and potato.

Put the shallots, garlic and cream in a small saucepan. Season with nutmeg, salt and pepper and bring to the boil. Simmer for one minute.

Oil a gratin dish with olive oil, then put in a layer of the sliced vegetables. Sprinkle with half the shallot cream, cover with another layer of pumpkin and potato and finish with a layer of cream.

Bake for 1 hour 15 minutes. (Serves 6)

Onion Confit Tart

Confit or caramelised onions are a big thing in Bordeaux, often made into a sort of chutney, but here they appear in a sumptuous little onion tart. It makes a good lunch dish.

50ml (2 fl oz) olive oil
30g (1 oz) butter
8 medium red onions, finely sliced
4 – 5 sprigs thyme
240g (8oz) puff pastry
50g (2 oz) grated gruyère
75g (3 oz) mascarpone
salt, freshly ground black pepper

Preheat the oven to 220°C (430°F).

Heat the olive oil and butter over a low heat, put in the onions and the shredded thyme, with tough stalks removed, and a pinch of salt. Cook for about 30 minutes, stirring once or twice, sweat them very, very slowly, letting the onions soften and caramelise without browning too much. Add a teaspoon or two of water half way through.

Butter a 20cm (8in) tart tin with a removeable base. Roll out the pastry and use it to line the tart tin, letting the pastry overlap the sides and hang over the rim.

Use baking paper or foil and dried beans to hold the pastry in place while it cooks. Turn down the heat to 200°C (400°F) and bake the tart shell blind for 20 minutes.

Remove the paper and beans.

Sprinkle the Gruyère over the base of the tart, spoon in the onions, and bake for 10 minutes. Dot the mascarpone over the top and bake for a further 15 – 20 minutes until the mascarpone is melted.

Remove the tart and let it cool a bit, then cut the extra pastry away with a sharp knife held flat to the rim of the tart tin.

Eat the tart while it is warm. (Serves 4)

Roasted Shallots

It would be nice to be able to roast the shallots in the hot ashes of a wood fire, to give them a smoky taste. Failing that, they can be roasted in their skins with butter which gives a delicious flavour. They can then be skinned and eaten.

30g (1 oz) butter
1 tablespoon sunflower oil
3 cloves garlic
500g (1lb 2 oz) shallots
3 sprigs thyme
3 bay leaves
100ml (3½ fl oz) white wine
50ml (2 fl oz) water
salt, freshly ground pepper

Preheat the oven to 200°C (400°F).

Melt the butter with the sunflower oil in an ovenproof gratin dish. Trim the roots off the shallots but do not skin them. Roll them about in the tin with the garlic, so that they are coated with the butter, stick the herbs in here and there. Season lightly.

Pour on the wine and water, cover the dish and roast them for 45 minutes. (Serves 4)

One way to serve the shallots:
Place the shallots in their skins in a dish with some fresh mint leaves, fresh white goats' or curd cheese and slices of country bread. Let people pop the succulent shallots out of their skins and eat them with the bread, cheese and mint leaves.

Chapter Ten

Desserts, Baking, Fruits and Nuts

It seems that desserts do not receive huge priority in the South West, and after the tapas, pinchos, plates of charcuterie and giant salads and generous main courses that seem to feature at every meal, it is hardly surprising.

However people do still eat dessert every day and generally choose variations on their own, very traditional particular favourites.

You will generally find *crème caramel* and *crème brulée*, which may be made with caramelised fruit juice, and anything with custard, particularly *Pantxineta* (a puff with custard), goes down well; tarts of apples (*tourtière Gascon* and *Croustade* come under this category) or tarts of plums, peaches, strawberries, greengages or pears; anything made with chocolate; ice creams and sorbets when its hot, with maybe some alcohol poured over the top, rum and vodka are popular; jelly, perhaps made with red wine; rice pudding and other milk puddings including Mamia, the pure white sheep's milk junket beloved by the Basques; Gâteau Basque; and various forms of cheese cake. To this can be added fruit crumble and clafoutis and any kind of éclair, particularly profiteroles. But I get the impression that most home cooks do not make any very complex desserts at home – why do so, when you can so easily pop round to the Boulangerie and get a stunningly beautiful ready made gâteau or tart?

Clearly, over the centuries people have developed the habit of going to the local pâtisserie to buy little treats, concocted with love, passion and artistry by the local Rageneau. The sweet tooth of the South West has resulted in some of the most beautiful, sophisticated and alluring pâtisseries, chocolate shops and tea shops in the world, with fripperies piled up in the windows and on the shelves in the most inviting way, ready to be enjoyed in between meals. Here are some of the local specialities.

Macaroons

Mini almond meringues for aristocrats – these are still baked in the Pays Basque by Maison Adam, who made them in May 1660 as a wedding gift for Louis XIV and Marie-Thérèse, the Infanta of Spain, when they were married in the lovely little church in St Jean de Luz. Maison Adam is still prospering and still has the chic-est shop in town.

But vying for the top place in macaroon stakes is Saint Emilion, where they were originally made by nuns who claimed a secret recipe, never divulged, that make their macaroons the best in the world.

In 1948, another superlative Basque Pâtissier at Chez Paries, invented the Mouchou – two macaroons stuck together with a creamy filling – he played with flavours, using pine nuts, hazelnuts or pistachios instead of almonds – and now they pile them up in pyramids of every flavour and hue. Try cassis and violet.

Chichis

These are really a street food to be eaten after visiting the market, while walking along – the same as Spanish churros – they are long, deep fried, fluted fritters dipped in sugar or in liquid chocolate.

Croquants, Tuiles au Noix

These are from the Dordogne. It makes sense for the bakers of Bergerac to invent a local delicacy out of walnuts, by putting them into crisp tuiles, sometimes with chocolate.

Pastis Bourrit

A Landaise pastry, a sort of fluted brioche without the little topknot, flavoured with rum, vanilla, orange flower water and anise flavoured liqueur such as pastis. Indispensible at weddings, first communions and hunting feasts. Michel Guérard calls Pastis Bourrit, 'The voluptuous half-breed, derived from the illustrious brioche and the famous Milanese panettone, but without the candied fruits'.

Rocher des Pyrénées

Also known as *Gâteau à la Broche*, Marriage Cake or Shepherd's Cake, this large cake looking a bit like a tall, spiky hedgehog, is a real curiosity, turning up at fairs and celebrations in the high villages of the Pyrenees.

It is cone shaped, cooked on a spit contraption over a wood fire. The batter, full of eggs, sugar and flour and flavoured with orange flower water, orange and rum, is slowly dribbled, layer after layer, onto a large horizontal cone covered with paper, revolving over the smouldering logs. The cake builds up and cooks gradually and takes on a delicious flavour of wood smoke – it takes hours to cook. When it is eventually presented, standing up like a cactus, it is devoured bit by bit, just as it is or with honey.

Pruneaux Fourrés

Agen prunes, mauvey, bluey-black and sticky, stoned and stuffed with more Agen prunes, what could be more luscious and jam-like.

Puits d'Amour

Little choux pastry tarts, filled with *crème pâtissière*, or even better, cream Chiboust – whipped cream lightened with Italian meringue –

and then sprinkled with sugar and caramelised – light as feathers, two or three are hardly enough.

Russe

Russe is an emblematic cake in the South West. Two layers of fine almond meringue held together with a layer of hazelnut butter icing and some crunchy praline – delicate and rich, the Russe is perfect with coffee.

Touron

Think pink, yellow, green, purple, chocolate and rose colour. Once again, the provenance of these sweets, sold in large slabs dotted with nuts and cherries, or in small bite sized rounds, seems to be a convent – this time the sisters of Toledo, who as long ago as the thirteenth century, made these to celebrate Christmas. They can be soft nut colours or blindingly bright and eye-catching, but are really just nougat, or is it sometimes more like marzipan? Perhaps a bit of both.

Guinettes

A variety of cherry with a tiny stone, soaked in kirsch and robed in chocolate. The cherries keep their stones and stalks. Pick one up by the stalk and dip it in your cup of coffee for a fraction of a second, as Guy Suire author of Le Petit Livre des Gourmandises et Friandises de Sud Ouest, tells us to do. Then close your eyes and lower it gently into your mouth.

Kanouga

A belle époque invention, chewy caramel combined with smooth chocolate, cut into squares. White Russian visitors to Biarritz at the turn of the nineteenth century were spending their money freely and had this sweet invented and named for them by Maison Paries, in 1905. The mouth watering caramels are still going strong.

Pantxineta – Puff and Crema

As the poet says in Rostang's Cyrano de Bergereac:

> "'…This puff
> Has so much cream its crying "Hold, enough!"'"

I experienced the feeling myself. A pastry puff filled with fragrant *crema pastelera* – custard – a delicate and airy dessert at the splendid Kaia-Kaipe Restaurant in Getaria, a historic fishing town east of San Sebastian. They serve it with vanilla ice cream and hot chocolate sauce.

They make individual cream puffs, but it is easier and more traditional to make one large one and cut it into slices. A more rustic topping is roughly chopped hazelnuts and almonds.

300g (10 oz) butter puff pastry

For the crema pastelera:
375ml (14 fl oz) milk or 150ml (5 fl oz) whipping cream and 225ml (7 fl oz) milk
1 small stick cinnamon
1 vanilla pod
1 strip of lemon rind
1 strip orange rind
3 egg yolks
50g (2 oz) granulated sugar
20g (1 oz) cornflour or rice flour
¼ teaspoon salt
1 extra egg yolk
1 tablespoon slivered almonds
icing sugar to sprinkle

Heat the milk or milk and cream, together with the cinnamon, vanilla pod and citrus peels, until small bubbles start to show round the edges. Remove from the heat and let it cool, stirring once or twice. Remove the cinnamon, peels and vanilla pod.

Beat the egg yolks in a jug. Stir in the cream and milk gradually until they are well blended.

Mix the sugar, cornflour and salt in a saucepan and very gradually whisk in the milk and egg mixture with a hand held electric whisk; go slowly to avoid lumps.

You will need to scrape into the corners and down the sides of the pan with a scraper to avoid lumps.

Heat the mixture gradually, stirring, over a medium-low heat and keep stirring, scraping the edges and bottom of the pan, until the mixture comes to the boil. This takes time, ten or fifteen minutes altogether.

When you see it is boiling, turn down the heat and continue cooking for 1 minute, still stirring, then remove the pan, and cool quickly by setting the pan in a bowl of cold water. Stir gently once or twice and when it is cool, cover in cling wrap, which has to be flush with the surface of the custard, to stop it getting a skin.

Chill in the refrigerator for 1 hour. It will keep 2 – 3 days in the refrigerator.

Now the tricky bit. Preheat the oven to 180C (350F).

Roll out the puff pastry into two rectangles 35cm x 20cm (14in x 8in). Place one sheet on a wetted baking sheet. Brush round the margins with beaten egg yolk. Spread the custard over the pastry, leaving the egg-glazed margin round the edge. Carefully place the other half of the pastry over the top, sealing the edges. Brush with remaining egg yolk and scatter with slivered almonds, and then sprinkle with icing sugar through a sieve. Bake for 30 minutes. Allow to cool a little before slicing. Serve with vanilla ice cream and, if you can believe it, chocolate sauce. (Serves 6 – 8)

Crema Pastelera

A quicker version of the pastry cream (custard really) that features in many Basque desserts.

100g (4 oz) granulated sugar
50g (1¾ oz) cornflour
¼ teaspoon salt
500ml (18 fl oz) milk, preferably creamy milk
2 large eggs
½ stick cinnamon
1 vanilla bean, split halfway, lengthwise

Put the sugar, cornflour and salt in a saucepan and mix well.

Add a few tablespoons of the cold milk and the eggs, and beat with an electric hand held beater.

In a separate pan bring the milk to the boil with the cinnamon and vanilla bean. Remove from the heat immediately it comes to the boil.

Slowly pour the hot milk into the mixture, stirring with a wire whisk. Place on a medium-low heat and keep stirring until the mixture thickens. Remove the pan and stir until smooth.

When cool, cover with plastic wrap, placed flush on the surface. Refrigerate – it will keep for 2 – 3 days but does not freeze well.

Les Noisettes – Hazelnuts

Nutella, a spreadable pâte of hazelnuts and chocolate (invented for children as blocks of chocolate in the 1940s, by Italian company Ferrero of Alba, and turned into the luscious spread when their refrigeration broke down), became wildly popular in Aquitaine, and the nut and chocolate spread was available everywhere as street food, on hot waffles, in pancakes, spread on strawberries or as a flavour for icecream. There was (and is) a huge factory making it, outside Paris, but mostly it came from Piedmont.

Cut to the 1970s – this is when the growing of hazelnuts started in the Lot, Dordogne and Tarn-et-Garonne – Cancon, near Villeneuve sur Lot, now claims to be the hazelnut capital of France.

It seems that the *coudrier*, hazel tree, can be grown very happily side by side with the *prunier*, plum tree. They like the same conditions and soil, but are harvested in different seasons. Some prune gowers are diversifying and there are now some 250 nut growers around the area of Cancon. They have formed a co-operative called Koki and already grow 95% of France's hazel nuts, producing more than 5,000 tonnes of nuts a year.

Koki have started to make a spread called La Chabraque d'Ecureuil, (Squirrel's Saddle?) which is made of chocolate and grilled hazelnuts and which comes in dark or milk form. One aficionado says it is so good it will make you swear off Nutella for life. Another great local product is Mutines, chocolate with caramelised hazelnuts.

The nuts can be milled to make a delicate hazelnut oil (be aware of a rather short shelf life) with a flavour just made for dressing a salad of young green beans.

Chocolate-Hazelnut spread
Pâte à Tartiner Chocolat Noisettes

It is possible make your own chocolate and hazelnut spread. Powdered hazelnuts are called for; you can buy them or make them in a spice grinder, in which case use blanched hazelnuts. This is a very chocolatey version – it works really wonderfully with dark chocolate (70% – 74%), but children may prefer a milk chocolate version.

50g (2 oz) of blanched hazelnuts or powdered hazelnuts
125g (5 oz) dark chocolate
100g (4 oz) butter at room temperature
½ tin condensed milk
1 teaspoon hazelnut oil (optional)

If using whole nuts toast the hazelnuts in a dry frying pan until light brown.

Allow to get cold. Grind the nuts to a fine powder.

Melt the chocolate in a bain marie – a pan inside a larger pan with 5cm (2 inches) of water in it.

Add the butter in small pieces, stirring it in after every addition. Stir in the condensed milk, nut oil and finally the powdered hazelnuts. Keep stirring until you have a lovely smooth texture. Pour into jars and allow to cool. Keep in the refrigerator but allow to come to room temperature before eating.

Pralines de Blaye

Almond pralines, brown, crunchy and rough, unlike smooth pretty sugared almonds, were, it is said, invented by the cook of the Duc de Choiseul, for certain dignitaries of Bordeaux, invited to lunch with the Duke at Blaye in 1649. But Marechal Praslin discovered these delights while on a mission to Bordeaux and left for Paris, stealing both the cook and the recipe.

Now we can find them everywhere, although those not made at Blaye are hard as pebbles and will break your teeth. Find the best examples at the Pâtisserie Brégier, Cours de La Republique, Braye.

Pruneau d'Agen

Also known as Prune d'Ente (which means grafted) this plum is actually grown mostly at Villeneuve sur Lot. Gaul had known some varieties of plums since the Greeks and Romans brought them into Languedoc, in the sixth century B.C. and after, but the particular type of prune that could be successfully dried, was originally grafted on native plum trees at the Monastery of Clairac, by the Benedictine monks. This variety was brought from Asia by the Crusaders and was soon found to be an excellent keeper when dried; prunes became very important as provisions for mariners, preventing them from getting scurvy from lack of fresh fruits.

These lightly purple and yellow plums, covered in a velvety bloom, are gathered when they are ripe, washed and then graded and put onto wooden racks and dried.

If the racks are heated by smouldering wood, the prunes acquire a smoky flavour.

Prunes in Rum

250g (9 oz) stoned Pruneaux d'Agen
200ml (7 fl oz) white wine
3 tablespoons rum
3 dessertspoons sugar
½ vanilla pod, cut in two lengthwise

Put the prunes in a bowl and add the wine, rum, sugar and vanilla. Allow to steep for one or two days. Serve just as they are, with or without cream, or use for making other desserts such as Clafoutis, (page 312) using prunes instead of cherries. They keep well in the refrigerator.

Prune and Hazelnut Tart with Armagnac

Originally from Bruno Loubet's collection of Bordeaux recipes. He pours the Armagnac over the hot tart as it comes out of the oven and sets it alight.

20 stoneless prunes
4 tablespoons Armagnac
100g (4 oz) butter
60g (2 oz) sugar
4 egg yolks
1 whole egg, beaten
250ml (9 fl oz) crème fraîche
1 vanilla pod
zest of ½ lemon
80g (3 oz) ground hazelnuts
300g (10 oz) puff pastry

Bring the prunes to the boil in a mixture of 4 tablespoons of Armagnac and 2 of water and simmer for 10 minutes. Let them cool and soak in the mixture for an hour or two. Drain them well and pat dry.

Heat the butter in small pan until hazelnut brown then pour it into a large bowl. Add the sugar, egg yolks and whole egg and whisk until smooth. Add the crème fraîche, the inside of the vanilla pod, the grated lemon zest and the ground hazelnuts and mix well.

Line a 20cm (8 inches) tart tin with pastry letting it overlap the sides. Chill in the fridge for 30 minutes.

Preheat the oven to 180°C (350°F).

Remove the tart shell from the fridge and bake it blind, lined with greaseproof paper and dried beans, for 12 minutes at 180°C (350°C), then remove the paper and the beans. Arrange the prunes all over the base then pour the hazelnut mixture over them. Put the tart back in the oven, lower the heat slightly to 170°C (340°F) for about 35 minutes or until golden brown. To test it push a skewer into the middle and see if it comes out clean. When it has rested for a while, trim off the overlapping pastry.

Chill overnight to firm up the filling. Dust with icing sugar.
(Serves 6)

Périgord Strawberries

May is the time for the strawberry festival of Vergt, capital of the strawberry growing country between Bergerac and Périgueux; from here, considered the best of all in Paris, come the elongated Gariguettes with their fresh and intensive flavour and Mara des Bois, with a whiff of perfume, or if you want very large, well flavoured strawberries that are intensely red all the way through, there is a variety called, incomprehensibly, Seascape.

Jean Christophe Gounou, who makes icecreams and sorbets and has a shop called Sucre-glace in Périgueux, will only use strawberries from Vergt for his strawberry sorbets.

Sorbet à la Fraise

500g (1lb 2oz) very red, ripe strawberries, colour is important
250g (9 oz) caster sugar
juice of 1 lemon

Wash and hull the strawberries. Drain them well, cut them in quarters and purée them together with the sugar. Add lemon juice to taste and mix thoroughly. Freeze in an ice cream maker.

Strawberry and Rhubarb Crumble

This recipe comes from Périgord – it was a surprise to me and I thought it original to combine rhubarb crumble with strawberries. It turns out to be a magical combination.

400g (14 oz) strawberries, cut in quarters
200g (7 oz) rhubarb, cut in small batons
75g (2¾ oz) sugar
1 dessertspoon grated fresh ginger

For the crumble:
200g (7 oz) flour
200g (7 oz) sugar
150g (5 oz) butter

Preheat the oven to 200C (400 F).

Mix the fruit with the 75g (2¾ oz) sugar and put it into an oven dish. Cover and bake for 25 minutes. Rhubarb and strawberries both make an enormous amount of juice, so pour off the juices and reduce them by half or more, in a small saucepan. Return this syrup to the fruit in the oven dish, stir in the ginger.

Mix the flour and sugar together in a bowl. Cut the butter into small pieces and rub it into the flour with your finger tips, until it has the consistency of rough breadcrumbs.

Cover the fruit with this mixture and bake for 30 minutes.
(Serves 4 – 6)

Crumble Fruits Rouges

Crumble is a very different thing in the Béarn, first of all it is pronounced 'crurmbler', and you will be corrected if you pronounce it wrong, and secondly it has been turned into a sort of pastry, to be served in slices, with a thin pastry crust, raspberry and strawberry filling and crisp crumb and nut top, embellished with plenty of sweetened whipped cream. This is how they serve it at the huge Brasserie de Berry in Pau; it is rather special and quite easy to make.

1 sheet, 350g (12 oz) – pâte sablé or shortcrust pastry
200g (7 oz) raspberries
200g (7 oz) strawberries, hulled and cut in half
squeeze of lemon juice
2 tablespoons sugar

For the crumble:
1 tablespoon each of sesame seeds, blanched almonds, pine nuts and blanched hazelnuts
75g (3 oz) butter
100g (3½ oz) plain flour
50g (2 oz) ground almonds
pinch salt
75g (3 oz) sugar
1 packet vanilla sugar

Preheat oven to 180°C (350°F).

Put the raspberries and strawberries in a dish and sprinkle them with a squeeze of lemon and 2 tablespoons of sugar. Let them sit in their own juices for half an hour.

Toast the sesame seeds in a dry frying pan.

Toast the nuts in the oven for 5 minutes, spread out in a tart tin. When they are cool, chop them very roughly.

Make the crumble by rubbing the butter into the flour with the ground almonds and a pinch of salt until the mixture resembles breadcrumbs, add the sugar and vanilla sugar and stir it through. Add the sesame seeds and nuts and mix them in with your fingers.

Sprinkle two tablespoons of the topping into the raw fruit and stir it round. It will absorb the juices and prevent the tart from being too wet.

Fill the pastry shell with the strawberry and raspberry mixture, with the juices they have made.

Cover with the crumble mixture and bake for 30 minutes.

Cut the excess pastry from the tart with a knife held flat against the rim of the tart tin.

Serve with whipped cream. (Serves 4 – 6)

Blood Orange Tart

Blood oranges have a short season; they colour up in cold weather, and so they are a winter fruit, which may explain the sharp flavour, perfect for a tart with the tang of a lemon, a hint of orange and a beautiful rose colour.

350g (12 oz) short crust or *pâte sablé* pastry
2 – 3 tablespoons pine nuts
2 eggs
1 egg white
100g (4 oz) caster sugar
grated rind of 2 blood oranges
4 blood oranges (125ml – 4 fl oz – blood orange juice)
juice of 1 lemon
125ml (4 fl oz) double cream
icing sugar

Heat the oven to 180°C (350°F).

Line a 20cm (8in) tart tin with pastry, letting it overlap and hang over the rim of the tin. Line with a sheet of baking paper and fill with some dried beans and bake blind for 15 minutes. Allow to cool a bit.

Toast the pine nuts lightly in a dry frying pan.

Beat the eggs and sugar together until thick and creamy. Very slowly incorporate the orange and lemon juice and zest.

Incorporate the cream. Fill the pastry shell with the mixture, place it on a baking sheet. Scatter the top with pine nuts and bake for 25 – 30 minutes. Allow to cool to lukewarm.

Sprinkle with icing sugar shaken through a sieve. (Serves 4)

Les Noix – Walnuts from Périgord and Quercy

Walnuts flourish in the Dordogne. Walnut trees, the branches covered with moss, the leaves translucent golden-green at sunset, flank the roads and the fields of maize and wheat that line the Dordogne river valley. It all looks so inviting in early October, when a fragile mist hangs over the river and the nuts start to fall with a patter onto the lanes that wind between villages. But these trees are likely to be closely guarded and belong to someone who will jump out at you, someone who harvests the nuts and does not want any passing stranger to pick them up.

Most of the nuts are sold on the markets or to wholesalers, some 5,000 to 7,000 tonnes per year, and some are turned into delicious walnut oil, a local flavour since the thirteenth century, now used mainly for salads.

But they may also appear in walnut bread and walnut tarts, as sweets and, particularly when the nuts are fresh, roquefort salad with walnuts.

There are forty indigenous French varieties – favourites are Marbot for early nuts, Grandjean for eating fresh and Franquette, small but reliable.

Although it is said that if you sleep in the shade of a walnut tree you will fall sick or melancholy, this tree was formerly essential to life here. Most of the staircases, floors and furniture were made of walnut, and the fires fuelled with fallen walnut branches.

At midsummer, the fête of Saint Jean, some of the leaves are picked and dried and made into an aromatic aperitif called *quinquina*, while in autumn the green outer shells from the ripe nuts are pounded and mixed with eau de vie, sugar and honey and then kept for a year or so until they develop the characteristic mahogany colour and medicinal flavour of *crème de noix*, a pleasantly tipsy-making medicine for old ladies.

The nuts themselves are allowed to fall, or are shaken from the trees, then collected and dried on racks. Once they are shelled, the shells, traditionally, are collected and ground, and used on the floor of bread ovens to prevent the loaves from sticking.

Caramelised Walnuts

Eat these delicious candied walnuts as they are or on ice cream or with *Mamia*, the delicate white Basque sheeps' milk dessert. If you make it with hazelnuts instead of walnuts, it becomes *la Noisettine*.

Some people put a tablespoon of butter in with the sugar and nuts when they make the caramel.

When the mixture starts to caramelise, you have to move quickly to spread out the nuts or they will all stick together; you have about 30 seconds to do it.

125g (4 oz) walnut halves
75g (3 oz) granulated sugar

Have a sheet of baking paper ready on a baking tray.

Put the nuts and sugar in a non-stick pan and put it over a medium heat. When the sugar starts to melt and caramelise, turn the nuts over and stir them round until they are coated with caramel, it takes just seconds.

Tip them out quickly onto the baking sheet and spread them out and separate them with two spatulas as fast as you can. They will go hard and crunchy in a minute. (Serves 4)

Chestnuts

Also known as *le pain du pauvre*, the bread of the poor, or *l'arbre à pain*, bread tree, or even *pain de bois*, bread of the woods, the sweet chestnut tree *(castanea sativa)* and its fruit sustained life itself in South West France through many famines.

In Périgord, 'For six months of the year at least, the country dwellers, share-croppers, domestic servants and labourers lived on almost nothing but the fruit of this tree, which more than once in this department has saved the poor from famine.'[1]

In the French Revolutionary Calendar, Sept 24th was known as the day of the chestnut 'Chataîgne'.

Cooked chestnuts were a sweet treat for nuns and monks, as well as the poor and served at the tables of noblemen, often as a fruit eaten for dessert.

They were, for example, eaten in rather high company; at a banquet held in Périgueux in 1773 for Comte Arlot de la Roque; after 33 courses came eight delicious desserts including lemon jelly, and almond tart. Then came some ragoût of ham, ox cheeks, pigs' trotters, truffles etc, followed by two dishes of waffles, four compôtes, two iced cheeses, marzipan, macaroons, cheeses and chestnuts. Together with 22 bottles of wine and 10 loaves of bread.'[2] Roasted chestnuts are sometimes sprinkled with new season's wine or orange juice and sugar, a delicacy much enjoyed by nineteenth century families.

When turned into desserts and confectionery the chestnut combines perfectly with chocolate, with cinnamon, with cream, with rum and with vanilla.

Pêches Roussane de Monein

A very ancient variety of peach that used to grow amongst the vines. It ripens at the beginning of August and is not really a commercial fruit, as it is very fragile, with juicy, perfumed flesh, and a skin which peels off easily.

The Béarnaise are very proud of this peach, an eighteenth century

[1] 1811, 'Description topographique de la France' Peuchet and Chanlaire.
[2] (LaVialle, Jean-Baptiste. *Le Châtaignier.* Paris: Vigot Frères, 1906)

early variety from the Jurançon, yellow and ruby red. It can be eaten as it is or made into a superb golden jam.

Confiture de Melon d'Espagne

Known in Bordeaux as *Pastèque de Confiture*, this is an autumn melon, (*citrullus lanatus*) a member of the watermelon family, with pale flesh and a tough skin mottled dark green.
It is used to make a marmalade-like conserve with caramelised pieces floating in its depths. It was once very much the taste of home for many children, who were given this very sweet jam for breakfast.

I *melon d'Espagne* of about 7kg (15½ lb)
2½ kg (5½ lb) preserving sugar
3 unwaxed lemons, keep the pips
I unwaxed orange, keep the pips
I vanilla pod
I or 2 small apples (optional but will help the set)

Halve the lemons and orange and slice them into thin strips. Cut the melon in half and then in quarters and remove the skin with a knife (this is the hard bit, be careful, it is very tough!). Cut into large chunks and put these in a preserving pan with the sugar, the lemons, the orange, the citrus pips tied in a muslin bag, the cinnamon and some of the seeds from the inside of the vanilla pod. Stir everything together.

Leave to steep overnight, the melon will release its liquid.

The next day stir everything and bring rapidly to the boil. Turn down the heat, add 1 or 2 grated apples and simmer gently for about 3 hours. The liquid should reduce considerably.

When the jam has thickened well, remove the bag of pips, plunge a hand held blender into the jam for a moment – keep a few bits whole.

Fill clean, warmed jars with the mixture while it is still very hot. (Makes about 12 pots.)

Gâteau Basque

You can't really be in the Pays Basque for many hours before encountering this modest looking, round, golden pastry, which, like a pie, has a hidden filling. It is said to date from the eighteenth century, when it had no filling and was more of a biscuit than a cake.

The Gâteau Basque, in its glorious cherry version, may have originated in the valley of the Nivelle river near the town of Itxassou, famous for its black Xapata cherries, which are eaten fresh or used for black cherry jam, which, mixed with rum, fills the middle of the cakes.

The other traditional filling is a cream filling, not dairy cream, but a fairly firm custard, flavoured with vanilla pods. (See recipe on page 297)

Since it is mostly pastry, this should be rich and light; it can be made with or without lemon zest, simple or complicated. The best are crumbly and contain almonds.

120g (4 oz), half a pot of Morello or black cherry jam
½ tablespoon of rum (or more to taste)
an egg yolk for glazing
butter and sugar for preparing the cake tin

For the pastry:
150g (5 oz) plain flour
30g (1 oz) ground almonds
90g (3 oz) icing sugar
½ teaspoon baking powder
good pinch salt
finely grated zest of a lemon
100g (4 oz) butter
1 medium egg, beaten

Mix the rum into the jam.

Butter and line the bottom of a spring-sided cake tin 20cm (8 inches) in diameter. Brush the sides and bottom with melted butter again and shake some granulated sugar around inside the mould, so it sticks to the sides.

Put the flour, almonds, sugar, baking powder, salt and lemon zest in a large mixing bowl. Add the butter cut in small pieces and either rub it in by hand or blend in a food processor, until it is like breadcrumbs. Add the beaten egg and work lightly with your fingertips until it has held together in a ball. Cover with cling film and leave for 40 minutes in a cold place or the refrigerator.

Heat the oven to 180°C (350°F).

Divide the pastry into two parts – make one a third of the whole and the other two-thirds. Line the cake tin with two thirds of the pastry rolled out into a disc on a floured board, be careful as it is quite sticky; make it large enough to come 4cm (1½ inches) up the sides of the tin.

Spread the jam over the pastry.

Roll out a second disc, smaller than the first and just about the same diameter as the tin, brush one side with beaten egg. Place it over the jam, egg side up. Roll the sides over and pinch and prod them together to seal the edges; this will keep the jam from bubbling through

Brush the top with more egg yolk beaten with a few drops of water. Bake for 40 – 45 minutes. Allow to cool to room temperature.

Coffee and Armagnac Cream
Verrines de Breuil Fermier au Café

Coffee shops in Aquitaine are cave-like, fragrant and enticing. They roast and sell coffee beans sourced from all over the globe; acid Kenya, perfumed Moka with scents of truffle and hay, Nicaragua with the faint smell of cognac are all favourites.

Ancient, brass-embellished torrefying machines turn the beans in heated trays and a great smell of roasting coffee fills the street outside.

There are several in Bordeaux, one in Bayonne, one in Bazas, one in Biarritz and one in St Jean de Luz. They like coffee strong here, *un petit noir* or *un café serré,* or if you want it with a dash of milk, ask for a *noisette.* Or an espresso with a bit more milk? *Un petit crème.*

300g (10 oz) *breuil fermier* (sheep's milk curd) or *fromage frais*
125ml (4½ oz) tablespoon double cream
140g (5 oz) icing sugar
1 vanilla pod, cut in half
1 packet of sponge fingers or *langues de chat*
1 cup of strong black coffee
1 soup spoon of Armagnac
4 squares best dark chocolate
1 soup spoon good quality cocoa powder

Mix the *breuil* with the sugar and add the seeds from the vanilla pod.

Whip the cream until light and fluffy and fold it into the *breuil* or *fromage frais*.

Put half the sponge fingers into small glasses or ramekins.

Mix together the coffee and Armagnac and pour half over the biscuits. Cover with half the *breuil*.

Repeat with a second layer of biscuits, coffee and Armagnac, and lastly the remaining *breuil*. Chill for one hour. Grate the squares of chocolate over the top, sprinkle with a little cocoa powder at the last minute.

Clafoutis

This is a modern version of a very old dish. I like the idea of lightening it with beaten egg whites, as it can be very solid.

75g (3 oz) plain flour
75g (3 oz) caster sugar
2 eggs, separated
300ml (10 fl oz) creamy milk
1 tablespoon Armagnac
300g (10½ oz) ripe black cherries

Heat oven to 150°C (300°F). Combine flour and sugar in large bowl. Whisk together the egg yolks, milk and Armagnac. Gradually whisk the mixture into the flour and sugar, to make a smooth batter. Whisk the egg whites to a soft peak and fold them into the batter.

Pour the batter into a round dish greased with butter, scatter in the cherries and bake for at least 60 minutes, until a skewer poked into the middle comes out clean.

Tourteau Fromager, Quesada or *Gâteau de Fromage*

On Biarritz market, standing up proudly on the corner of the cheese stall of Madame Olga, the biggest cheesecake ever seen attracts the customers. It is a giant and about 24cm (10 ins) tall with an exciting dark brown top; in fact it looks much like a giant cep.

Madame Olga recommends that you serve it in slices, at room

temperature, with a translucent, ruby-coloured *coulis*, actually more of a flowing jam, of cooked raspberries and red currants. This is similar to her version of cheesecake.

500g (1lb 2 oz) *faiselle* (see below) or use *ricotta* or *fromage blanc*
75g (3 oz) sugar
4 eggs, separated
75g (3 oz) butter, melted
100g (3½ oz) flour
½ teaspoon baking powder
1 packet of vanilla sugar or the seeds scraped from half a vanilla pod.
You can also add, to your own taste:
zest of half a lemon, 1 tablespoon Armagnac and a pinch of cinnamon

Heat the oven to 150°C (300°F).

Butter the inside of a deep springclip mould, and line the bottom with baking paper.

Mix the cheese with the sugar and vanilla, beat in the egg yolks, melted butter, flour and baking powder. Add lemon zest, Armagnac and cinnamon to taste. Whisk the egg whites and fold them in. Pour the mixture into the mould and bake for 90 minutes.

Faiselle, Fromage Frais or Requeson

Faiselle is a fresh white cheese. It is easily made with milk, cows', goat's or sheep's, fermented and then strained in a mould called a *faiselle*, hence the name of the cheese. These moulds can be bought on cheese making sites on the internet, as can the curdling agent, rennet and a mesophilic ferment which you can use to start the process off. Or you can start it off with a little help from 2 Petits Suisses or 2 Yeo Baby *fromage frais*; these will give the right flavour and bacteria. After that you can actually use the whey from your own cheese as a fermenting agent.

It takes a couple of days, and the temperature varies at different stages, so you need a cool larder to start with and a warmish room to complete the cheese.

All your bowls and utensils and your hands, must all be very clean.

To make *faiselle*:
1 litre (34 fl oz) whole milk, cow, goat or sheep
2 little *fromage frais* such as Petit Suisse or Little Yeo, natural flavour/or
buy a mesophilic ferment on the internet. After that you can use some of
the whey from your own *faiselle*.
3 drops rennet (obtainable from chemists or on line).

Mix the *fromage frai,s* ferment or whey into the milk in a saucepan and
leave it, covered in a cool place (15 – 20°C or 60 – 70°F) overnight to
develop its flavour.

Now heat the milk and cheese mixture to 38C (body heat)(100F)
and stir in the 3 drops of rennet. Quickly pour into a mould with holes
and an outer container to hold the liquid or into lots of small moulds.

Cover and leave to set at room temperature 20C (70F), for 12 – 24
hours. Forget it, it must not be moved, and do not put it into the fridge.

When it has set, chill it for 2 hours. Pour off the liquid whey (if it is
not too sharp you can keep it if to use as a starter for your next batch).

If you want to turn the *faiselle* into *fromage blanc*, beat it with a little
single cream.

Mamia

Basques are very fond of milk puddings, and the favourite is definitely
Mamia, bowls of snowy white. rich ewe's milk (or failing that goats' or
cows' milk), set, like junket, with rennet.

Serve the *Mamia* with honey, although some people will say that the
taste is purer if you just sprinkle the top with sugar.

Sheep's milk is available from farm shops (look up the British Sheep
Dairying Association) and from goats' milk from Whole Foods Market.

1 litre (34 fl oz) ewe's, cow's or goat's milk
pinch fine salt
4 drops of rennet per bowl.

Have 4 bowls ready, distribute 4 drops of rennet to each of the bowls.

Put the milk in a saucepan, add a pinch of salt and bring it to the
boil. Remove it from the heat. (If using non-pasteurised raw milk it
should be boiled for 8 minutes, taking it off and putting it back on the
heat several times so it does not boil over.)

Let the milk cool to 37 – 38C (around 100F). Pour it into the bowls, stir once and leave, without disturbing, to set. Chill. Serve with sugar or honey.

Bordeaux Batter Cakes
Cannelés

Makes 30 small ones or 15 large – make the batter at least one day and up to 4 days ahead.

These heavenly little caramelised cakes rise in tiers in the windows of every Bordeaux pastry shop. Deep glossy chestnut brown in colour, they should be soft and chewy inside and crisp and caramelised on the outside. I prefer smaller ones, which can be eaten at a bite. They will keep for a day or two.

My recipe is based on one from the brilliant cook Rachel Khoo, a great champion of French food, who recommends cooking them in a silicone mould with 8 holes or in muffin tins – traditionally these little upright cakes are prettily fluted like miniature jelly moulds. I use little nonstick steel moulds bought in Biarritz.

500ml (17 fl oz) whole milk
50g (1¾ oz) butter
1 vanilla pod, split
100g (3½ oz) plain white flour, sifted
225g (8 oz) icing sugar, sifted
1 level teaspoon salt
2 eggs plus 2 egg yolks
60ml (2 fl oz) rum

Heat the milk and butter together with the vanilla pod until just simmering, then remove from the heat and allow to cool.
Sieve the flour, sugar and salt together into a bowl. Mix well.
Beat the eggs and yolks lightly.
Remove the vanilla pod from the milk and keep it for later.
Add the milk and eggs to the flour and beat lightly.
Strain the batter through a sieve, add the rum and return the vanilla pod. Cover and keep in the refrigerator for 24 hours or longer, to

develope the flavour.

Preheat the oven to 240C (460F). Remove the vanilla pod from the batter and give it a stir.

Fill the moulds three quarters full with the batter, using a jug or small ladle. Place the moulds on a baking tray and cook for 15 minutes. Turn down the heat to 190C (375C) and cook for a further 25 minutes for small cannelés or up to an hour for large.

They will rise a bit and get very brown. Remove from the moulds and leave to cool and crisp up on a wire rack.

Gâteau des Rois, Couronne des Rois

In the South West, at Christmas and through January the pastry shops are filled with *Gâteaux des Rois* (which during the French Revolution were renamed *Gâteaux de l'Egalité*). They are made of brioche, ring-shaped and flavoured with crystallised orange peel and orange flower water. The top is decorated with crystal sugar, crystallised peel and a gold cardboard crown. At one time they had a bean inside and the person who got the bean could be king for the day. Now they have small china favours.

Start the dough 24 hours ahead.

For the dough starter:
50g (2 oz) flour
6g (teaspoon) instant yeast
50ml (2 fl oz) tepid water

For the syrup:
50ml (2 fl oz) water
50g (2 oz) butter
60g (2oz) icing sugar
pinch salt
120ml (4 fl oz) rum
a few drops of orange flower water

For the dough:
200g (7 oz) flour

1 large egg
1 egg for glazing
75g (3 oz) candied orange peel
50g (2 oz) pearl or nibbed sugar

Make the starter:

Mix the flour with the yeast granules. Add the water and form a dough. Knead for 10 minutes and leave to rest and rise for 50 minutes.

Make the syrup:

Put all the ingredients in a saucepan with a heavy base, stir to dissolve the sugar and bring to a simmer. Cook gently for 10 minutes. Let it cool. If you have a thermometer, ideally the temperature of the syrup when you add it to the dough should be 40 °C (just over 100°F).

Make the dough:

Place the flour and one egg in a bowl and make soft pliable dough, incorporating three-quarters of the syrup a little at a time. Add a little tepid water if the dough seems too firm, it should be soft and pliable. Chop half the candied orange peel into small pieces.

Work the remaining syrup into the starter, combine the starter mixture, and the chopped crystallised orange peel, little by little, with the dough. Form the dough into a ball and put it into a bowl with enough room for it to swell.

Cover the bowl well with cling film and place in the fridge overnight.

The next day:

Remove the dough and allow it to come back to room temperature. Let it rise if it has not done so – it should be at least double its original size. This can take some hours.

Cut the remaining candied peel into 8 strips.

Work the dough into a ball and pierce the centre, turning the inside, where it is pierced, downwards and through the hole you have made, towards the outside as if you were turning the whole thing inside out ,and tuck it slightly under to form a crown or ring (dough nut style) 25cm (10 inches) across, with a smooth, rounded top.

Preheat the oven to 210°C (410°F).

Cover a baking sheet with buttered baking paper and place the crown on this. Brush the crown with beaten egg and sprinkle with pearl or nibbed sugar. You can make this by smashing some sugar lumps.

Place 8 strips of candied peel around the ring, like the spokes of a wheel.

Cover lightly with cling film and allow to rise in a warm place for 30 minutes.

Bake for 20 – 25 minutes; keep an eye on it. Serve sliced, warm or reheated, spread with butter if you like.

Brioche French Toast
Pain Perdu au Rhum

This is a very grown up version of a popular children's dessert, originally a way of using up left over bread. You can use bread but it is much lighter if made with brioche. At Café du Commerce in Biarritz it is served with custard and salted caramel ice-cream

1 tin-shaped brioche loaf
500ml (18 fl oz) full cream milk
1 vanilla pod
125ml (4 fl oz) rum (or more)
pinch of salt
1 egg, beaten
2 tablespoon flour
2 tablespoon sunflower oil, or 1 tablespoon oil and 1 tablespoon butter
1 dessertspoon caster sugar, plus sugar to sprinkle
ground cinnamon or good quality cocoa powder to sprinkle

Cut 4 brick shaped pieces of brioche about 8cm (3in) by 4cm (1½ inches) by 3cm (1 inch), removing the crust, (or simply use thick slices, crusts removed).

Bring the milk to boiling point; you can put a vanilla pod in if you like the flavour, and allow to cool. The time honoured Gascon way of stopping it boiling over is to put a pebble in the middle of the pan. Remove the skin from the top.

Mix in the rum and a pinch of salt. Transfer the mixture to a shallow bowl.

Beat the egg on a plate. Sprinkle the flour over another plate.

Have ready a frying pan in which you have heated 1 – 2 tablespoons oil or the oil and butter.

Dip the pieces of brioche into the milk-rum mixture and let it soak through, then pick up a piece carefully and give it a gentle shake.

Now dip each piece in egg on all sides, shake again and lastly dip in flour, which should visibly coat it.

Make sure the frying oil is hot and fry the brioche on all sides until golden.

Drain on kitchen paper, sprinkle with sugar and cinnamon and serve with caramel ice cream and, if you like, custard (*crème Anglaise*) or cream.

Black Cherry Jam

Black cherries are grown at Itxassou, in the Pyrenees, the Beltxa cherries being the best variety, not too sweet.

This is the jam to eat with farm made sheep's milk cheeses such as Ardi Gasna, sometimes called the Farmer's Dessert, and the same jam is used in Gâteau Basque.

Stoning cherries is not easy, so it is worth investing in a cherry-stoning gadget. Start the jam the day before as the cherries need to steep in the sugar, in order to stay whole in the jam.

1 kg (2 lb) stoned black cherries
1 kg (2 lb) preserving sugar

Put the stoned cherries in a bowl with the sugar and leave overnight.

Transfer them to a pan with their juices and bring to the boil. Skim the foam. Simmer until the jam is beginning to gell. Test it by putting half a teaspoonful on a cold plate, after a minute, when it has cooled, pull you finger through the jam. If the two halves stay separate and do not run, then the jam is ready.

Ladle into clean, warm pots while it is still hot. (Makes 4 pots.)

White Fig Jam

White figs are really greeny-gold; they are delicate, sweet and quite small. Some people put walnuts into this delicious jam, which is popular with cheese. French style jams are usually softer and more fluid than ours.

1¼ kg (2¾ lb) green figs
1 lemon, sliced
1 vanilla pod
1kg (2¾ lb) preserving or granulated sugar

This jam takes two days to make, start in the morning. While you are cooking the jam, which is done in stages, use a heat diffuser and do not stir the figs.

Heat a large pan of water to boiling point and plunge in the figs for 30 seconds, do not stir them. Drain them gently, the idea is to keep them whole. Turn off the heat.

Now place half the figs in a preserving pan, cover with the lemon slices and put in the vanilla pod. Sprinkle with half the sugar.

Put the remaining fruit on top and sprinkle with the remaining sugar.

Leave to macerate for five hours, without stirring.

Place the pan over a low heat and wait until the sugar has almost all dissolved. Then remove it from the heat, cover the pan and leave it to sit overnight.

The next morning bring the fruit to the boil once more and simmer for 1 hour. Remove it from the heat, cover and allow to steep again.

Finally in the afternoon prepare your jam jars. Bring the jam back to the boil and cook until it reaches a jam-like consistency, it should be a golden colour. Remove the vanilla pods and ladle into pots while it is still hot.

Quince Paste
Pâte de Coing

Formerly a great speciality of Périgord Noir, the quince paste was formed in the shape of palm leaves and dried in the wooden drying racks (clayes) used for drying chestnuts.

It is eaten, as an alternative to black cherry jam, with sheep's cheese, hard sheep's cheese like Ardi Gasna, not the fresh kind. The paste should be a deep copper colour, if it is a pale orange, the quince has been mixed with apple.

Find it at Mille et un Fromages, on the Biarritz market or Chez Chailla in the Halles de Bayonne.

Marvels
Merveilles

Mervailles, little wonders with a long history, these deep fried pastries, often made for children, were traditionally eaten on Mardi Gras, and could come in every sort of shape, diamonds, triangles, slashed rectangles, little people, animals, ribbons and so on. They are delicate and very moreish.

300g (10½ oz) flour
1 teaspoon baking powder
pinch of salt
75ml (3 fl oz) milk
1 vanilla pod
40g (1½ oz) butter
100g (4 oz) sugar
2 eggs
1 tablespoon rum
icing sugar

Mix the flour with the baking powder and salt in a bowl.
Heat the milk with the vanilla pod and add the butter and sugar. Stir until both have dissolved.
Beat the eggs together with the rum.
Pour the butter and milk mixture and the eggs into the flour, stirring them in to make a pliable dough. Do not make it too wet, you must be able to knead it and roll it out.
Knead well and allow to rest for 2 – 3 hours.
Cut the dough into four pieces and roll into balls.
Roll one piece out into a thin rectangle or oval, 4 – 5 mm thick; the dough is very elastic so it takes a bit of perseverance to roll it.

Now cut it into shapes – use a sharp knife (or a fluted cutter if you like), and cut strips like wide ribbons, which you then cut diagonally, into long diamond shapes. Make a further little slash about one third of its length, down the middle of each diamond, so that you can slightly pull open the diamond shape.

Heat deep frying oil to 170C (340F) and drop the diamonds in. Fry until brown underneath, then turn them carefully with tongs. When they are brown all over transfer them with tongs to kitchen paper and then to a plate. Sprinkle with icing sugar and serve while still warm. (Makes about 50.)

Bibliography

D'Abartiague, Lewy. *On the origin of the Basques,* 1896 (a study made at the request of the London Geographic Congress of 1895)

Béraud-Sudreau, Stéphanie, *Le Carnet de Cuisine de Bordeaux* (Bordeaux, Éditions Sud Ouest 2007)

Béziat, Marc, *Recettes Paysannes du Pays Basque* (Rodez, Les Éditions du Curieux 2000)

Cazamayou, Marie-Luce, *Mes Recettes Pyrénéennes* (Clermont- Ferrand, Christine Bonneton 2011)

Cazeils, Nelson, *La Grande Histoire de la Pêche au Thon* (Rennes, Éditions Ouest-France 2004)

Coulon, Christian, *Le Cuisinier Médoquin* (Bordeaux, éditions confluences 2000)

Darroze, Hélène, *Les Recettes de mes Grands-Mères* (Paris, le Cherche-Midi 2014)

Doussy, Michel *La Cuisine du Bassin d'Arcachon* (Portet-sur-Garonne, Nouvelles Editions Loubatières, 2008)

Ducasse, Alain, *L'Esprit Bistrot, Meilleures Recettes de Benoit.* (Levalloir-Perret, Alain Ducasse Éditions 2012)

Duluat, Claudine with Pouget, Jeanine, *Recettes de Quercy* (Carlucet, France, les Éditions du Laquet 1991)

Escurignan, Maïté, *Manuel de Cuisine Basque, Cuisine Traditionelle et Nouvelle Cuisine* (Hélette, Éditions Harriet, 1997)

Ezgulian, Sonia, *Cuisinière Béarnaise, les meilleures recettes des Pyrénées-Atlantiques* (Lyon, Éditions Stéphane Bachès 2010)

Flaubert, Gustave, *Voyages* (Paris, Arléa 1998)

Guérard, Michel, *La Cuisine Gourmande* (Paris, Éditions Robert Laffont 1978)

Guérard, Michel, *Le Jeu de l'Oie et du Canard* (Eugénie-les-Bains, Compagnie Fermière et Thermale d'Eugénie-les-Bains 1998)

Hart, Sam and Eddie with Nieves Barragán Mohacho, Barrrafina, *A Spanish Cookbook* (London, Penguin Books, 2011)

Hirigoyen, Gerald with Cameron, Hirigoyen, *The Basque Kitchen, Tempting Food from the Pyrenees* (New York, Harper Collins 1999)

Koffmann, Pierre with Timothy Shaw, *Memories of Gascony* (London, Headline Book Publishing 1991)

Kurlansky, Mark, *The Basque History of the World* (London, Jonathan Cape, 1999)

La Mazille, *La Bonne Cuisine de Périgord,* (Flammarion, Paris 1983)

Lorfeuvre-Audabram, Régine, *Souvenirs Gourmands du Bassin d'Arcachon* (Lyon, Éditions Stéphane Bachès, 2012)

Martin, François, *Connaître la Cuisine Bordelaise* (Bordeaux, Éditions Sud Ouest 2011)

Martín, Pedro, *Les Meilleures Tapas de Donostia* (Donostia, ediciones Ttarttalo 2004)

Noël, Noëlle, *La Cuisine du Midi,* (Nimes, Éditions Lacour, 1993)

Pardies, Françoise, *Manuel de Cuisine Landaise* (Bayonne, Éditions Harriet 1987)

Penton, Anne, *Customs and Cookery in the Périgord and Quercy* (Newton Abbot, David & Charles 1973)

Pinaguirre, Catherine, *Mes Recettes du Pays Basque* (Paris, Christine Bonneton 2007)

Progneaux. J.E., *Recettes et Specialités Gastronomiques Bordelaises et Girondines* (Les Rochelles, Quartier Latin 1969)

Stendhal, also known as Henri Beyle, *Voyage Dans le Midi de la France 1838* (Paris, Encre 1984)

Rostand, Edmond, translated Christopher Fry, *Cyrano de Bergerac* (Oxford, Oxford University Press 2008)

Suhas, Jean, *Les Trois Cèpes de Michel, Histoires Gourmandes du Sud-Ouest et d'Ailleurs* (Bordeaux, Pleine Page 1970)

Suire, Guy, *Le Petit Livre des Gourmandises et Friandises du Sud Ouest* (Bordeaux, éditions confluences 2012)

Valeri, René, *Le Confit et son rôle dans l'alimentation traditionelle du Sud-Ouest de la France* (Kristianstad, Nya Civiltryckeriet 1977)

Wells, Patricia, *Bistro Cooking* (New York, Workman Publishing, 1989)

Wells, Patricia, *The Paris Cookbook* (Kyle Cathie, London 2001)

Wolfert, Paula, *The Cooking of South West France* (New York, Harper Perennial, 1988)

Index